Dreaming of Jeannie

TV's
Prime Time
in a
Bottle

Text by Steve Cox

Photographs: Howard Frank Archives

nnie

TV's Prime Time
in a Bottle

ST. MARTIN'S GRIFFIN
NEW YORK

Also by Steve Cox

The Hooterville Handbook: A Viewer's Guide to Green Acres
Here's Johnny!: Thirty Years of America's Favorite Late Night Entertainment
The Addams Chronicles
The Beverly Hillbillies
The Munsters: Television's First Family of Fright
The Munchkins of Oz
The Abbott & Costello Story (with John Lofflin)
Here on Gilligan's Isle (with Russell Johnson)
Cooking in Oz (with Elaine Willingham)

ISBN 0-312-20417-5

First Edition: March 2000

10 9 8 7 6 5 4 3 2 1

BOOK DESIGN BY RENATO STANISIC

Contents

Acknowledgments ix

Introduction xi

1. All Systems Go: Launching a TV Series 1

2. I Dream of Jeannie—The Nightmare 25

3. The Jeannie Theme 41

4. The Bottle 45

5. The NASA Files 57

6. Not All Smoke and Mirrors 67

7. Sex and the Censors 75

8. Camp Runamuck: Jackie Cooper and TV's
Transcendental Entities 81

9. Geniealogy 87

10. No "Laugh-In" Matter 109

11. Master of the Game: About Sidney Sheldon 117

12. Barbara Eden 127

13. Larry Hagman 134

14. Bill Daily 143

15. Hayden Rorke 149

16. Emmaline Henry 155

17. Barton MacLane 161

18. Vinton Hayworth 165

19. The Maid Did It:
The Unsolved Murder of Herb Wallerstein 169

20. Feminism and the Jeannie by Susan J. Douglas 175

21. Bill Daily on Almost Everything 181

22. The End 189

23. Reentry 193

24. Episode Guide 209

25. Strictly Taboo 269

◆

Acknowledgments

✦

To be honest, this is a book our friends put us up to . . . we don't know whether to love 'em or to hate 'em. We'll decide that later. Right now, we'll just thank 'em.

To those members of the cast, crew, and creative team who conjured up the television series *I Dream of Jeannie,* we are grateful for your insight, your warmth (applicable to some), your time, and your recollections: Larry Hagman, Barbara Eden, Sidney Sheldon, Bill Daily, Hayden Rorke, Robert Purcell, Dick Albain, Tom Ward, Ross Bellah, Clarence Peet, Gene Nelson, Jackie Cooper.

The authors wish to thank the following individuals and organizations for their support, enthusiasm, patience with our more-than-occasional prodding, and various kinds of research assistance.

Academy of Motion Pictures Arts and Sciences, Anil Ajodah, Animation Sensations, Scott Awley, Oscar Aviles, Richard Barnes, Kathy Bartel, Carol Brady (St. Louis County Library), Ken Beck, Edward Bernds, Butterfield & Butterfield, Carl Canizares, Steven Colbert (an exemplary research consultant), Columbia–Screen Gems Television, Jerry and Blanche Cox, Ned Comstock,

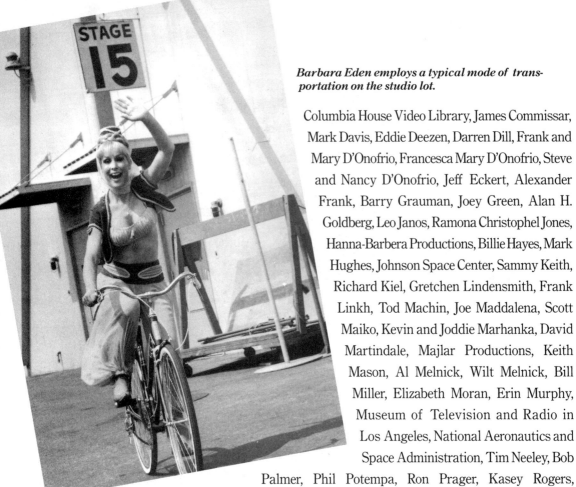

Barbara Eden employs a typical mode of transportation on the studio lot.

Columbia House Video Library, James Commissar, Mark Davis, Eddie Deezen, Darren Dill, Frank and Mary D'Onofrio, Francesca Mary D'Onofrio, Steve and Nancy D'Onofrio, Jeff Eckert, Alexander Frank, Barry Grauman, Joey Green, Alan H. Goldberg, Leo Janos, Ramona Christophel Jones, Hanna-Barbera Productions, Billie Hayes, Mark Hughes, Johnson Space Center, Sammy Keith, Richard Kiel, Gretchen Lindensmith, Frank Linkh, Tod Machin, Joe Maddalena, Scott Maiko, Kevin and Joddie Marhanka, David Martindale, Majlar Productions, Keith Mason, Al Melnick, Wilt Melnick, Bill Miller, Elizabeth Moran, Erin Murphy, Museum of Television and Radio in Los Angeles, National Aeronautics and Space Administration, Tim Neeley, Bob Palmer, Phil Potempa, Ron Prager, Kasey Rogers, Glenn Rosenberg, Ray Savage, Bill Ross, Wayne Schulman, Lester Shurr, Louis "Doc" Shurr, Shirley Sumbles, Sony Pictures Entertainment, Derek Tague, Jack Townsend, U.S.C. Special Collections, Daniel Wachtenheim, Alex Wallerstein, Elaine Willingham, Marc Wood, Dave Woodman, Chuck Yeager, and Johnnie Young.

A great big thank-you to the folks at St. Martin's Press: Gordon Van Gelder, Bryan Cholfin, Gretchen Achilles, Naomi Shulman, and Jim Kapp.

Most of the outtake, behind-the-scenes and portrait photographs, and color plates are culled from the collection of Louis "Doc" Schurr, whose agency handled Larry Hagman in the 1960s. This extraordinary private collection is now maintained by Howard Frank, cousin of Schurr. (For information about these and other entertainment photographs, send an SASE to Howard Frank Archives/Personality Photos, Inc., P.O. Box 300050, Midwood Station, Brooklyn, N.Y. 112230–0050.)

The authors are donating a portion of the royalties from this publication to the National Make-a-Wish Foundation.

Introduction

"A Thousand Pardons"

On July 4, 1997, NASA received the first images from their probe known as the Mars Pathfinder. Dispatched into space was a robotic land rover, *Sojourner,* which landed and grazed the surface of the placid red planet, Mars. Simultaneously, astounded earthlings, in unison, viewed on their television sets all the panoramic images relayed directly from Mars. But why study Mars, take photographs, and reconstruct the geological surface?

In our own tiny world, another question arose: Why do we study television—including this near-fossil known as *I Dream of Jeannie*? Why study its surface and dig deeper into its past? Posterity?

Astronaut Buzz Aldrin beautifully described the moon as "magnificent desolation"; the same could be said summing up the series *I Dream of Jeannie.* Truthfully, we've asked ourselves more than once why anyone would write a book about *I Dream of Jeannie.* The show isn't *that* funny. No great guffaws or out-loud belly laughs or snorts of uncontrollable hysteria in these shows. The program never possessed pathos to trigger a gulp or a tear. *Jeannie* never won industry accolades or overwhelming praise from critics, the way some of its contemporaries did. It won no Emmy Awards. It never topped the ratings during the

1960s. In fact, it never burst into the Top 25 ratings average for any of its five seasons.

Is this not pathetic?

The answer must be *nostalgia*. While the 1960s were a unique period in television history, *I Dream of Jeannie* was in there somewhere in the mist and smoke, conjuring up humor all its own; it was appreciated by the masses, yet its curious appeal was never really recognized or explored. The show was as mysterious as magic itself, you might say. More than three decades have passed since *Jeannie* was introduced to viewers, and the show remains a genuine TV artifact of the sixties. Everything becomes new again, and, let's face it, who doesn't like to reminisce? (We thought Larry Hagman wouldn't, but thankfully we were wrong.)

At best, this was a feel-good show; it was escapism. (We hope the book serves its master at least as well.) Simply, *I Dream of Jeannie* is a show about a curvaceous genie in scant clothing who was something to behold then, and still is. In this book we explore just how this creature from ancient legend personified sixties television sitcoms in the most luscious and lustful of ways. Surely Howard Stern won't be the only one to publicly, or privately, admit that Barbara Eden was an object of sexual allure

to the pubescent—and, for some, a source of release. Even a fully dressed Eden was a beauty to behold in this sitcom. Imagination is what really drives the libido; producer Sidney Sheldon knew that all too well. And so did some of us, whether we realized it or not. We watched Jeannie week after week, night after night. We keep watching Jeannie . . . and dreaming.

Is this what they mean by "milking the scene"?

1

All Systems Go: Launching a TV Series

◆

Throughout the sixties a procession of martians, witches, genies, talking ani-
mals, ghosts and robots would invade the tree-lined streets of Sitcomland.
Entire families of monsters would move into the neighborhood: the Addamses,
the Munsters, the Partridges. An undeniable trend toward supernatural blink-
ing and twitching would render a cartoon-like video hallucination that was per-
haps not entirely inappropriate to a culture that was experiencing the shock of
a sharp rise in recreational drug use among its middle classes.

—David Marc

he stars in the heavens were aligned and Sidney Sheldon's telemetry was dead-on perfect when he created *I Dream of Jeannie,* a television comedy designed to be escapist and not much more. Truly one of the standout psyche-delic shows of sixties television, *I Dream of Jeannie* was also considered by

Bottle Opener: Sidney Sheldon having a word with Larry Hagman on location
at Zuma Beach, where the opening scenes of the pilot episode were filmed,
December 1964.

Beached Blonde: By the end of 1964, a glowing Barbara Eden had a brand new television series, and a baby on the way.

many to be the ultimate male fantasy. (These days, we're free to mention that the show probably tickled a few females in the right way, too.) This comic tale of a genie and her master, like the ancient story of Aladdin, has been retold countless times, but this one has the distinction of being recognized as a genuine TV artifact.

You are hereby granted the opportunity to uncork the secrets of TV's most delectable supernatural being: Jeannie, the remarkably well-preserved 2,000-year-old genie from Baghdad. There was no television persona like her, and there never has been. She speaks with no contractions. She grants any wish for her master. Well, most of the time.

The show's creator was Sidney Sheldon, one of the most prolific writers of our time. The famed scribe put *this* story on film, for posterity. As the legend has it: Unwittingly set free from a bottle by astronaut Tony Nelson, a gorgeous genie appears and instructs her master, "Thou may ask anything of thy slave." From that moment on, the evening of September 18, 1965, every American male yearned for one.

Actually, the genesis of this genie was not some deep-seated figment bottled up in Sidney Sheldon for decades, or anything as romantic as that. Sheldon is a highly competent talent who, in the mid-sixties, had created and was writing and producing a popular sitcom called *The Patty Duke Show.* Screen Gems, the company whence his paychecks came, really didn't care whether he was overworked or not, because they approached the one-man production team and asked if he'd like to dip into the well again and come up with another concept.

"The network didn't have a lot of confidence in *The Patty Duke Show,*" Sheldon says. "I got a call from executives at Screen Gems to develop another show for them. I had an idea about a genie that was different from other genies. Usually, you know, you have Burl Ives come out of a bottle . . . but I enjoy writing about women. Women are more interesting than men. A woman in danger is more vulnerable than a man in danger. I hate the stereotype of the dumb blonde. I write about women who are more capable than men at what they are doing."

Over a weekend, Sheldon wrote the pilot script. All the while, he had the young actress Barbara Eden in mind to portray Jeannie. "She had the exact qualities that I wanted," Sheldon explained. Although Eden had done some television and a few motion pictures, it is safe to say that Sheldon had spotted her in the film *The Brass Bottle*—all about a plump genie played by Burl Ives. Sheldon's inspiration for *his* genie stemmed from many sources and a variety of concepts mushed together; however, he does admit that *The Brass Bottle* had a little something to do with the timing. No mistaking, *I Dream of Jeannie* was not a copy of *The Brass Bottle.* Nor was it a direct ripoff of TV's *Bewitched,* which had already

Possibly Sidney Sheldon's chief inspiration for I Dream of Jeannie *was a 1964 motion picture based on a novel by F. Anstey.* The Brass Bottle *starred Burl Ives as an overstuffed genie of the lamp; Barbara Eden costarred in this typical Tony Randall romp.*

been on for half a season when Sheldon rolled his sleeves up to design *Jeannie.*

Bewitched, like *Jeannie,* was inspired by a motion picture: *Bell, Book and Candle* (1958). Bill Asher, husband of Elizabeth Montgomery, was involved with *Bewitched* from the first twitch. He was an experienced producer (he staged President Kennedy's inaugural gala with Frank Sinatra in 1961) and a talented television director. For a while, Asher even worked closely with Sidney Sheldon on *The Patty Duke Show.* "Sidney was polite about it all," says Asher. "He came to me and asked me, 'How would you feel if I did a show for Screen Gems about a genie?' And I told him I didn't care." Granted, there were to be supernatural similarities, and the fact that both shows were produced on the same studio lot added to the parallels and common personnel. But *Jeannie* can hardly be labeled a replica.

Oh yes: A beautiful female lead was another enticing element shared by both sitcoms. Barbara Eden was approached by Sheldon and, having accepted the role eagerly, she was the first one hired on the program. A battery of actors were considered and tested for the costarring role of astronaut Tony Nelson. Robert Conrad was seriously considered, as was Darren McGavin—who turned the role down. Actors Gary Collins and Jack Warden together tested for the roles of Tony and Dr. Bellows—but the prizes ultimately went to Larry Hagman and Hayden Rorke. The young stand-up comic Bill Daily, with all his nervous tics, was hired as Tony Nelson's sidekick, and the main cast was complete.

Larry Hagman was interviewed about his new role late in 1964, not long after he received it. "It's crazy," Hagman told writer Erskine Johnson, "how one thing can lead to something entirely different in show business. My wife had been supporting me for three months and I was down to thirty cents in my pocket when I was sent the script of an Alfred Hitchcock show with an offer to play the leading role for $1,500."

Hagman flew from New York to Los Angeles to film the episode, but he had his reservations about the job. It was an especially twisted drama and he predicted to his wife that though it might get made, it would never air.

"It was about a young fellow and his bride held captive by a gang of bearded hoods who finally torture the wife to death in front of the bound-and-gagged hus-

ABOVE: *Larry Hagman: "The question is, who was the slave and who was the master?"*
OPPOSITE PAGE: *One of Barbara Eden's first television appearances was on* I Love Lucy *(1957).*

The house facade used for the home of Major Nelson, as seen today on the Warner Bros. ranch facility lot (formerly the Columbia ranch) in Burbank, California.

Dreaming of
Jeannie

band. I figured I had nothing to lose and I needed the money," he said.

Hagman's intuition was right. The show was in the middle of shooting when the episode itself got gunned down. No matter to Hagman, who was happy to get a buyout and not have to work. Since he was already on the West Coast, his agent immediately had him test for some upcoming TV roles, one of them being Tony Nelson. It also didn't matter that this genie show had little prestige and was going to be the only one on NBC not filmed in color; it was a starring role, which would provide some stability in Hagman's career—for a while, anyway.

The entire series (outside of rare location shooting and stock footage) was shot on Soundstage One at the old Columbia Pictures lot on Gower Street in Hollywood. The outdoor house exterior was located on the Columbia Pictures Ranch Facility (now the Warner Bros. Ranch) in Burbank. The house used for Tony Nelson's residence throughout the series was just a shell, located on a "neighborhood street" at the ranch. The houses in a row were fixtures on the tiny lot for many years, used in countless films and television shows. The Tony Nelson middle-class home had served years earlier as the Bumstead residence in many *Blondie* films starring Penny Singleton and Arthur Lake.

It had also been seen on *The Donna Reed Show* and was Mr. Wilson's house on *Dennis the Menace.* Today, it still stands, right alongside the Partridge Family abode and a few others. The Sam and Darrin Stephens property is down the road, at the corner, still there as well, as if time had stopped.

When *Jeannie* hit the air, it became a likable—even believable—and cute little program, but it was never a giant success . . . ratings-wise, anyway. Sidney Sheldon was constantly being ribbed by critics wielding the same damned phrase at him: It's a one-joke-show.

"Sure," he admitted at the time, "I do one-joke series. *The Fugitive* is a one-joke show. *I Love Lucy* was a one-joke show. It's what you do with it each week that counts." And as long as the Madison Avenue sponsors kept buying these popular one-joke shows, writers like him were going to keep dreaming them up. That's how things operated back then—with great influence from the sponsors themselves.

Dreaming of
Jeannie

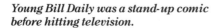
Young Bill Daily was a stand-up comic before hitting television.

It's doubtful that Sidney Sheldon dreamed of the problems *Jeannie* would sprout. Simply put, the pilot and the first season were rough for many reasons, one being that Sheldon's golden boy, Larry Hagman, was more than he had bargained for. "His contributions have always been underestimated," Sheldon says, "but it was very hard for him to play that type of character." One brief moment stands out in Sheldon's mind:

"I remember returning from the desert where we shot one of the early episodes. We stopped at a red light and Larry rolled down the window of the limousine and yelled out, 'Someday you're all gonna know who I am!' " Well, of course, Hagman meant it. But at the moment, this attitude of his concerned the producer.

Bill Daily noticed it, too. "Larry was a little of an egomaniac," Daily says. "I think that made him insecure. He wanted to be the star and everything went to Barbara. He wanted to be noticed, so he did other things like a naughty boy. He would do things to get noticed."

Leon Adams, author of *Larry Hagman: A Biography* (St. Martin's Press), put it into perspective this way:

> Larry Hagman was a star. The show paid him $150,000 a year and afforded him instant visibility. . . . Larry and Barbara Eden never brawled, but it was hard not to feel any resentment toward their respective situations. Major Nelson, after all, had to be on camera during some eighty percent of the scenes, and his role required the most work, since the dimensionality of the show couldn't be expected from the role of Jeannie. But Barbara Eden was the star, the glamour girl, and Larry Hagman essentially played straightman to her antics. It wasn't easy.

Sidney Sheldon can't forget the initial days of the pilot's production, because trouble started brewing. "The first day was hell," he says. "The director, Gene Nelson, called me to say, 'Sidney, I'm quitting.'

"So I said, 'I'll be right down.'

"When I got to the set, he said, 'I can't work like this. Larry Hagman doesn't know his lines. Bill Daily doesn't know his lines.' So I said, 'Let me talk with them.' And I went in and asked Larry why he didn't know his lines. He said, 'What are you talking about? I know every line of the script. Now that I have the gist of the character, I'm just expanding it a little.'

"Expanding it! I told him, 'This is

RIGHT: *Hayden Rorke and Larry Hagman going over lines during a break in filming, December 1965.* BELOW: *Shooting an early episode on the loft set.* Jeannie, *like many shows of the day, was a one-camera production put on film—not videotape.*

television. You can't do that.' And Bill Daily said, 'I'm a stand-up comic, I don't know how to memorize lines.' So we got Bill a little tape recorder and he used to listen to the lines over and over to get them."

Bill Daily vividly recalls those nervous days. "I did have difficulty memorizing my lines," he says, "no doubt about it. Because I didn't know how to learn and wouldn't learn. I had an improvisation and Second City background. I like to wing it. If the scripts had been good, I would have stayed with it. Even today, when I don't like the script, I can never memorize it.

"So it boils down to this," Daily continues, "if those scripts had been great scripts, there wouldn't have been any problems with Larry, or Gene Nelson, or anybody. They were just terrible scripts. The problem with Larry was he didn't handle it well and he hurt Sidney a lot. You don't say out loud that you hate the scripts. What you do is say, 'Hey, I've got an idea. Why don't we do it this way or try it this way?' Larry would just tear up the script and walk out."

As time progressed, things got worse for Hagman, and by the end of the first season, he was ready to fall apart. The pressures built to the extent that he was nauseated every day. "I was screaming and yelling, vomiting and crying," he explained later. "It was nervous breakdown time. I was so far gone." Crew members on the production were getting fed up, and patience at the network levels had diminished as well. Eventually, Hagman sought a psychologist's assistance to soothe the beast within. (Obviously Dr. Bellows's sitcom psychobabble wasn't doing the trick.)

Dreaming of
Jeannie

For the most part, Hagman was outspoken and didn't care if he was difficult. He tried every way he knew to fight for quality on the show. He told the *L.A. Times* in 1966, "For instance, I insisted on seeing daily rushes. I was told it wasn't done. Why wasn't it done? Because it wasn't. When that happens, we have that person replaced. Then we try it. Or we try something else. And maybe it can't be done, but at least we try."

Larry Hagman recently explained what he felt was his biggest headache on the show:

The repetition of the scripts. I now understand it, but I didn't understand it at the time. You know, when you've got a formula and it works, you don't fuck with it. Every fourth week we'd get the same script again. We had kind of four basic things: Jeannie gets locked up. Jeannie can't help. Jeannie has a sis-

OPPOSITE PAGE: *Eden and Hagman in a scene in Tony's loft office.*

ter. Jeannie has a dog. They all worked, but it seemed like nobody really ever
wanted to explore much beyond that. Sometimes they did, but generally, that
was it. We were shooting like 33 shows a year, really cranking them out. I
didn't know it was extraordinary and in those days it wasn't extraordinary.
This was a one-camera show. Today it's different.

Bill Daily agrees. In a matter of time, he explained, he and Hagman were able to
devise a system of their own to patch up the scripts. They experimented, trying a little
of this and testing a little of that, until they were more comfortable with each other's
style of working. Barbara Eden mainly just went along competently and peacefully.

"We were out there fighting with an average script and no jokes, trying to make it
work," Daily explains. "Sidney, hell, he was gone half the time. If it weren't for Larry
and me working them out and adding some business, we would have just been talking
to each other for twenty pages. Larry used to say, 'Come on! This is moving pictures.
Moving! Let's *do* something!'

"So we actually began directing everything we did and just made it up as we went
along because Sidney Sheldon wrote the whole thing and left. We'd be standing there
for fifteen minutes and talking and Larry would say, 'Why don't we do this and that?'
And the directors would allow us to do it. Today, that wouldn't happen."

The actors were constantly thinking on their feet, trying to modify and improve the
already frenetic performance they blocked in each scene. Notice that nearly every
episode moves along at a frazzled, frantic pace. *If it moves quickly enough,* they

Sitcom Hit: After the critics' smoke cleared, viewers tuned in, and the cast of Jeannie *was flying high. It is doubtful the show's initial prime-time ratings accurately reflected the program's loyal following.*

thought, *maybe no one will notice the script isn't too funny.* "We'd rewrite during a freeze!" Daily adds. "We'd freeze and then we'd say, 'Hey, let's come back over *here*.' And most of the time it worked out."

Hagman concludes, "After a while, everybody meshed. Barbara and I were fine together. Billy, he was wonderful. Hayden was great to work with and we had the cream of the character actors to come on the show."

B.Y.O.B.

Larry Hagman was complicated. Even he admits it. But it was his eccentric nature that really confounded people. He once said in a *Playboy* interview, "Well, I am eccentric to the extent that I collect funny hats and costumes and flags and have marches on the beach. But what the fuck? I mean, eccentric more than what? Outrageous is more like it. I just like to live out my life a little more than most people."

On any given day during production of *Jeannie,* Hagman might show up at the studio dressed as a gorilla, or in overalls like a farmer, maybe a clown. Some people thought he verged on psychosis, but he always maintained that everything was in check. Hagman just plain liked variety, and he liked to be outwardly outrageous; more often than not, he was at his zaniest when friends least expected it. Not to mention strangers.

Sean Cassidy, son of the titanic actor Ted Cassidy (famous for his portayal of Lurch on *The Addams Family*) was a kid, but he vividly remembers Larry Hagman coming over to the Cassidy home to visit his father, who was a friend.

"I opened the door to greet Larry and he was standing at our front door in pink granny glasses with a yellow chiffon kind of cape—a shoulder-to-floor cape," says Cassidy. "The rest of the outfit was orange and red. It was just the wildest Peter Max kind of outfit. I was blown away because this was Major Nelson from *I Dream of Jeannie.* I used to watch the show. It was no gag, he was just dressed that way. He came in and spent the evening or whatever it was."

Hagman enjoyed experimenting with all kinds of things, including the popular mind-altering drugs of the day—such as LSD. What's more, he professes he loved every minute of it. "I guess it was just about the best thing that ever happened to me," he said. "It changed my way of looking at life, and more important than anything else, it changed my way of looking at death. . . . It was just one of those little drawers. I had my experience and was ready to go on to something else."

Hagman's ongoing vice, initiated during those years, was the tickling taste of fine champagne. It became as tasty as cherry Kool-Aid. "Oh, I stuck around Larry a bit," says Bill Daily, "and one thing about his drinking—nobody knew it. He drank champagne in the morning, he drank all the time. But he never missed a line, he was always on time, and it didn't seem to be a problem. Larry was a food gourmet and he loved the taste of champagne."

Hagman drank nowhere near as much as, say, actor Forrest Tucker, who was soused almost every day while shooting *F Troop* during the same years. Stories of nips and Tucker at work are famous in Hollywood. The star, who played the Irish sergeant O'Rourke on the sitcom, was mighty proud of his customized golf cart with a minibar built onto it. He scooted around the Warner Bros. lot with a drink in one hand and the other on the wheel. When he wasn't dealing with Agarn and the Hakowee Indians, he was enjoying a blast of Jack Daniel's on the sidelines. But the most amazing thing was

The Brass Bottle, *as Sidney Sheldon has admitted, inspired him in creating* I Dream of Jeannie. *In this light comedy, Tony Randall plays an unsuccessful architect, Harold Ventemore, who bids at auction and wins a "kum kum"—an antique brass vaselike bottle. It's an "authentic relic with ancient hieroglyphics around the seal," he observes. Ventemore decides to transform the relic into a lamp with a shade, and inadvertently releases an ancient alum of the green djinn amidst a cloud of (green) smoke.*

15
Dreaming of
Jeannie

"Yea, verily!" Fakrash Alamash (played by Burl Ives) sings ancient praises to his new master. The genie attempts to explain his presence and history, which involves an angry King Solomon who commanded he be "imprisoned in a bottle of brass and cast into the sea, there to abide the day of doom." Fakrash tries to present the unbeliever with gifts, such as rubies the size of pigeon eggs, but Ventemore thinks the hefty intruder is a lunatic.

Of course, the events that follow disrupt the architect's entire existence—his love life, his work, his home—until Ventemore is restrained in a straitjacket and placed in an asylum due to Fakrash. Behold . . . he must have Fakrash prove himself an authentic genie in a court of law.

Burl Ives is the jubilant genie Fakrash Alamash in the film The Brass Bottle.

Some of Barbara Eden's earlier television appearances included **Father Knows Best, I Love Lucy,** *and* **The Andy Griffith Show.**

that he never displayed drunkenness. Never missed his cues. Always showed up on time, and rarely lost his temper. He was a model actor.

Hagman's demeanor while drinking was much the same as Tucker. Who knew that his champagne consumption would eventually become as uncontrollable as his eyebrows? His "enjoy life" and "live life to the fullest" mind-set ended up haunting him decades later, and he's lucky to have survived.

These days, Hagman is a mellower man. He has nothing to prove. His talents are on film, a life's work to be proud of. *TV Guide* noted, "He's lost that mercurial edge, uncocked the hammer that used to set off the irascible side of his personality." And it seems, he's even reconciled himself with his own career . . . and *I Dream of Jeannie.*

"The best thing that came out of doing those shows are watching the reruns," Hagman says today. "They are still funny and I laugh at myself. I look at it and say, 'My God, is that me?' I cannot believe it.

"I am getting so much mail on the show," he adds. "Maybe a hundred and fifty letters a week, just regarding *Jeannie.* Much bigger than *Dallas,* because *Jeannie* is on so often. There's a whole new generation of kids out there and they all know me as Major Nelson, not J.R. They look at me and say, 'Boy, you've changed.' "

If you dissect the machinery in this TV show, you'll find a few obvious parts used in building the engine that kept *I Dream of Jeannie,* well, staggering along in the second half of the sixties. The show was part wish-fulfillment, part fish out of water, part hallucinogen. All the pieces were affixed to one another haphazardly with lug nuts that didn't always fit. What flew was this odd contraption, a show which never found a comfortable corner in the network lineup or in viewers' living rooms.

Naturally, a book like this is apt to ponder and speculate on what makes a television program tick. The sensible question here is, What *resuscitated* this show each year? In some ways, *Jeannie* was like a network hemorrhage miraculously clotting each season at the eleventh hour. After the first season, Barbara Eden's breasts were not the only buoys keeping the show afloat. The effective—and necessary—transformation from black and white to vibrant color was as rewarding to the eyes as it was on *Gilligan's Island.* (In fact, *Jeannie* was NBC's last show to be filmed in black and white, and had it remained in duotone, it would have died right there on the table.) But don't let anyone try to tell you that the show wasn't a power fantasy aimed at men. (And for some reason, after decades, the show has attracted a faithful gay following as well. Jeannie/Barbara Eden is a TV diva in the minds of many.)

Sure, Sidney Sheldon's snappy write-in contests each season prompted postal employees to haul in sacks of mail—concrete evidence of the existence of the viewers out there. This key kept the show from being locked out, and anyway, there was not much use in citing ratings. Critics at the time bunched *I Dream of Jeannie* with what they labeled "meatless sausages," the look-alike, sound-alike TV comedies churned out by Hollywood during the era. They all seemed to have a superficial sameness, although many sitcoms noticeably strived for independence, not excepting this one. It's astounding that *Jeannie* was not stung with the bitter venom of cancellation sooner. In the end, what does it matter? *Jeannie* was a survivor . . . five seasons is nothing to scoff at, even with mediocre ratings—numbers that most programs today would kill to earn.

At the time, *Jeannie* and her audience seem never to have been given the opportunity for a nice courtship. The program was moved five times in five years, and was never allowed to take root before being pulled from the soil and replanted in another time slot. Consider its prime-time leaps and bounds:

> *Sept. 1965–Sept. 1966, Saturday 8:00–8:30*
> *Sept. 1966–Aug. 1967, Monday 8:00–8:30*
> *Sept. 1967–Aug. 1968, Tuesday 7:30–8:00*
> *Sept. 1968–Aug. 1969, Monday 7:30–8:00*
> *Sept. 1969–Sept. 1970, Tuesday 7:30–8:00*

Each year, news of the program's fate came late, in the form of a telephone call from Sidney Sheldon. So much anxiety and uncertainty plagued the *Jeannie* ensemble that eventually some of the players became numb from the fire drills. By the fourth season, Barbara Eden publicly declared her indifference and even described her cure for the blues. She was already lining up other things to do, expanding her horizons, exploiting her newfound TV fame with additional gigs. During production hiatuses, she appeared on TV variety shows, starred in a stage production of *Kismet,* and polished her nightclub act, which headlined at Las Vegas's Frontier. In a March 1968 *Variety* column, Eden described her most recent period in limbo, waiting to find out about the future of her folded-arm tricks. She told the reporter:

> I had a poignant feeling because this is like a family, our group. But it was all
> so ambiguous. First they told me we were back because of my popularity,
> that they had taken polls, which proved this. This happened while I was in
> New York guesting on the Bob Hope show. I returned here and was taping a
> special at NBC, when an NBC man told me I was off their schedule.
>
> That night I got three calls from Screen Gems and NBC, saying don't
> believe it, you're not off. I thought that's nice, but I didn't believe we were back
> until I got the official notification from Sheldon, who is a calm man in a storm.

If you thought disappointing ratings and the unsettling path the show took were ambiguous, then examine the program itself. Its premise was always puzzling and unclear. There was rarely a fluid, genuine chemistry between the two main characters. At best, their on-camera relationship was amicable and tolerant, and lacking in magic and depth—even the love they were supposed to achieve at the time of their marriage lacked realism. There seemed to be insincerity near the surface.

Face it, the program's title is off kilter: Tony Nelson wasn't dreaming of Jeannie during most of the series; he would have been content to meet an old girlfriend after so many years, or to escort the general's gorgeous niece around Cocoa Beach. A trip to Hawaii *without* Jeannie was a godsend for him because he could watch the babes on the beach hassle-free. No genies.

If you watch *I Dream of Jeannie* with any regularity, you may have noticed the inner struggle going on. What was the show *really* about? Was it about a naive blond genie who wreaked havoc, impetuously blinking up problems for her master, in whom she was romantically interested? Should the show have been called *I Dream of Tony*? Or was the show actually about an astronaut, a well-known Air Force pilot who worked and trained at NASA and had to dodge a genie with whom he was cohabiting? Tony Nelson was a respected citizen of Cocoa Beach, a virile male explorer with "the right stuff" for the sixties. Eventually, his character evolved into kookiness, and he stumbled around most of the time making excuses to the ranks and spending nearly every waking hour avoiding Jeannie's bizzare catastrophes.

Back during the show's original run, if someone had dared to pose the question, point-blank, "What *is* this show all about?" to the show's stars, Barbara Eden and Larry Hagman, it's likely that they would have been given very different answers. This show's true premise was difficult to define then, and even now it's hard to discern.

Sidney Sheldon explained in 1966 that the show was symbolic of the relationship between "masterful man and his supposedly servile woman that exists in real life," he said. "They may both claim that he's the boss, but in practice it doesn't usually work that way." The paradox, whether or not it was intended from the start, took shape. Was the title of the show misleading? Keep in mind, however, that *Jeannie* was not a deep institution, and those who worked on it weren't a think-tank aiming to disseminate cultural wisdom via the TV airwaves. (Even Dr. Bellows's psychobabble was minimal to nonexistent.) There were no messages in this bottle. These scripts were written by people who were simply trying to get a laugh; any further analysis would be irrelevant.

Me, Myself, and
I Dream of Jeannie

Sidney Sheldon flew solo when he created, wrote, produced, and cast Jeannie. *He worked best while secluded in his customized soundproof office, pacing and dictating scripts right off the top of his head into a microphone for his secretaries to transcribe. Sometimes he wrote out his concepts in longhand on yellow legal pads, and it was up to his assistants to decipher the scribblings.*

For Sheldon, paradise was to "go into conference with myself," he said in 1966. "If I like the story, I write it and I'm the final authority on whether to give it a polish or send it to mimeo," he said. "If what I create comes up short, I take the rap."

Some writers crave the attention of another human being to bounce ideas off; their talents shine when they work with a partner. Some writers work more effectively in groups, building on one another's concepts. And some writers demand solitude. Sheldon was one of those. He often resorted to methods such as meditation and self-hypnosis to push the creative juices and conquer deadlines.

NBC network and Screen Gems execs knew it was best simply to leave him alone to absorb himself in his hectic schedule. To help him focus, Sheldon had the studio's top art director, Ross Bellah, design and install an enormously solid double door for his office. "It was pretty thick, with deadening in it," Bellah recalls. "He didn't want to be disturbed."

Screen Gems executive Jackie Cooper recalls Sheldon's solitary nature. "His office was in an old wooden building," he says, "and I remember Sidney was way at the end of the hall. He wanted a room between him and his receptionist as well as the soundproofing in the walls and this huge double door. Sidney wanted to be with Sidney.

"The fact that Sidney was allowed to do his work without interruption was good," Cooper says. "We had to trust Sidney. He didn't want you close to him. But doing it his way was the right thing because he had the material."

As a solo scribe while the show got on its feet and sprinting, producer

Sheldon had the "write stuff" and was doing it all: He pumped out some forty consecutive scripts during the first couple of seasons, and when he collaborated with a few writers, he ultimately rewrote much of this dialogue, adding jokes and bits of business. During Jeannie's first season, there were weeks when Sheldon amazingly churned out three scripts—occasionally writing a Patty Duke episode and a Jeannie in the same day.

"I was writing I Dream of Jeannie. I created I Dream of Jeannie and I was also producing the show and getting screen credit for all these and it became such an ego trip," he told an audience at the Museum of Television and Radio recently. "So I called the Writers Guild and told them I was going to write under these names, which I gave them, and they said that would be okay."

The pseudonyms Sheldon adopted for many Jeannie scripts were Christopher Golato, Allan Devon, and Mark Rowane—names he created and liked because of their ring. Sheldon was nominated for an Emmy Award (1966–1967) in the category of "Outstanding Writing Achievement in Comedy," but lost to Buck Henry and Leonard Stern for their work on the popular NBC spy spoof Get Smart.

If only for the sheer volume of his output Sidney Sheldon deserved to take home the golden lady.

Sidney Sheldon and Larry Hagman talking with an official from the Northrop aeronautical facility in Southern California, where some filming took place.

The show had one thing going for it: Somehow, it appeared at just the right moment in TV history. Wouldn't you agree that today, an episode about a visit from Jeannie's uncle Tariq Aziz and humorously hostile granduncle Saddam Hussein all the way from Baghdad would not go over so well?

More important, *I Dream of Jeannie* was perfectly wedged into its place in the annals of man's space exploration. It was one of the few space programs able to take full advantage of the here and now, what with real-life NASA breaking new barriers every year during the decade. It is probably the only long-running program to exploit to any extent the American space program; it was the most popular one in the sixties, anyway, and the only one to last. There were others, you know.

Dreaming of
Jeannie

Remember a sitcom of the mid-sixties called *It's About Time,* created by Sherwood Schwartz, which for some reason ran out of time after clocking in just one season? (In TV Schwartzica time, the show came directly after stranding seven castaways on *Gilligan's Island* and just before he introduced America to a bunch of Bradys.) Like all of Schwartz's shows, it had a great theme song. It starred Jack Mullaney and Frank Aletter as NASA astronauts who had broken the time barrier; their misguided space capsule crash-lands in prehistoric time. Among the friendly cave dwellers are Gronk and Shad, played by Joe E. Ross ("Oooh, oooh") and Imogene Coca. In one episode, airing January 22, 1967, the time-space travelers manage to repair their ship and return to the twentieth century—bringing along Shad, Gronk, and family. The prehistoric cave people had more difficulties adjusting to modern times than the astronauts did during their journey to Jurassic TV.

Can we forget Sid and Marty Krofft's soft Saturday morning TV comedy, *Far Out Space Nuts*? Starring in this brief 1975 show were bumbling Bob Denver and bombastic Chuck McCann as NASA employees who accidentally launch a space probe. (While stocking the spaceship with food, Bob Denver's character accidentally pushes the LAUNCH button instead of the LUNCH button.) Hopelessly lost, the unwilling space travelers pick up a strange little furry alien creature named Honk (Patty Maloney) and take it along for the ride.

Television, especially with *I Dream of Jeannie,* was teetering between fact and fiction in the sixties. On one hand, we knew there were no genies; on the other hand, space travel was a reality and we saw it was no television stunt in 1969 when Neil Armstrong made a "giant leap for mankind" and planted a flag on the virgin moon with all the earth as witness. (The historical event was not without humor. After Armstrong, Buzz

Aldrin carefully stepped down out of the *Apollo 11* lunar module—"making sure not to lock it on my way out," he said live to the worldwide audience. Nobody remembers *that* line.) Civilization's meeting with the moon also marked the end of *I Dream of Jeannie.* Even if the program had continued for one more season, it couldn't have possibly survived the real-life *Apollo 13* misadventure, which put NASA itself in a state of flux for years.

Credit *is* due. During the sixties, NASA created heroes out of daring American males, but not many hit TV shows. President Lyndon Johnson knew that America could not afford to be second best in the space race, and fulfilled John F. Kennedy's commitment during this decade. America saw NASA take the lead and reach the moon first. Who knows how many young boys and girls were inspired to pursue the space program as a career or become scientists after watching the moon landing . . . and *I Dream of Jeannie?* (Not to shatter your force field, but *Star Trek* probably inspired more adolescents than both of the former combined. C'mon—Bones is, without a doubt, cooler than Bellows.) Fiction ultimately prevailed on the tube; before and after the *I Dream of Jeannie* era, TV shows with a space travel themes simply bypassed NASA and invented their own mother organizations. *The Jetsons, Lost in Space*, and *Star Trek* fast-forwarded centuries and made little to no mention of NASA back here on earth.

Even given the limited quality standards of sixties television, *I Dream of Jeannie* rarely hit the mark in attempting to represent NASA at Cape Kennedy. It was hardly a scientific portrayal of the space program. The show displayed little authenticity, especially with respect to the actual vastness of the American space program. Using bland stock footage, the TV show hardly captured the tropical essence of Cocoa Beach, Florida, and the surrounding area, either.

Basically, a show that took place on and around the NASA base had little to do with most Americans. At least on *Bewitched,* you knew the show wasn't about an ad agency, but the subsetting of Darrin's duties lent itself to many funny situations. In *Jeannie*'s NASA subplot, the situations were far less recognizable to viewers, hardly familiar, and rarely believable. After watching any handful of episodes of *Jeannie,* a stranger might have believed that NASA revolved around this demanding, old, slick-haired psychiatrist who ran the base out of his small, brown-paneled office, which had no secretary.

And so, *I Dream of Jeannie* is a survivor, and it is what it is. But as we all have learned, everything depends on what the definition of "is" is.

I Dream of Jeannie—
The Nightmare

♦

Larry Hagman was a bit of a problem. He wanted to be a star, but when you're in a show with a half-naked actress saying, "What would you like, Master?" the audience isn't looking at you. So I tried to write scripts that would build him up.

—*Sidney Sheldon*

Sure, this was an innocuous little show, a sweet sitcom about a gorgeous genie, but production was not immune to grave difficulties. Right from the start, egos were uncorked and clashes took center stage. Near fistfights.

In what turned out to be his final interview, director Gene Nelson sat confidently in a booth at a North Hollywood restaurant and began to describe the "hellish" first weeks he experienced while helping mold the series.

Nelson, a superb tap dancer who worked in many Warner Bros. musicals (he played cowboy Will Parker in the film version of *Oklahoma!*) eventually unlaced his Capezios and became a television and film director, with Elvis Presley's *Kissin' Cousins* (1964) and *Harum Scarum* (1965) to his credit. He had

been in the entertainment business for many years when he accepted the assignment of directing the *Jeannie* pilot and the first ten episodes of the series. When interviewed, Nelson said he was planning to write his autobiography, which would include a chapter called "*I Dream of Jeannie:* The Nightmare." He died months later, in August 1996, having never completed that book. Somehow, I don't think he'd mind that I borrowed the title.

Before *Jeannie,* Nelson had directed some low-budget Lippert films, several TV pilots, and episodes of *The Rifleman, The Donna Reed Show,* and *Farmer's Daughter.* He even stood at the helm for some half-hours of *Gilligan's Island.* "I was on the upswing of becoming one of the top ten directors in television," he said. "Things were really starting to move along when I got the call from Sidney Sheldon. He sent me a script. I made notes and got together with him."

Director Gene Nelson, a former actor and tap dancer, talks with Barbara Eden during production of an early episode. (Courtesy of Gene Nelson.)

It was the first time Nelson had worked with—or even met—Sidney Sheldon, but he was aware of the producer/writer's skills. "Sidney wrote very fast," recalled Nelson. "He told me once, 'When I write something, I turn it over to my nine-year-old daughter. If she likes it, then I know it's good.' That's exactly what he told me. I was impressed with him, though. Here's the guy who won the Academy Award for *The Bachelor and the Bobby-Soxer.* He was like a child, he looked so young. He had a lot of enthusiasm, which I loved."

Obviously, Sheldon's daughter okayed the pilot script for *Jeannie* because it landed at NBC; the network purchased it and funded its filming in association with Screen Gems Television, a branch of Columbia Pictures. "They had already tested two or three actors for the cast and I was given final choice," Nelson said, "but I gather that this thing was in progress before I got there. They showed me some of the tests."

Nelson said his initial speculation about the two characters and how they would blend turned out to be accurate. "Hagman had this marvelous energy and kind of nervousness about his character that really registered on the film," he said, "and Barbara played right into that with Jeannie as the calm one. There you had a balance.

The masking tape on the floor helps the actors hit their mark in a scene and ensures proper placement for lighting and focus. Notice the flowing, sheer fabric draped around Eden's midriff to disguise her pregnancy.

"Larry Hagman," he concedes, "had a wonderful, natural timing. He was what I call a courageous actor. He wasn't afraid to experiment. What I didn't realize when we hired him is that his courage could make him a pain in the ass. But there was no denying he was good and contributed to the success of the show."

According to Nelson, another key figure in the show's initial appeal was the director of photography, Fred Jackman, an inventive cameraman who came up with fresh ideas as they filmed. In addition, Nelson noted, everyone involved made a conscious effort to stay away from anything that might seem to rip off *Bewitched*.

"NBC was cheap as hell," Nelson said, "and they wanted to do this pilot with all this special-effects business. So not to go over budget, we had to do as many of the special effects [as we could] in-camera to keep the postproduction bill to a minimum. On top of that, Barbara Eden was pregnant and we had to have at least five shows ready in September to release as a new season of this new series. And this meant we had to work through the summer."

"The schedule was hectic," he said, "but we got our team in place. It was really a cooperative effort. We were pushing it. One day reading and rehearsal, and the next day we were doing the show. It got so we had no time for rewrites. We had lunch together and reworked things that needed to be rewritten."

Gene Nelson took a sip of coffee and inhaled deeply before describing the first day with the ensemble on *I Dream of Jeannie*.

"The first day of reading, okay? Larry Hagman is full of piss and vinegar. Ready to go. At that time, he was getting back into the

ABOVE: **Showtime** *magazine cover, circa 1965, introducing* I **Dream of Jeannie.** *(Sidney Sheldon Collection, USC Cinema-Television Library.)* OPPOSITE PAGE: *Jeannie summons her grandfather, an ancient Djinn (J. Carrol Naish), to meet her new master in the episode "Djinn and Water."*

The Guarding of Eden

Things didn't always go as planned in the filming of I Dream of Jeannie's first episode, late in 1964. Barbara Eden can attest to that.

The first day of shooting the pilot—which took place on a desolate beach location about thirty miles from Hollywood—was one of those rare frigid December days in Southern California. This was winter, even there. Eden, dressed only in her sheer harem costume, stood and knelt in the sand, hour after hour, take after take, while everyone else was in heavy sweaters, jackets, and coats. Hagman's wardrobe was a long-sleeved NASA space jumpsuit. But the chilly wind at the beach turned Eden's flesh from pale pink to mood-ring purple after several hours outdoors.

Nearing the end of the day, while Eden was squatting close to the water, her back to the approaching waves, the surf struck. She was soaked in chiffon, shaking, and ready to pack it in for the day—but she remained a trouper.

Later in the shoot, the script called for a scene in Tony Nelson's living room. Eden was to jump in the air and land on a sofa next to her costar, Larry Hagman. The flying was a cinch. After all, don't all of us remember jumping up and down on our parents' great big bed—or on a trampoline—when we were kids? No problem.

On cue, Eden took an assisted launch by jumping from the springy seat of a nearby armchair. The landing was a bit tricky, however. Hagman was seated with one leg folded under him, and Eden had to land on her stomach with her face looking up into his and into the camera just beyond.

When director Gene Nelson rehearsed the action, it went smoothly and Nelson ordered the cameraman to begin grinding away for the take. Eden took her leap, jumped on the chair, catapulted into the air, and aimed for the sofa. The cameras zoomed in for the landing.

The cast and crew gave a little gasp as she landed and raised her angelic face upward with a small stream of blood trickling from her mouth. Eden had landed with her chin squarely on Hagman's knee, gashing her lip.

That was it. The day's shooting was over, and Eden was taken away for medical attention. She returned the next day, ready for more vaulting, but it took some careful makeup artistry to conceal her swollen lower lip.

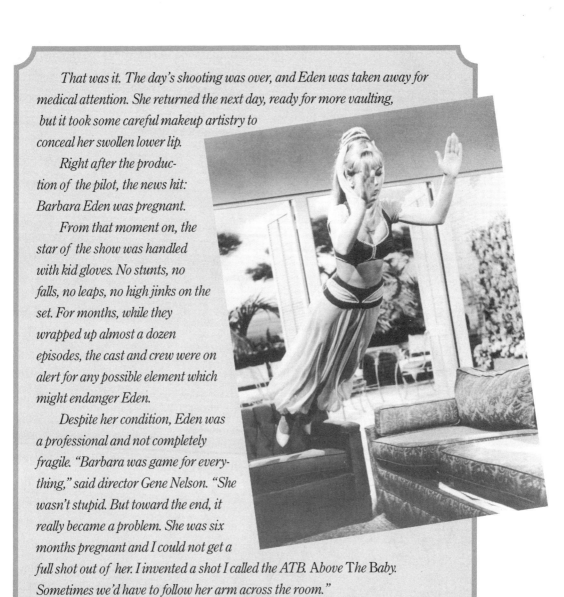

Right after the production of the pilot, the news hit: Barbara Eden was pregnant.

From that moment on, the star of the show was handled with kid gloves. No stunts, no falls, no leaps, no high jinks on the set. For months, while they wrapped up almost a dozen episodes, the cast and crew were on alert for any possible element which might endanger Eden.

Despite her condition, Eden was a professional and not completely fragile. "Barbara was game for everything," said director Gene Nelson. "She wasn't stupid. But toward the end, it really became a problem. She was six months pregnant and I could not get a full shot out of her. I invented a shot I called the ATB. Above The Baby. Sometimes we'd have to follow her arm across the room."

good graces of his mother [Mary Martin]—it was a strange situation. A lot of his drive and enthusiam was to show that she was not the only star in the family. His whole motivation for a lot of it was this.

"At the end of the reading, we were *all* enthused and excited," Nelson said. "Before lunch, we were going to go back to the studio and start blocking and Larry asked me,

'Where is the fan mail department?' And from that moment on, in *his* mind, it became *The Larry Hagman Show* and he set out to make it that. From that point on, it was hell.

"The more he got complimented, it got to the point where, you know, he and I would get into it about something in the scene or the way I was directing it or what he wanted to do or what he didn't want to do," Nelson said. "Not being known for my patience, I had to muster up every ounce I ever had. He would have taken over the show. And he'd do so many self-disturbing things. If Bill Daily had a kind of funny line—he'd want it."

According to Nelson, Hagman's peculiarities were not limited to the rehearsal stage. "When Larry got really mad," Nelson said, "he'd go down to the set and piss all over the set. Really. I understand that eventually, NBC had to hire an on-the-set psychiatrist to be with him every day."

If Hagman's behavior infuriated the director, it was Barbara Eden's complacency that pushed him over the edge. "I remember once when Larry went into one of his tantrums," Nelson said, "we were standing there with the lights on, ready to go. He's vomiting all over the goddamned set with his expounding about all this and that and the other thing. Never once did Barbara say anything. She'd walk off the set and go to her dressing room. She didn't want to be part of that. I resented that. I felt she was the star of the show and if she couldn't contribute anything besides her acting—in regards to harmony on the set—I felt there was something initially wrong with her character. She never came to my defense or said anything to Larry.

LEFT: *Ad from a Mexico City newspaper, circa 1966. (Sidney Sheldon Collection, USC Cinema-Television Library.)* OPPOSITE PAGE: *Once again, Tony must convince Dr. Bellows that neither of them has gone berserk.*

She Wore Pink Velvet

Barbara Eden's breezy pink and maroon harem outfits—now considered the standard for any respectable femme genie—were created by the Academy Award–winning costume designer Gwen Wakeling. The delicate outfit, with its bolero-style top and Arabian pantaloons billowing around the legs, was constructed of chiffon and velvet; its special braided-cording trim was imported from France. The pink-and-gold satin shoes Eden wore were made in India.

Originally from Detroit, Wakeling began a career in silent films (The King of Kings, *1927*), quickly establishing a reputation as one of Hollywood's top fashion stylists. Studio head Darryl Zanuck personally appointed her the designer for many films at 20th Century Fox, including most of Shirley Temple's finest. Wakeling took home an Oscar in 1950 for Best Costume Design in a Color Motion Picture (Samson and Delilah). Although she worked primarily in films, Eden's Jeannie creation was one of her final projects before retiring. The costumes in Elvis Presley's Frankie and Johnny (1966) were Wakeling's last.

Gwen Wakeling's death in 1982 at the age of eighty-one went relatively unnoticed by the entertainment industry.

"This happened so often," Nelson said, "it became part of the day's work. Him wanting to have control of the show, or at least, control of his character. His motives were always self-serving."

Nelson's contract called for him to direct the pilot and the next ten episodes; he had an option to continue. About halfway through, he says, Eden's pregnancy was becoming more evident, and "she needed to be handled more carefully all the way around," he said. "My impatience grew out of Larry's behavior and her lack of behavior, and all of the elements squeezing us so tightly to get this done before she looked pregnant," Nelson explained. "That's the only excuse I have for any indiscretions I might have caused on a day-to-day basis."

With just a couple of shows left to direct, things came to a boiling point between Nelson and Hagman one afternoon on the soundstage. During the production of the episode "Djinn and Water," which costarred the veteran character actor J. Carrol Naish as Jeannie's great-grandfather, forces collided.

"J. Carrol Naish was this marvelous, seventy-eight-year-old actor, and they had a patch on his eye," Nelson said. "He was really not well. Yeah, I had to spend a little extra time with him. On closeups, sometimes it was line-for-line. He knew what was happening. He was such a professional, it bothered him a lot.

"The scene was up in the attic," Nelson added, "and as I recall, Jeannie was there and she left the scene and it was just J. Carrol and Larry. Then Larry started groaning and saying, 'God, this guy is old.' I think I did Larry's closeups first. Then we turn around and we're on J. Carrol. At one point, after he blew his lines a few times, Larry, in front of the crew, said, 'Jesus Christ! You call yourself a professional?' and all that. I grabbed him by the tie and literally dragged him out by Bronson Avenue and said, 'You son-of-a-bitch! I gotta talk to you!'

"We were down a couple of steps from the stage, but on the street and sidewalk," Nelson said. "I threw him against this wall. I said 'Never speak to an actor like that! If there's anything to be said, *I'll* say it, or I'm gonna tear your head off!'"

Unbeknownst to Nelson and Hagman, assistant director Herb Wallerstein had already run to the telephone and alerted Sidney Sheldon about the imminent skirmish. Sheldon dropped what he was doing and ran to the side of the soundstage looking for the two men, hoping to find a bloodless confrontation.

"I was just about to nail Larry when I hear 'No! Stop! Stop! No!' It was Sidney running toward us and he was waving his hands," Nelson said.

Dissolve now to a meeting in Sidney Sheldon's office days later. The producer and the director are trying to figure out a solution. "I told Sidney this," recalled Nelson. "I said, 'I'm looking into my crystal ball here. And I'm telling you. If this goes, it's going to be the most expensive series you've ever worked on, and the most troublesome, the most unhappy, and the most miserable.' "

Nelson outlined to Sheldon a possible solution. "I have a suggestion," Nelson told his boss. "Take it or leave it. You write a show where the bottle gets lost. Somebody throws it in the garbage can by accident and it goes down the street and falls off the truck near another actor."

Sheldon sat at his desk and shook his head at the notion of axing Hagman. "No, no," he said. "NBC loves Larry."

Somehow, cast and crew muddled through one more episode and wrapped for a few months. "After we finished that last show, I wasn't speaking to Larry unless I had to," Nelson admits. "During our period off, Sidney called me into his office and showed me a letter he had received. He said, 'I want you to read this.' It was from Florida, or wherever Larry was. It was one page. In essence, it said, 'Don't expect me back if Gene Nelson is associated with the show.'

"He was testing his power and he was willing to gamble," Nelson said, still with bitterness. "I ended up writing a letter to Hagman apologizing, attempting to appeal to his professional sense and asked if we could put this behind us. Still, I got fired and my option was not picked up. All during this, Bill Daily and Barbara Eden never came to my aid."

Bill Daily admits that the first string of shows was quite tense, but rather points the finger of blame at the director. "Gene Nelson was an asshole, uptight all the time," Daily says. "He was stoned all the time and Larry got him fired for a very good reason. I agreed. If I was bigger, I would have had him fired, but I wasn't that important on the show.

"Barbara, she rarely stood up for anyone," Daily further explains. "She just sat there. She's a lovely lady, but she never stood up for Larry when he complained about the scripts or any of that. He had to be the heavy all the time. When Larry did get in some really hot water, I think she did finally save his ass. He was gonna get fired and I think she stepped in somehow. But that was rare."

It was obvious to Sidney Sheldon that he would have to find just the right individual to direct his show. After he tried out a flood of very competent directors, two talented men floated to the surface—or survived—and became regulars with the production: Hal Cooper and Claudio Guzman.

Dreaming of
Jeannie

"Claudio was a genius," says Bill Daily. "He let Larry do his thing and he was able to handle Larry. Hal Cooper was just as brilliant, but Hal had everything planned out in his mind. Larry and I just wanted to do it like theater. He wanted to work it out and have them block it around us. We worked well like that."

Michael Ansara as the Blue Djinn and Barbara Eden as Jeannie.

The Animated Opening

Although he has gone unrecognized for his contribution to I Dream of Jeannie, *his artistry appears in every episode. The man's name is nowhere to be found in the show's credits.*

Let it be known: The opening sequence, which tells the cartoon story of the dancing Jeannie's uncorking, was the handiwork of the legendary animator and director Friz Freleng.

The late Isadore "Friz" Freleng was described by the L.A. Times *as "the blithe spirit who helped give life to a menagerie of such madcap merrymakers as Bugs Bunny, Daffy Duck, Sylvester and Tweety Bird . . . and became the personification of Yosemite Sam." Freleng, who died in 1995, was a primal force, a pioneer with few peers in the history of filmed animation.*

Freleng began his career drawing and animating in Kansas City, Missouri, and moved to Hollywood in 1927. He worked for Walt Disney for a couple of years before founding the Warner's animation studio as head artist in 1930 along with Rudolf Ising and Hugh Harman. Freleng's first Looney Tunes cartoon, "Sinkin' in the Bathtub," was produced the same year. One of the characters he introduced was a stuttering pig named Porky in the cartoon "I Haven't Got a Hat" (1935).

In 1937, Freleng moved over to Metro-Goldwyn-Mayer, but eventually he returned to Warner Bros., staying with Bugs, Porky, and the rest of the Looney gang until the early 1960s, when television minimized the need for theatrical

cartoons and the animation units at the big studios were downsized.

In 1963 Freleng, along with partner David H. DePatie, established DePatie-Freleng Enterprises; they began producing animation for television, and some feature films. Their greatest invention was the Pink Panther, originally used to introduce films featuring the bumbling Inspector Clouseau, portrayed by Peter Sellers. The Pink Panther took on a life of his own and became the star of a Saturday morning television show.

It was during Freleng's years in the "Pink" that he animated the opening of I Dream of Jeannie, producing the brief sequence at his DePatie-Freleng studios. For the second season of Jeannie, produced in color, DePatie-Freleng expanded the sequence to forty-five seconds and incorporated a space capsule and an astronaut. (It has been mistakenly reported over the years that the same studio created both Jeannie and Bewitched cartoon openings. The animated opening of Bewitched, however, was produced by Hanna-Barbera Studios, which, at the time, was in full swing with The Flintstones. An animated Samantha and Darrin Stephens even appear in one episode of the prehistoric prime-time show.)

Barbara Eden recently recalled Freleng's thoughtfulness following the birth of her son, Matthew, in 1965: "The man who drew the opening was so kind. He had the studio send over these wonderful pictures and cutouts of the Pink Panther and we decorated my son's room with the cartoons."

Multiple Oscar–winner Freleng won the only Academy Award bestowed upon Bugs Bunny crowning (you might say), a cartoon called "Knighty Knight Bugs." The animator was honored by the Motion Picture Screen Cartoonists' Guild, the British Film Institute, and the International Animated Film Society. One of Freleng's most talented contemporaries, fellow animator Chuck Jones, wrote: "No student of animation can safely ignore the wizardy of [Freleng's] cartoons—if he can stop laughing long enough to seriously study their beauty."

Dreaming of
Jeannie

OPPOSITE PAGE: *An actual hand-inked and -painted animation cel of Jeannie used in the title opening of* I Dream of Jeannie. *(The image of the bottle was laid in separately with this cel for display purposes.) In 1994, this cel sold for $1,500 at auction. (Courtesy of Howard Lowery Gallery.)*

3

The Jeannie Theme

✦

Sidney Sheldon's obvious choice for a theme song for his new show might have been Stephen Foster's "Jeanie with the Light Brown Hair" (more commonly referred to as "I Dream of Jeanie") which dates way back to the middle of the nineteenth century. But Sheldon didn't want anything too obvious for his bottle baby.

When you contemplate the various submissions for new themes that have survived in Sheldon's personal production files, it seems evident he toiled over the selection. Sheldon hand-wrote several versions of his own lyrics on a long yellow legal pad, scratching out and reworking. Eventually, he scrapped the notion of using his own lyrics. He decided to go with music composed by Richard Wess for the theme and pilot score.

The Dick Wess theme, a nice instrumental jazz waltz, was used for the first season, but his option was not picked up for the rest of the series. At the conclusion of the show's first season, many elements were on the brink of change.

For the second season Sheldon shifted to a new sound to go along with the expanded, full-color animated opening and title sequence in the second season. Again, Sheldon opted to buck the trend and utilize just a melody with no lyrics. At the time, having lyrics to accompany the themes played during sitcom openings was a popular way of introducing the story and creating an instant, audible key (for instance, lyrics were used for *Gilligan's Island, The Beverly Hillbillies, The Addams Family, Green Acres,* and *The Flintstones;* the list goes on).

The new theme, simply titled *Jeannie,* was written by Hugo Montenegro and Buddy Kaye. But an awkward situation occurred: The music was written by Montenegro, with accompanying lyrics by Buddy Kaye. Sheldon's decision to strike the lyrics sent Kaye's actual contribution into near oblivion. Almost no one has ever heard these lyrics (and unfortunately, they are too expensive to reprint here).

Under an agreement outlined in Sheldon's files, Buddy Kaye received screen credit for publicity purposes (and to mark his unused contribution), but he has never shared in performance royalties of the *Jeannie* theme. Those profits have always gone to Hugo Montenegro, sole composer of the bouncy tune.

Montenegro (1925–1981) was an accomplished and prolific composer, arranger, and orchestral conductor for both film and television, and of course he released several albums of his work. Montenegro mastered a big, romantic string sound, utilizing unusual instruments such as the electric violin and electric harmonica.

Barbara Eden holds up her own Jeannie T in 1996. (Photo by Steve Cox.)

Hugo Montenegro's years scoring the *Jeannie* episodes were among his busiest professionally. He combined his orchestra and chorus and recorded Ennio Morricone's theme from the Italian film *The Good, the Bad, and the Ugly.* The record shot to number 2 in the United States and England, selling well over a million copies.

*Stuffed deep in Sidney Sheldon's personal production files for
I Dream of Jeannie is a mysterious piece of hand-written sheet
music, which, if utilized, could have altered the whole feel of the
sitcom.*

*In 1964, while deciding on a theme song for his new television
show, Sheldon considered several submissions from a variety of
songwriters, even composing—and scrapping—lyrics of his
own. Finally, after making his choice, Sheldon had his secretary file all the compositions away. Most notable is one original
score in the stack—either overlooked or rejected—titled "Jeannie," words and
music by Gerry Goffin and Carole King.*

*Through her personal representative, pop music singer-songwriter Carole
King recently said she had no recollection of the piece . . . it was too long ago
and so far away.*

Some of Montenegro's best film work includes the score for Otto Preminger's
film *Hurry Sundown* (1967) and music in the Dean Martin "Matt Helm" films *The
Ambushers* (1968) and *The Wrecking Crew* (1969). Montenegro provided music for
Frank Sinatra's film *Lady in Cement* (1968), the Elvis Presley Western *Charro!* (1969),
and John Wayne's *The Undefeated* (1969).

Selected Discography of Hugo Montenegro

* *Original Music from* Man from U.N.C.L.E. (1966)
* *More Music from* Man from U.N.C.L.E. (1966)
* *Hang 'em High* (1968)
* *Moog Power* (1969)
* *The Best of Hugo Montenegro* (1980)
* *Plays for Lovers* (1981)

Several of Montenegro's LP albums have been digitally remastered and
released on compact disc.

4

The Bottle

✦

Much like Judy Garland's mystique-surrounded ruby slippers of Oz, the incandescent carafe recognized as the TV home of *Jeannie* totes with it an allure unlike any other television prop. What is it about this gleaming receptacle, an *objet de* pop art that commands from both casual television viewers and hardcore Hollywood preservationists? Susan Douglas, a writer and professor of media and American studies, goes so far as to label the bottle phallic: "It doesn't take a shrink to decipher why Jeannie's bottle was shaped the way it was . . ."

It's doubtful that notion ever came into play when Sidney Sheldon, or whoever, decided this unusual glass bottle would be the lodestone for the television series. After more than thirty years, no one is absolutely positive how this particular bottle came to be the chosen vessel, Jeannie's resting place. Take note, however: The bottle itself was part of an existing article of merchandise before it became a television prop.

Over the years, it had been assumed that Sidney Sheldon was the man who first saw potential in the decanter. Over those same years, credit for the bottle's discovery has also been given to personnel in the Screen Gems art department. In 1996, director Gene Nelson claimed it was *his* find:

"We were getting ready for the pilot. I happened to go into a liquor store and here this damned thing was, filled with some kind of liquor. I bought it, showed it to Sidney and he liked it. We took it to the prop department, who painted it with gold leaf, and we thought it was terrific."

Commonly known now as the "Jeannie bottle," it was actually a Jim Beam liquor decanter containing "Beam's Choice" scotch whiskey. Marketed exclusively in 1964 as one of many general-issue bottles from the two-hundred-year-old Kentucky distilling company, the green smoked-crystal decanter caught someone's eye and eventually wound up becoming part of a television show. There was no formal association between the Jim Beam Company and Sidney Sheldon Productions or Screen Gems.

In those days, Beam's decanters came in many different shapes, commemorating all sorts of things. The "Jeannie bottle" was one of 800 different styles produced by the distillery over decades. (Beam ceased production of special decanters in the early 1990s.) "The decanters were produced strictly as a means to market the company's bourbon," says Shirley Sumbles, administrator of the International Association of

TOP: *Larry Hagman clutching his first-season bottle for an early publicity portrait session.* LEFT: *Jim Beam Company distributed these special gift-box decanters labeled "Beam's Choice" and "Gilbey's." The stylized green smoked-crystal decanters contained Jim Beam scotch whiskey. It was these liquor decanters which were painted and used as "Jeannie bottle" props on the program. (Courtesy of Daniel Wachtenheim.)* OPPOSITE PAGE: *The original design blueprint for the Jim Beam liquor decanter, a k a the "Jeannie bottle." (Courtesy of Oscar Aviles and the T.C. Wheaton Company.)*

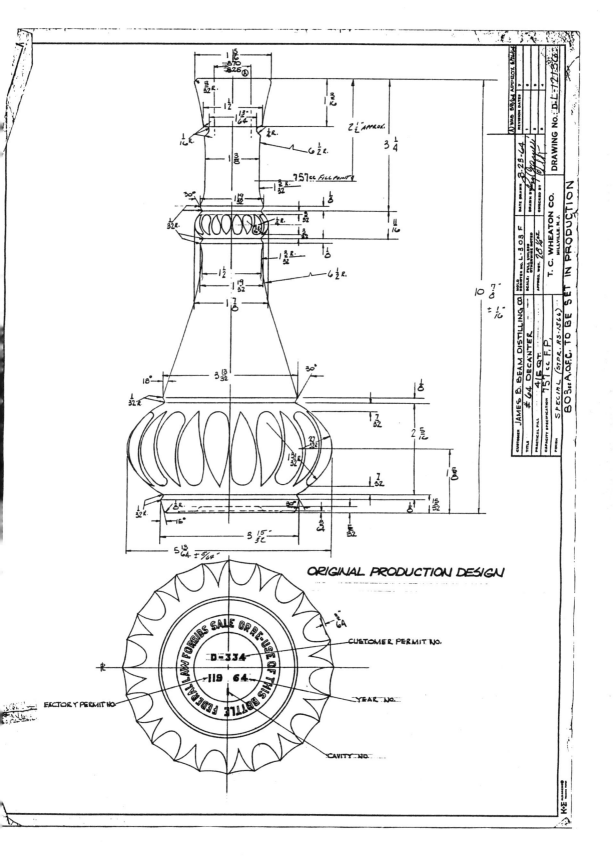

ORIGINAL PRODUCTION DESIGN

CUSTOMER PERMIT NO.

FEDERAL LAW FORBIDS SALE OR RE-USE OF THIS BOTTLE

D-334
119 64

FACTORY PERMIT NO.

YEAR NO.

CAVITY NO.

CUSTOMER JAMES B. BEAM DISTILLING CO.
TITLE # 64 DECANTER
PRACTICAL FILL 4/5 QT.
CAPACITY SPECIFICATION 757 cc F.P.
FINISH SPECIAL (SPEC. RS-/364)

MOLD REGISTER NO. L-303 F
SCALE: FULL UNLESS OTHERWISE NOTED
APPROX. WT. 28 4/2.

T. C. WHEATON CO.
MILLVILLE, N.J.

DATE DRAWN 8-25-64
DRAWN BY
CHECKED BY

DRAWING NO. DL-12136.

803 cc A.O.F.C. TO BE SET IN PRODUCTION

Vac 59/64 APPROX.
REVISIONS DATES

Who can forget Ferris Bueller's Day Off? The 1986 mega-hit motion picture starred Matthew Broderick as a cocky teen who cleverly cuts school and makes an adventure of his day off. Remember the scene in his bedroom where he gets jiggy with the I Dream of Jeannie theme?

Jim Beam Bottles and Specialties Clubs. "I get calls all the time from *I Dream of Jeannie* collectors looking for that decanter. To our collectors, glass bottles are not highly desired. Ceramic bottles are primarily what they collect."

The glass bottle itself was designed in 1964 by Jack Becker for the Wheaton Bottle Company. Becker, now retired, says he saw a similar cut-glass bottle on a visit to Germany; later, while working for Wheaton Bottle, he patterned a similar concept and had artist Ray Cramer put it in blueprint form on paper. Uncorked, the bottle stands eleven inches; with a cork it stands a little over fourteen inches. The bottle's topper and base feature an elliptical teardrop indentation design around them.

Artists at Screen Gems took the bottle, removed the round labels, and, for the first season only, painted a simple gold-leaf design on it. For the second season—which introduced the show in color—it was decided to make the prop a little flashier for the camera. Bob Purcell, an artist at Screen Gems' art department, redesigned the bottle and gave it an overall metallic or pearlescent purple sheen with assorted colors (turquoise, orange, brass, and pink) and intricate gilt highlighting. This "second season" design was retained throughout the rest of the program's run and is most recognized as the Jeannie bottle.

Thanks to extensive research, I'm able to offer answers to a few commonly asked questions about the Bottle.

How many bottles were used in the production of the show?

No one knows exactly; however, several members of the production have estimated that approximately six to eight bottles were painted and used in the series over the years. (Dick Albain, the show's special effects supervisor, used one bottle specifically for floating, smoking, and a variety of other special effects.)

Do any authentic bottles survive today?

Yes. Barbara Eden has a "second season" bottle which she took home when the show ended. (Believe it or not, Sidney Sheldon says he did not think to rescue one for himself when the show was canceled.) A couple of bottles were broken during production. A few bottles—first- and second-season versions—have surfaced over the years and been sold at auction; however, in some cases, questions have arisen regarding provenance and authenticity.

Was the same prop bottle used in the "reunion" movies?

No. An artist named John Moffitt was hired to paint a dozen Jim Beam bottles with a similar design. Utilizing a template, Moffitt applied great detail to these bottles, which are slightly darker in color than the originals. Close examination of the arches and other minute details reveal the distinctions.

What are the unpainted Jim Beam decanters worth?

Current collector's guides list the price as $25–$50 per bottle if the bottle is in good shape, with its original cork stopper. Many fans have been known to pay more than this for "naked" bottles. Check your local thrift shops, flea markets, and *Jeannie* websites for these gems. (Keep in mind that a similarly shaped blue crystal Jim Beam decanter *with a handle* was released as well, and in 1980, a red version—again with a handle— was marketed.)

Astoundingly, a few TV prop bottles have sold at auction, fetching some shockingly high bids. In 1995, a first-season bottle with the gold-leaf design sold through Odyssey Auctions in Hollywood; the fan whose wishes were granted took the bottle home after writing a check for $10,000. Later that year, a colorful second-season bottle, auctioned through Butterfield & Butterfield, went for $12,650. In 1998, a first-season bottle auctioned by Profiles in History fetched $15,000. These days, experts estimate

At Home with the Bottle

When Jeannie lounged in her one-room inner sanctum, somehow viewers weren't strangled by claustrophobia despite the fact that everyone knew these had been her cramped quarters for 2,000 years. Wouldn't you have loved to have the plans for the interior of Jeannie's bottle and build a luxurious bejeweled playpen or a fort of your own? Or, the ultimate, to own the actual set itself?

Larry Hagman took that opportunity.

The studio was disposing of the original interior bottle set (used in the first dozen episodes) in order to construct a more elaborate, dazzling interior; upon hearing this, Larry Hagman had the doomed fiberglass dome shipped to his residence in Rustic Canyon, Santa Monica, California.

"I put it in my backyard," says Hagman. "It made a wonderful sound chamber. Before we had boom boxes, we had just little portable radios or record players . . . remember records? It was wonderful to sit inside that thing and play music. It was like being inside a speaker."

For more than a year before the giant dome was eventually trashed, Hagman used the three-quarter enclosed coop as his own private sea of tranquillity, for meditation or whatever. Hagman and his friends had found a perfect refuge "to sit out there and have a party," he says. "Then some kids came around and they stepped through it and ruined it. They didn't do it intentionally, they were playing and jumping up and down. It was sitting out in the sun and getting pretty brittle and the kids stuck their feet through it in several places."

OPPOSITE PAGE: *Jeannie's mod, comfy, crystal home.*

that $20,000 is the benchmark for an original *Jeannie* bottle. The difficulty lies in positively authenticating such props.

Bill Miller, the CEO of the Odyssey Group, which owns the Odyssey auction house, says a few bottles popped up in the 1980s. "I was told that it was much like the discovery of the ruby red slippers," he says. "When they were going to do the TV special, a number of [bottles] were found in the prop department when they

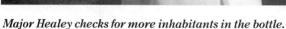

Major Healey checks for more inhabitants in the bottle.

were looking for a pattern to copy or duplicate."

What disturbs Miller, as well as many other dealers in Hollywood artifacts, is the number of obvious fakes that are being produced and passed off as original props from the television program. "The thing about props and costumes—unlike autographs, which are like DNA, with patterns which are always consistent—is that much of what makes the prop and costume market is faith. Unless Elvis walks up and hands you that jumpsuit, is it really his?"

Joseph Maddalena, president of Profiles in History, a Beverly Hills auction house, pointed out a detail of the rare, authentic first-season bottles. "These bottles have gold paint and an overlay," he says, "with a fine wash of mint green which mutes the gold. It's opaque, and it looks like that green translucent color. It's just enough of a painted overlay to get rid of the reflection on the gold leaf." (It's possible the Screen Gems art department applied the misty overlay not only to compensate for the strong lighting on the set, but also to provide an aged, worn appearance.)

According to Oscar Aviles, a New York schoolteacher and artist who became fascinated with the *Jeannie* prop, the first thing people do when they pick up one of the Jim Beam bottles is unplug the cork and sniff inside.

As a child watching the program in the 1960s, Aviles was so curious about the bottle's shape and design that he actually cut-and-pasted a homemade Jeannie bottle out of construction paper. Years later, he discovered a Jim Beam bottle while browsing through a antique shop. Eventually, he spent years researching the history of the vessel and setting his own hand to the bottles, perfecting the color and design schematic on replicas. "It took a little bit of mathematics to figure out the geometrics of the design to make it perfect," he says, referring to the intricately painted arches ("fourteen of them") around the bottle. With the help of Barbara Eden as well as others, Aviles has examined a few original bottles, noticing that even the props "weren't painted so precisely as to perfectly match each other," he says. "There are slight variations."

Aviles spent years experimenting, mixing enamel paints, testing the true colors on bottles in both sunlight and artificial light, attempting to replicate the prop for fun. It takes the artist many

Artist Oscar Aviles applies fine detail to a Jeannie bottle reproduction. (Photo by Steve Cox.)

While it's interesting to ponder the variety of great guest stars who popped in and out of I Dream of Jeannie, *it's even more fascinating to ponder the ones who didn't.*

An official NBC third-season sales and planning "press" book that was distributed to affiliates boasts the following names slated for guest appearances: Annette Funicello, Soupy Sales, and Willie Mays. The pamphlet goes on to reveal: "In addition, Mary Martin, Jerry Lewis, Kirk Douglas, Mickey Rooney, Desi Arnaz, Dick Shawn, and Caterina Valente all have told Sidney Sheldon that they plan to appear on Jeannie *during the upcoming season, subject to the successful working out of scheduling logistics."*

What happened?

hours of painstaking concentration to complete a replica Jeannie bottle. With photos and designs spread in front of him, he meticulously reproduces the fine detail, colors, and contours of the original. Impressed by the artist's handiwork, Larry Hagman commissioned a replica from Aviles for his own collection.

"I'm an artist, and really it's a beautiful bottle," Aviles says, "and I know it opens things up for fraud. I mean, anyone can replicate these things. Look at the little box used on *The Addams Family* for Thing. How does anyone know that the box someone may have is actually the box used on the program, or just made to look that way?

"People should be very careful about this," he warns. "I have seen bottles in auction catalogs which claim to be authentic, and I know that I painted it. I know my own work. I can tell. . . . There it is, mistakes and all. But I have never tried to pass off a bottle as an original. Larry Hagman purchased one from me and I have seen him with it and he always explains it is a replica. I am like a painter-for-hire. For the most part, if people are willing to pay what it costs for a good replica, I'm happy to do it, but what people do with them after I paint them up is up to them. It bothers me to see the fraud out there."

Aviles traced one bottle, for instance, back to a customer on the West Coast who ordered a replica. Years later, the collector turned around and sold the bottle to Planet Hollywood, where it is now on display—implying that it is an original prop used on the television show.

A Latin phrase applies here: Caveat emptor, "Let the buyer beware."

5

The NASA Files

✦

What we do in Jeannie *is what NASA is currently doing. We're not going to pile fantasy on fantasy. We'll stay with them, not go ahead of them. When they get to the moon, we'll go with them . . . if the series is still on.*

—Sidney Sheldon
January 27, 1966

idney Sheldon designed *I Dream of Jeannie* during an explosive phase of American space exploration. The United States National Aeronautics and Space Administration was in the throes of a race to touch the moon first and fulfill the late President Kennedy's mandate. All the while, Sheldon was manning a mission of his own in an attempt to land a genie on television and create one of television's most famous sitcom astronauts. The space program was enormously

Associate producer Sheldon Schrager (left), producer-director Claudio Guzman, an unidentified NASA official, and Sidney Sheldon (far right) take a firsthand look at aeronautical equipment while touring the Johnson Space Center in Houston. (Courtesy of NASA.)

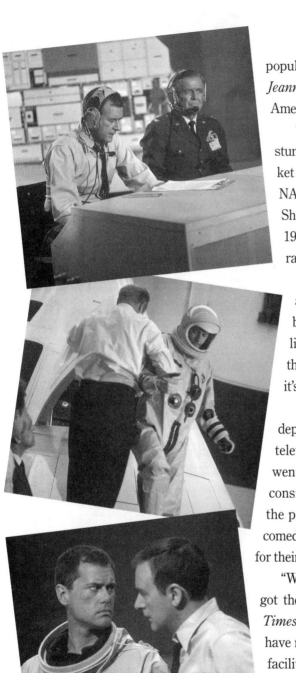

popular in America in the 1960s, and *I Dream of Jeannie* was the first television series to star America's rising new breed of heroes—astronauts.

That was why Sheldon had an astronaut stumble upon this genie's bottle—not a supermarket clerk or a postman or a car dealer, but one of NASA's best, Tony Nelson. "I just asked myself," Sheldon explained to *Showtime* magazine in 1966, "what kind of man would be most embarrassed by having a genie?

"Well, it might not make much difference to a man in an ordinary job, but it would make a big difference to a scientist, because a scientist likes to explain things in rational terms and if there's anything you can't explain scientifically, it's a genie."

Sheldon chose to avoid an antagonistic depiction of NASA and the U.S. Air Force in his television sitcom. From the beginning, Sheldon went through the proper channels; he acquired considerable cooperation from NASA, assuring the powers that be that this peculiar television comedy would actually prove to be a positive force for their cause.

"When NASA saw what we had in *Jeannie,* we got their full cooperation," Sheldon told the *L.A. Times* in 1966. "I know some of the military forces have refused to allow film companies to use their facilities because the stories involved tend to hurt their images. But we're not out to ridicule anyone. We merely use a service to play against a situation."

LEFT: *Shooting at the Northrop aeronautical facilities in Southern California, May 1965.*

Edwards Air Force Base, in southern California, provided full use of its NASA facilities to the *I Dream of Jeannie* production team. Sidney Sheldon personally took a "flight" in the *Gemini* simulator to share astronauts' experience in weightlessness. He even sampled the dehydrated food supplied to working astronauts. ("It was terrible," he said at the time. "I ate some fruit and couldn't tell what it was. It was almost apple, almost banana. It made me nauseous.")

Sidney Sheldon routinely sent scripts to NASA for suggestions, recommendations, and corrections in dialogue, protocol, and so forth. (Whether the scripts nauseated NASA officials is classified information.) During production, Sheldon maintained communication with Edward S. Barker, a "protocol officer" based in Houston, Texas, as well as Edward Orzechowski in NASA's Public Information Division at the Western operations office.

It was NASA's wish to demilitarize the television show, replacing military officers with NASA technicians and such. An official communication, dated May 4, 1966, that survives in Sidney Sheldon's production files states:

Barbara Eden and her husband, Michael Ansara, touring the Johnson Space Center in Houston during the series. (Courtesy of NASA.)

Looner Descent
Notes on an Alan Shepard Interview:
June 15, 1995, Pasadena, California

I caught up with astronaut Alan Shepard on a summer day. On May 5, 1961, Shepard became the first American to fly in space—a brief, monumental event that tripped America's thrusters in the famous space race with Russia to reach the moon. Just think of it: Shepard reached the moon himself during the Apollo 14 mission and drove a golf ball on the big ball of cheese for all to see.

Years later, back on earth, Shepard was handling massive crowds and signing copies of his book, Moon Shot. I nervously orbited the spaceman and when the time felt right I made a descent to ask him a few questions regarding I Dream of Jeannie—just what he wanted, I'm sure.

Cox: Do you remember meeting Sidney Sheldon back when he was making I Dream of Jeannie?

Shepard (instantly recognizing Sheldon's name): Yes. I remember the show vaguely.

Cox: Did you watch the show?

Shepard: Oh, I used to watch it now and again.

Cox: Outside of a genie, did the show accurately depict astronauts?

Shepard (laughs out loud): No, I don't think so.

Cox: Bill Daily said his character was patterned after you.

Shepard (looking disgusted): Who? Bill Dana?

Cox: No, no. Bill Daily. You know, Bob Newhart's neighbor. Major Healey on I Dream of Jeannie. Was he playing you on TV?

Shepard: I've never heard that. It may very well be. I had nothing to do with that TV show. I don't know who's giving you this information. I really don't know what the hell you're talking about.

Is it true astronaut Alan Shepard was the inspiration for a character on I Dream of Jeannie? *(Photo by Steve Cox.)*

I must have caught him off-guard with the question, or else he'd been pre-
pared with that answer for an awfully long time. Shepard had a glazed look in
his eyes, as if he was still in reentry.

One book-buyer approached and spoke to him of bravery. Shepard replied,
"A lot of people thought we were crazy in those days." A variety of people
swarmed. He was surprisingly patient with some really eerie fans. Gave the
thumbs-up sign and a big smile to a young male about to head to Pensacola to
earn his own wings. He signed very little space memorabilia, only books,
inscribing quickly on each: "A Shepd."

A wide-eyed kid just wanted to say hello to an honest-to-goodness man who
had been to the moon. With his right hand Shepard kept up signing as books
passed in front of him while extending his left hand for one of those awkward
but warm sideways hand grasps. "You gonna be an astronaut when you grow
up?" Shepard asked him.

"No," the kid answered flatly.

—Steve Cox

We wanted to assure you that we will appreciate as much authentic information about the manned space flight program as you can inject into the series. . . . We would like to see a decreasing emphasis on military roles. We try very hard to project the image of the program as a peaceful, scientific exploration of space. This is an important aspect of our international relations.

Walter E. Whitaker
Office of Public Affairs, NASA
Washington, D.C.

Several NASA operations and military affiliates around the country put out the welcome mat for Sheldon. Along with his associate producers, some cast members, and key production people, Sheldon toured the Northrop Corporation and Edwards Air Force Base, the Kennedy Space Center in Florida, and the Johnson Space Center in Houston, before and during production of the series. At Cape Kennedy, Sidney Sheldon and Claudio Guzman met several of the *Mercury VII* astronauts, part of the original team who pioneered the American space program. Sheldon recalls shaking hands with Alan Shepard and Gordon Cooper. And it was rumored that moonwalker Alan Shepard—known for his unusual personality and for being the first and only person to hit a golf ball on the moon—inspired the offbeat character Roger Healey. Actor Bill Daily confirms the rumor.

"I think you've heard the right story," Daily says, "but [Alan Shepard] probably doesn't really know because nobody wants to tell him. In the beginning, when I came in with my off-the-wall style, Sidney Sheldon didn't like it. But then he met Alan Shepard a few more times and the more he saw him, the more he thought I was right on the mark. It's true."

Bill Daily met Shepard once in the sixties: "I saw him down at the Commander's Palace in New Orleans at some big fund-raiser. He was sitting across from me and I told him the story and he didn't know what I was talking about."

Because the setting for *I Dream of Jeannie* was a NASA base at Cocoa Beach, any visit from the Hollywood folks to an actual NASA locale usually got them the red-carpet treatment and press coverage. Astronauts Walter M. Schirra and Frank Borman were asked to appear in an episode in 1969, but both declined.

Dreaming of
Jeannie

During the show's fifth season, when Tony Nelson finally weds Jeannie, some of the filming took place at Cape Kennedy and around the town. When a mock wedding took place at the Cocoa Beach City Hall with cast and crew, it attracted a great deal of attention. Also present were Florida's governor, various Air Force brass, representatives of the McDonnell-Douglas Corporation, and Cape Kennedy officials, as well as members of the city government.

During the years when the show was in full swing and NASA was shooting for the moon, Barbara Eden was the darling of Cape Kennedy. During one memorable event in Cocoa Beach in June 1969, the town celebrated "Barbara Eden Day" with enormous press coverage, special dinners honoring the star's presence, luncheons with the mayor, proclamations, the issuance of a key to the city, the whole shebang. This visit also prompted a photograph that appeared on page one in major newspapers across the nation. The press ate it up.

"Buzz Aldrin gave me this great big kiss," says Barbara Eden, "and it was on the front page of all the local papers. The press men kept saying, 'Barbara, give the moon man a kiss,' and so I gave him a nice kiss on the cheek. But he said, 'Aw, I can do better than that,' and he grabbed me and gave me that real kiss, a big kiss, and everybody cheered. You can tell from the pictures in the papers that I was really shocked."

OPPOSITE PAGE: *A publicity photo of Eden sitting in Colonel Chuck Yeager's office at Edwards Air Force Base.*

COL. CHUCK YEAGER

A Few Words from General Chuck Yeager

He's been called the greatest test pilot of 'em all. The man with the right stuff. He was the first man to fly faster than the speed of sound, a World War II fighting ace who thrust the art of flying into the supersonic era.

Although there is no mention of Larry Hagman or Barbara Eden in this daredevil's bestselling autobiography (*Yeager*, written with Leo Janos), maybe it's about time somebody revealed that this aviation legend appeared in an episode of I Dream of Jeannie. Strangely, Colonel Yeager did not receive screen credit for this sitcom fly-by. In 1997, General Yeager was gracious enough to reminisce about his rare television appearance.

How much involvement did you have in the Jeannie episode?

All we did is have Larry Hagman and Jeannie, or Barbara Eden, in my office and also we had Hagman simulating flying an F–106. I don't recall meeting Sidney Sheldon.

Was this out on an airfield?

If you want to call Edwards Air Force Base an airfield.

Why did you receive no screen credit for the appearance?

They only needed me for a few minutes. I didn't pay any attention to getting credit or not. As a military guy, you don't get paid for things like that. I didn't pay a hell of a lot of attention to the program at the time, but lately, people have come up to me because they saw the reruns.

At what point in your career was this television appearance?

I was the commandant of the astronaut school and we were training guys for space and were very busy and doing a hell of a lot of flying. The one episode that they shot at Edwards was shot around the school.

You've appeared in other things, haven't you?

I had more activity in The Right Stuff; I played the bartender all the way through it. And one of the Cannonball Run movies with Hal Needham.

We've found a photograph of you with Barbara Eden. . . .

I'll bet she's settin' on the edge of my desk. I remember that. Barbara is a neat gal. I remember we were just sitting there talking. Both her and Larry Hagman were very interested in airplanes and flying.

How was Larry Hagman's portrayal of a pilot?

Not bad, but that's just TV. We laugh about that. It's like the movie Top Gun. *Being in combat and having fought in a few wars, we say that guy would last about two seconds in a real war.*

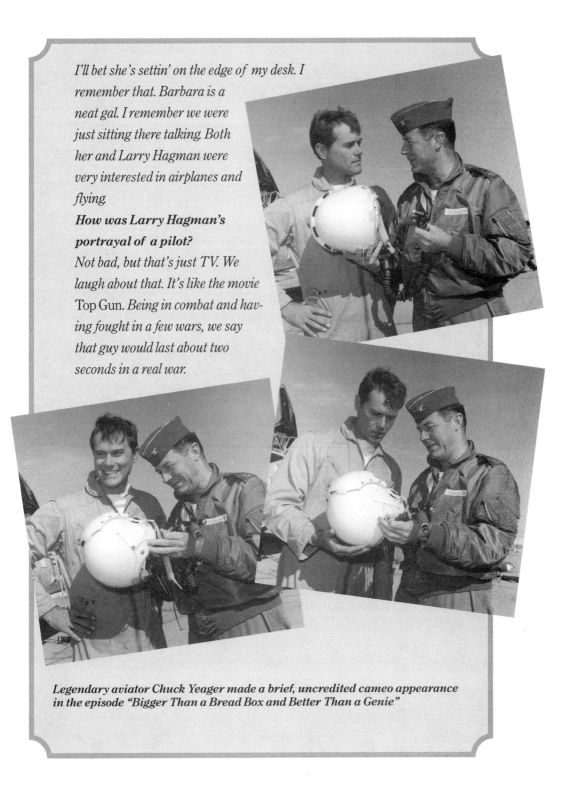

Legendary aviator Chuck Yeager made a brief, uncredited cameo appearance in the episode "Bigger Than a Bread Box and Better Than a Genie"

PHONOGRAPH

Solid State

4 SPEEDS

6

not All smoke
and mirrors

◆

As special effects go, the visuals orchestrated for *I Dream of Jeannie* were far from high-tech. There was no place in the budget for sophistication, and for this sitcom, it wasn't necessary to achieve grandiose effects that would astound an audience. Besides, a weekly program had no time for advanced film graphics and refined, intricate setups.

The most common special effect, used in every episode, was the freeze. It is not a technique commonly employed during everyday thespian chores in films or (especially) on television shows. But on the sets of *Jeannie* and *Bewitched*—as well as other shows such as *Topper* and *My Favorite Martian*—it was absolutely commonplace. The technique actually became routine for the *Jeannie* ensemble. However, to those guest stars who joined the cast for just one or two days of production, it could be a confounding process, not a simple task to grasp and perform effectively.

Rarely has it been mentioned, but Larry Hagman was a master on the

One of the nightmarish, gargantuan props.

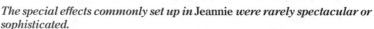

The special effects commonly set up in Jeannie *were rarely spectacular or sophisticated.*

show in more ways than one. Throughout his work on *Jeannie,* Hagman became quite adept at performing physical comedy; he executed some stunts so artfully, Buster Keaton would've been proud. Many of Hagman's pratfalls were prompted by freezes that resulted in his sudden stumblings into and over objects. There were times when Hagman had to flip backward over the side of a couch. To avoid wrenching his back or just landing improperly wasn't always easy to do, and required some rehearsal.

Just how *did* Jeannie pop in and out of a scene? How did visitors or objects appear and disappear suddenly? And how did Tony Nelson land in a foreign setting without warning? All this was accomplished quite easily. However, it took the cast a brief period to master "the freeze" and perform it with little or no effort—a feat to which they became accustomed.

Suppose Jeannie was to pop magically into the Nelson living room, right next to her master, while Tony and Roger are in the middle of a conversation. The director would call for action, and actors Larry Hagman and Bill Daily would begin their dialogue. When the director called for them to freeze, Hagman and Daily would pause, keeping as motionless as possible for a few seconds while Barbara Eden, who was ready just outside the shot, walked into the picture and stood between them. (Usually, the director would keep the camera rolling, and edit out Eden's walk-on in postproduction.) Once the director called for the freeze to end, Hagman and Daily would instantly react with a quick jerk of amazement at Jeannie's sudden intrusion. Get it?

There were times, however, when more elaborate costume changes were required or more individuals joined the scene during the freeze—say, when Jeannie popped in

Jeannie hides in a cup of java.

with some guests from ancient Baghdad. To do this, the director would call for a freeze, and it was up to the actor (and a crew member) to take note of his or her exact body position and placement on the set (occasionally marking the floor with masking tape). Then the actor would relax awaiting the change, after which filming resumed. When animals appeared suddenly in the shot, the director had to call for a freeze; stop filming; wait while the trainer led the elephant or horse onto the soundstage, steadied the animal, and positioned it; and then resume filming.

The freeze required precision and good mental note-taking on the part of the actors, director, and cameramen. Even today, it is not a task in which most actors are trained, because it is unique to "magic" productions. For instance, when a freeze was called, Larry Hagman might have been carrying his hat in his left hand, while holding Jeannie's bottle near his waist, in his right hand. *Also,* Major Healy might have been sitting on a chair, with his legs crossed and a cup of coffee in his right hand. At times, the precise action could be difficult to mark and re-create once filming began again later in the day. Continuity was all-important in filming *I Dream of Jeannie.*

The first season, filmed in black-and-white, featured a visual created by the special-effects veteran Dick Albain. It was up to Albain to create the traveling smoke emitted by Jeannie's bottle. For this effect, Albain used a small swatch of material soaked in salt-peter, which could be ignited to create billows of smoke. The swatch, called a smoke cloth, was attached to the end of an "invisible" wire (fishing line) with a little drill motor at the top of the wire to spin the line. A technician standing on a catwalk or a plank about ten-feet above the set would use a fishing-pole mechanism to move the smoke around the set. So, once the smoke cloth was ignited in the neck of Jeannie's bottle and pulled out by the wire, the drill motor would spin, creating a swirling cloud of smoke. The technician—hovering above, much like a puppeteer—moved the wire around the set to create the image of Jeannie's movement. Then . . . poof! A blast of black powder was ignited for Jeannie's appearance. (Albain also used carbon dioxide to create the blast of billowy smoke, but the residual smoke flakes often created more hassles.)

The second season—filmed in color—posed many challenges to Albain and his assistants. In 1966, *TV Guide* described Albain's new process for creating, for instance, the pink smoke that preceded Jeannie's transitions:

OPPOSITE PAGE: *Out on the veranda, Jeannie (actually her stand-in) catches some rays on a "floating" beach towel.*

I Dream of Jeannie contains some puzzling inconsistencies which, it seems, just slipped by. . . .

   ❋ If Jeannie was held captive in her bottle for two thousand years, how does she explain her relationships with famous personalities through the ages?

   ❋ If genies cannot be photographed (as Jeannie explained to her master), then how could her picture appear in the newspaper in the Laugh-In *episode ("The Biggest Star in Hollywood")?*

   ❋ Jeannie informs her master that she will forfeit her powers if she marries a mortal; so, when they are finally wed in the fifth season, how does she retain her magic?

   Is this not screwy, Master?

After many experiments, the special-effects men settled on a system of colored lights, dry ice, and steam to produce the desired cloud formations. Dry ice is placed in a five-gallon can on the floor; then steam or water is applied to the ice. The mixture creates smoke which billows upward. Colored lights are aimed up through the make-believe smoke. And mirrors placed around the area give the scene a perspective which seems to stretch off into infinity.

For some puffs of smoke, specially devised and filmed for Jeannie's entrances or exits, several different glorious colored lights (about 10,000 watts) were aimed simultaneously at the smoke to provide the palette sought by Albain.

Charles Ford, one of Albain's assistants in creating and implementing the effects on *Jeannie,* held an explosives license while working at Screen Gems. "Steam looks just like smoke on film," Ford says, "so we'd add smoke to the steam. Or we'd use a bee-pumper. We'd heat the beeswax with a little fire inside the pumper and blow out some smoke that way." Ford was, he says, often the guy on the other end of the fishing tackle, hovering above the set to move the floating teacup across the room. "Sometimes we actually used an ordinary fishing pole."

OPPOSITE PAGE: *Filming a scene with Barbara Eden's stand-in, Evelyn Moriarty (left), in which Eden also portrays Jeannie's brunette sister, Jeannie II.*

7

Sex and the Censors

♦

It is true: Jeannie was not supposed to expose her navel. But that didn't really cause as much uproar as the Cleavage Control and the Dialogue Censors who swooped down like network vultures.

Granted, to some degree there probably was cause for alarm. Barbara Eden's scenes in the pilot episode, when she wore nothing but one of Tony Nelson's clean white business shirts, were meant to grab attention. When she suddenly grabbed Tony, embraced him, and planted a nice kiss on his lips, it was noticed.

And then there was the eyebrow-raising fact that Tony Nelson and this luscious woman were actually cohabiting. Oh, my God! *TV Guide* noted: "*I Dream of Jeannie* is actually one of the most daring shows on TV. It is the only show, for example, in which an attractive unmarried girl has the free run of a bachelor's apartment." (The situation was reversed the very next television

"The star of this blithering comedy is Barbara Eden's cleavage. Latter gets excellent support from the other points of interest on her fine anatomy, all of which are perused throughout the half hour by a remarkably dedicated camera." —Variety *(review), September 22, 1965.*

season, when NBC's popular sitcom *The Ghost and Mrs. Muir* was broadcast. It was about an unmarried wraith of a sea captain who had full run of an attractive widow's home.)

The show business trade paper, *Variety,* put it quite bluntly in a review of the pilot for *Jeannie* (September 22, 1965):

> Miss Eden plays a genie who materializes out of an Egyptian jug to badger an astronaut, making his commanding officers believe he's off his rocker, driving his fiancée up the walls, and teasing viewers with dirty minds with innuendo (like at the climax of the initialer, what was happening behind the camera in astro boy's bedroom?).

Producer/creator Sidney Sheldon was the man at the helm of the show, the man who answered to the network's Office of Standards and Practices. "From what I've seen, Rowan and Martin and the Smothers Brothers get away with more than other shows," Sheldon shot back during the show's prime-time run. "I had a brief encounter with the NBC censors on 'Jeannie' when they objected to an unmarried couple living together. I won my point when I proved to them it was done tastefully and not a leering display of sex. The memos were long at first, but finally fizzled away."

Sheldon was referring to a flurry that started the moment his dialogue was ripped out of the typewriter. When the pilot episode was mimeographed and a copy of the script began making the rounds with executives at NBC, Sidney Sheldon waited in his office with a pen in his hand . . . readying himself. All writers, producers, and executive producers have learned to be prepared to defend their content. (In *Jeannie*'s case, Sheldon was all of them in one, and up to bat.)

Then it arrived. The NBC Broadcast Standards Department issued an edict, dated November 17, 1964, emphasizing certain details:

✷ NBC cautioned against any "open-mouth kissing between Tony and Melissa [Tony's fiancée]."

✷ NBC warned it would be "unacceptable in Scene #56 to see Jeannie's smoke disappearing under Tony's bedroom door."

✷ And this beaut: ". . . avoid the seductive and sexual innuendos when Jeannie

OPPOSITE PAGE: ***Nearly revealing her navel, Jeannie was sure to conjure a few fans.***

says, 'And I am going to please thee very much.' It would be helpful here to have her mention some specific pleasures such as jewels or money . . ."

A few steamy details were rewritten in the pilot script. For instance, notice Jeannie doesn't actually remain in Tony's bedroom when he retires for the night at the close of the show. Imagination played a huge part in the pilot. It was more alluring and effective than any nudity could have possibly achieved. Sidney Sheldon knew how to heighten curiosity, at least in his male viewers. But he had not yet begun to fight.

In an April 5, 1965, response to Thomas McAvity, the general program executive of NBC-TV, Sheldon offered a well-composed explanation of the direction *I Dream of Jeannie* would take. In part, he wrote:

In your letter, you refer to Jeannie as a pest. We should both have such a pest in our lives. At no time does Jeannie maliciously do anything to annoy or hurt Tony. Her actions are based on the reactions of any woman in love.

He continued:

In terms of the emotional relationship between Tony and Jeannie, I agree that there should be a strong attraction on Tony's part, and this will be expanded. Tony is laboring under the problem that no astronaut can have a girl genie and still remain in the space program, but in each script we will have a warm

Jeannie Gem

If *you'll look closely, you'll notice, near Barbara Eden's bosom, a sparkling teardrop jewel on a herringbone chain, just dripping seductively into her cleavage. It's there in nearly every episode of* I Dream of Jeannie. *The exquisite diamond, one of her favorites, she says, was a gift from her then husband, Michael Ansara. The "lucky" gem actually became part of her costume, you might say. Eden even wore it in the* Jeannie *TV reunion movies in the 1980s. Pragmatically, it made things simple for Eden. Having only one necklace made it easy to remember which piece of jewelry she had worn when she was matching shots from the previous scene or the previous day.*

Similarly, Elizabeth Montgomery wore a favorite diamond-studded heart pendant throughout most episodes of Bewitched. *Early on in the series, after she misplaced the original diamond heart, a nervous Montgomery had two pavé rhinestone replicas made, which she wore in some scenes as well. When* Bewitched *ended, the star presented the two rhinestone replicas to friends who worked on the show.*

79

Dreaming of **Jeannie**

moment between the two of them, instead of Tony constantly telling her to get out. By doing this, we can deepen the emotional content of the stories so that the audience is more strongly rooting for Tony and Jeannie to get together.*

Barbara Eden has always taken exception to those who assume Jeannie was too flirtatious and provocative. "I never approached Jeannie in that way," Eden says. "I always thought of her as a tomboy. She wasn't a vamp."

In March 1995, Larry Hagman and Barbara Eden reunited for a nostalgic look back at *Jeannie* on a segment of NBC's early-morning *Today* show. Pert host Katie Couric asked Larry Hagman to answer the three most commonly asked questions about the show.

Hagman offered, "One . . . yes, Barbara Eden is as beautiful off screen as she is on. And two . . . yes, she does have a navel. And three," he said, laughing, "no, I never did."

*Reprinted courtesy of USC Cinema-Television Library, Special Collections.

Camp Runamuck:
Jackie Cooper and TV's
Transcendental Entities

Talk about a Hollywood career to brag about.

In silent films he was one of the original *Our Gang* kiddies, with a Depression cap and pouty eyes; he was a cute blond kid vying for Miss Crabtree's affections in a handful of Hal Roach shorts. A brilliant child actor, he could cry with the best of them. At age eight, he costarred in the original film version of *The Champ* (1931) with Wallace Beery; in his adolescence, he dated teenaged Judy Garland right around her days of *Oz*. Young Jackie Cooper became one of the most successful, most recognized child stars in the movie heavens. His hand and foot prints at Grauman's Chinese Theatre in Hollywood have, quite literally, cemented his place in Tinseltown.

During the 1960s, all grown up, this Rascal traded his pair of suspendered shorts for fine business attire. Jackie Cooper was a fortysomething actor-

Actor and Screen Gems executive Jackie Cooper visits the star of one of his network programs.

turned-executive at Screen Gems, respectably elevated on the totem pole at this television division of Columbia Pictures. Cooper's TV experience was a plus: He had already starred in a couple of successful series, *The People's Choice* (1955–58, NBC) and *Hennessey* (1959–62, CBS). Under his management as vice president in charge of Screen Gems Television for several years, more than a handful of successful programs were produced—some eventually acquiring status as pop-culture lodestones of the sixties: *The Days of Our Lives, The Wackiest Ship in the Army, Gidget, Camp Runamuck, Hazel, The Farmer's Daughter, The Flintstones, The Donna Reed Show, The Flying Nun, Bewitched,* and *I Dream of Jeannie.*

His job was much like a traffic cop's. "We were trying to build the company," says Cooper, reflecting in a rare interview about his career. "We had six or seven shows. Screen Gems was hungry. By the time I was in my third year, I think we had some ten shows on the air."

Cooper set up office at Screen Gems on the Columbia lot, for the most part. His responsibilities varied, depending on what needs sprang from the growing stable of ongoing productions and pilots. "I believe it was me who talked Sidney Sheldon into Larry Hagman," Cooper says.

Dreaming of
Jeannie

He spent energy searching for talent, seeking material, helping producers look for writers, keeping the machine well-oiled and moving forward effectively. Today, Cooper quickly points out, however, that his direct, day-to-day involvement with Screen Gems productions was strictly limited, and that this hands-off stance was necessary in order to keep him out of the hair of producers and other supporting personnel. Creatively, it was the right move, as Cooper understood, especially since he was a seasoned actor and well into a directing career of his own. He knew the spectrum.

"Sometimes, I'd give a criticism, if it was welcomed," he says, "and sometimes when it wasn't. Once in a while the producers would try to go too far, like with *The Monkees.* I knew the network wouldn't agree and I'd tell them, 'You just can't do that.'"

Handling *Bewitched* was tricky. Much like a character on the show, Cooper suddenly found himself somewhere he didn't want to be. He was forced into the ring with the show's star, Elizabeth Montgomery, who had delivered the first punch. The star's sudden demands in the beginning nearly got her replaced and the entire tense situation quickly tested Cooper's abilities as an executive.

As he described it in his outspoken, best-selling autobiography, *Please Don't Shoot My Dog* (1981), Jackie Cooper had a showdown with the witch. Montgomery was not

Oh, come on, you knew there would be a Brady nexus somewhere. Here's the story: In the I Dream of Jeannie *episode entitled "My Master, the Doctor" (1966), a young, pre-Marcia Maureen McCormick appears briefly as a hospital patient known as Susan, whom Jeannie showers with affection. Fast forward exactly three decades. Barbara Eden makes a surprise appearance as Jeannie in the final scene of the acid-trip flick* A Very Brady Sequel *(1996) and delivers the last line of the movie.*

even the first choice to play Samantha: Tammy Grimes was seriously considered, but went on to have a show named for her instead. Nevertheless, Montgomery discussed her wishes over dinner with Cooper and tried to stare him down with those big blue eyes of hers ("which could become steely blue when she wanted"); she made it known that without the implementation of her wishes—such as approval on directors and approval on all casting—she would not participate in the series. "It's too bad," she told him stubbornly, "it would have been a nice little show." She was quitting.

Cooper explained:

I had our casting office begin looking for another girl, of the same general age and type as Liz Montgomery. I didn't tell the press (neither did Liz, I was happy to see), but there was a leak. In those days all the columnists in town had people in every studio on their payroll, at so much a tip, and there was no such thing as a secret. . . .

We found three girls we felt were good enough to test for the part of Samantha. We arranged for the tests to be filmed three days hence, and we hired a director, selected the scene, arranged for sets and costumes, brought in Dick York (already set for the costar) to work with the girls.

All things considered, Cooper felt this was simply a power struggle and decided it would be better to replace Montgomery than acquiesce to her list of ultimatums. One day before the tests, the matter was resolved—an action initiated by a seemingly calm Montgomery. It is not known whether she was aware of the plans in progress to retest actresses, but the retests were called off, and once again *Bewitched* starred Elizabeth Montgomery. (It's too bad tests were not made; in retrospect, the footage would be fascinating.) Cooper had won the fight and "kept everybody happy" in the end. That's what his job entailed. Moreover, when Montgomery hung up her broomstick and walked away, 250-some episodes later, she was a very wealthy woman with part ownership of the show and a healthy syndication deal in hand.

Cooper and Screen Gems stars on a press junket in Mexico, 1968. (Courtesy of Kasey Rogers.)

Cooper, now seventy-seven with graying hair and a penchant for race horses and blissful retirement, regards his association with Sidney Sheldon's *Jeannie,* and the production as a whole, as "efficient and enjoyable." Might he be holding back?

"Without sounding like I'm knocking any of the other Screen Gems shows, *Jeannie* was one of the most pleasant, professional experiences for me," he says. "I think the whole [*Jeannie*] company was happy, everybody cooperated, and everybody was realistic. Those shows didn't look like the cheapest shows in town. We wanted the energy out of these people and we wanted everybody to look good and we didn't want to work them to death. *Jeannie* was not *ER,* but it was very commercial, entertaining material, and show business, even today, needs that. There is that audience out there.

"Barbara Eden was an angel," he says without hesitation. "She was a woman and a half, without being a Marilyn Monroe, short fuse or anything. She was pretty, she was professional, intelligent. Still is all those things. She was learned and still listened. She had wonderful qualities."

Larry Hagman wasn't as timid with the bosses. At the height of the Vietnam War, the outspoken Hagman took several opportunities to publicly denounce our country's military involvement. Screen Gems officials warned him to keep his mouth shut—

especially since he was portraying a major in the U.S. Air Force on television. Of course, that mandate from the blue suits was just what Hagman needed to blow his top the next time he collided with a reporter. According to Hagman, Screen Gems even requested that he entertain the troops in Vietnam as some sort of restitution for his candor in the press. The actor declined.

In an in-depth 1980 *Playboy* interview, Hagman reiterated his position: "Even the press was not fond of my belief that the war was a criminal act and that those responsible should be put in jail. A lot of them thought I was crazy and, in fact, many journalists I knew personally would not print what I said because they liked me. I knew I might be damaging a product I was trying to sell, but frankly, I thought it was less important than killing our own children, servicemen, and a lot of others for no reason I could comprehend."

Despite the fact that Hagman had loud quarrels with Screen Gems officials and some of their decisions through the years, Cooper insists he was "a good boy" who did not need chiding. "He was an unusual guy, but he was never late for work and he knew his lines. Once in a while he'd have some objection. 'Do we *have* to do this? Do we *have* to do that?' And I'd say, 'Larry, do we *have* to pay you?' and he'd laugh."

Going into Cooper's seventh year at Screen Gems—with a few years left in his contract—all the laughs halted as matters became quite serious in the organization. Up until this time, Cooper had been considered quite an asset to the company, bringing in most of the shows *under* budget, saving vast amounts of money. Now, however, he made a select few in other Screen Gems divisions very nervous.

"We knew how to spend the money and we weren't stealing it—we were putting it into the shows. But there was a guy in New York who had had enough," Cooper reveals. "It was too hard for him to steal. I caught him."

Actually, a whole array of questions was pushed to the surface by Cooper. Folks began to sweat. Further, Cooper prompted some of the company's actors to seek financial accounting for their own series, which put the entire company in question, as well as one particular executive (as of this printing, the man is still alive).

In the end, Cooper left Screen Gems amicably, with a handsome buyout on his contract. Read into that what you wish, but rest assured, Cooper was quite content when he left the organization, and some executives were extremely relieved by the parting.

And yes, he did work in this town again. So this is the tale of a slice in the life of Jackie Cooper . . . another seven-year day in Hollywood.

THREE BRAVE HEARTS...
ADVENTURING IN A WONDER WORLD!

ADVENTURE OF
THE MASKED MEN!

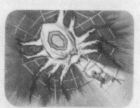

ADVENTURE OF
THE WONDERFUL WEB!

ADVENTURE OF
THE ALL-SEEING EYE!

Alexander
KORDA
presents

THE THIEF OF BAGDAD

In Magic Technicolor

with CONRAD VEIDT · SABU · JUNE DUPREZ

John Justin · Rex Ingram · Mary Morris

9

Geniealogy

The legend of Aladdin, his fateful rubbing of a magic lamp, and the powerful genie who emerges, has thrilled generation after generation. According to Funk and Wagnall's *Standard Dictionary of Folklore, Mythology and Legend* (1984), the tale originated from a learned young woman named Scheherazade, the wife of an Arabian king. Through the centuries, her "Arabian Nights" stories have been widely translated: From Arabic into French by Antoine Galland in 1704–17, and into English by John Payne, and also Sir Richard Burton in the nineteenth century. Andrew Lang, a respected English writer and editor, provided a translation for children to enjoy.

The ancient folklore was probably not even intended for children. The genie in the lamp has become a part of fairy tales, permeating every culture since it first arose eons ago. The adventures of Aladdin—originally a story about the son of a poor tailor who extricates a genie and a magic ring—have provided a lush and varied backdrop for film, television, and video since the advent of these media. For decades, the tale has been twisted and tweaked by Hollywood in more than a few adaptations—even including a pornographic version, *Bi Dream of Jeannie* . . . but let's not get into that.

Fred MacMurray stumbles upon a genie (Gene Sheldon) in **Where Do We Go from Here?**

In tracing the supernatural being of Arabian folklore through its countless variations, you find an array of multifaceted genies, male and female, black and white, short and tall, young and old, fat and skinny—and yes, straight and gay (oh, you'll know).

The compilation herein is by no means a complete gathering of every film and television presentation involving a genie, but the following checklist will offer a nice range of genies, or *jinnis,* if you wish.

Motion Picture Genies

✳ *The Thief of Bagdad* (1924) Starring Douglas Fairbanks, Julanne Johnston, Anna May Wong, Sojin, Snitz Edwards, Charles Belcher. "An imaginative silent film with awesome sets by William Cameron Menzies." Directed by Raoul Walsh.

❋ *The Thief of Bagdad* (1940) Starring Tim Whelan, Michael Powell, Sabu, John Justin, June Duprez, Conrad Veidt, Rex Ingram, Mary Morris. Oscar-winning Technicolor photography in this British-made version. Sabu finds a bottle on the beach and unleashes an untrustworthy genie (wearing an orange diaper). Rex Ingram, a tall, beefy black actor with a booming voice, plays the ill-tempered genie in this definitive adaptation of the Arabian Nights tale. This multiple Academy Award–winner earned statuettes for special effects, color cinematography, and color art direction—the most Oscars awarded to a picture in 1940.

❋ *Where Do We Go from Here?* (1945) Starring Fred MacMurray, June Haver, Joan Leslie, Anthony Quinn, Carlos Ramirez, Otto Preminger. Actor Gene Sheldon stars as the bearded genie in this silly musical comedy about MacMurray's journey's through American history. Includes an Ira Gershwin–Kurt Weill score. Directed by Gregory Ratoff.

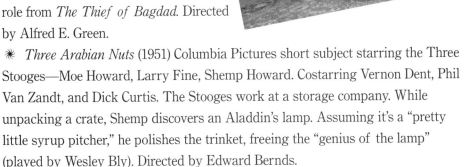

❋ *A Thousand and One Nights* (1945) Starring Cornel Wilde, Evelyn Keyes, Phil Silvers, Adele Jergens, Dusty Anderson, Dennis Hoey. Colorful production has Rex Ingram re-creating his genie role from *The Thief of Bagdad.* Directed by Alfred E. Green.

❋ *Three Arabian Nuts* (1951) Columbia Pictures short subject starring the Three Stooges—Moe Howard, Larry Fine, Shemp Howard. Costarring Vernon Dent, Phil Van Zandt, and Dick Curtis. The Stooges work at a storage company. While unpacking a crate, Shemp discovers an Aladdin's lamp. Assuming it's a "pretty little syrup pitcher," he polishes the trinket, freeing the "genius of the lamp" (played by Wesley Bly). Directed by Edward Bernds.

The Three Stooges unleash a genie (Wesley Bly) and use their third wish to conjure women and money in the Columbia short subject Three Arabian Nuts (1951).

✳ *Aladdin and His Lamp* (1952) Starring Patricia Medina, Richard Erdman, John Sands, Noreen Nash. One reviewer called it "poppycock, based on the juvenile fable, that will bore even the least discriminating children."

✳ *Bowery to Bagdad* (1955) The Bowery Boys are at it again in this, one of forty-eight comedies they made between 1946 and 1958. Horace Debussy "Sach" Jones (Huntz Hall) buys a lamp in a New York secondhand store and gets involved with the Mob, which is after the lamp. The genie (Eric Blore) refuses to grant any wishes to the mobsters, who have stolen the lamp. He sends the Bowery Boys back to Bagdad, where they are confronted by the Caliph, who claims rightful ownership of the lamp. Costarring Leo Gorcey, Bernard Gorcey, Bennie Bartlett, David Condon, Joan Shawlee, Robert Bice, Rick Vallin, Jean Willes, Charlie Lung. Veteran comedy director Edward Bernds noted this was his favorite Bowery Boys film to steer. "I loved the idea of the unconventional genie, the bored, snooty Englishman," Bernds said. "I think that was my idea. I had worked with Eric Blore some years before when I was a sound man on a picture called *She Couldn't Take It* [1935] with Joan

The Bowery Boys got into hot water in Iraq when Sach (Huntz Hall) becomes master to an English genie (Eric Blore) in Bowery to Bagdad *(1955).*

Bennett, George Raft, and Billie Burke. Eric Blore played an egotistical ham actor—a house guest, and I thought he was just great. In *Bowery to Bagdad,* the concept was that this genie was a cynical, insulting, supercilious limey," Bernds explained. "When he finds out he is now working for Sach and Slip, he says something sarcastic like 'Oh, *this* is going to be jolly.' I loved the idea and how it worked out."

✳ *The 7th Voyage of Sinbad* (1958) Starring Kerwin Mathews, Kathryn Grant, Richard Eyer, Torin Thatcher. An adventure-fantasy pitting Sinbad against a magician (Thatcher) who has miniaturized a princess. Richard Eyer as the genie. Visual

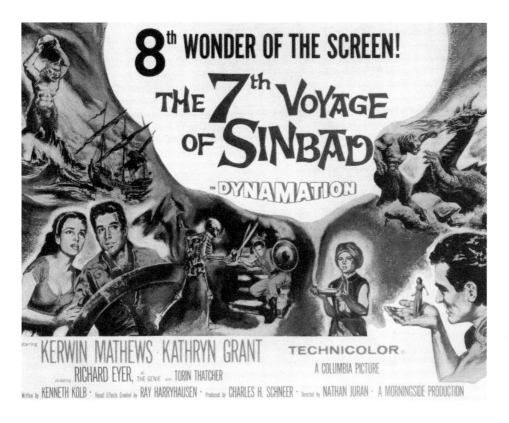

effects by Ray Harryhausen, including a memorable duel with a skeleton. Directed by Nathan Juran.

✳ *The Boy and the Pirates* (1960) Starring Charles Herbert, Susan Gordon, Murvyn Vye, Paul Guilfoyle. A children's adventure about a boy who is magically transported to the days of pirates and the high seas. Directed by Bert I. Gordon.

✳ *The Wizard of Baghdad* (1960) Starring Dick Shawn, Diane Baker, Barry Coe, John Van Dreelen, Robert F. Simon, Vaughn Taylor. Dick Shawn is a lazy genie who is worried about losing his power. A lazy movie, filmed in CinemaScope.

✳ *The Thief of Bagdad* (1961) Starring Steve Reeves, Giorgia Moll, Arturo Dominici, Edy Vessel. Directed by Arthur Lubin; filmed in CinemaScope.

✳ *The Wonders of Aladdin* (1961) Donald O'Connor stars in this children's fantasy. Costarring Noelle Adam, Vittorio De Sica, Aldo Fabrizi. Directed by Henry Levin; filmed in CinemaScope.

✳ *The Brass Bottle* (Universal; 1964) Burl Ives is Fakrash Alamash, a stout green djinn eager to assist his new master, Harold Ventemore (Tony Randall). Randall, in

*Dick Shawn is a genie
who has lost his powers
in the film* The Wizard
of Baghdad.

one of his early film roles, unfortunately underplays the comedy. A Felix Unger type of delivery might have been funnier. Come to think of it, Don Knotts would have been a better casting choice than Randall.

The film's special effects shine, especially at Fakrash's entrances and exits. One interesting visual has the overstuffed genie disappear by falling into a pool of water with no splash, only silent absorption. Based on the novel by F. Anstey, the film costars Barbara Eden, Edward Andrews, Kamala Devi, Richard Erdman, Kathie Browne, Ann Doran, Parley Baer, and Herb Vigran. Directed by Harry Keller. Critic Clive Hirschhorn calls it "a tale to appeal to the young at heart, if not the downright childish . . . a simple-minded story."

✳ *A Thousand and One Nights* (1968) Starring Jeff Cooper, Raf Vallone, Luciana Paluzzi, Perla Christal, Reuben Rojo. A tongue-in-cheek Spanish version of the Arabian Nights fantasy with all the familiar tapestry: flying carpet, genie, sinister vizier, etc. Directed by Joe Lacy.

✳ *The Thief of Bagdad* (1978) Starring Roddy McDowall, Peter Ustinov, Kabir Bedi, Frank Finlay, Marina Vlady. Directed by Clive Donner.

✳ *Priceless Beauty* (1988) Italian film starring Christopher Lambert, Diane Lane, Francesco Quinn, J. C. Quinn, Claudia Ohana, Monica Scattini, Joaquin D'Almeida. Former rock star feels guilty over the death of his brother. He finds a magic lamp in the ocean, and the beautiful genie inside tries to rebuild his confidence and ability to love. Directed by Charles Finch.

✳ *Miracle Beach* (1992) An obvious and liberal rip-off of *I Dream of Jeannie*— with many borrowed elements, right down to the purple bottle. This sophomoric sex comedy, however, is certainly more risqué. Starring Ami Dolenz, Dean Cameron, Felicity Waterman, Alexis Arquette, Brian Perry, Martin Mull, Vincent Schiavelli, Allen Garfield, Pat Morita. Dolenz stars as Jeannie, sent from the heavens to earth on a "goodwill mission." A downtrodden beachcomber finds a bottle and takes it into the bathroom. He rubs the bottle—but nothing happens. While he is standing at the urinal, the genie appears. Eventually, Jeannie falls in love with her master. Very few special effects, but plenty of nudity. In an early career gig, actor Dean Cain (TV's *Superman* in the '90s) is a volleyball player on the beach.

✳ *Kazaam* (1996) With the genie played by basketball star Shaquille O'Neal. Film critic Gene Siskel put it succinctly in his review on TV's *CBS This Morning:* "*Kazaam* is not magical at all. I think everyone will just remember it as part of

[Shaquille O'Neal's] basketball deal after this picture is long gone, including Shaq himself. . . . This is a bad film in every single way imaginable. I'll count the ways. . . . *Kazaam* wastes the congeniality and genuine charisma of Shaquille O'Neal in a positively boring story about a little boy who really needs a father figure. The film's first problem: it makes Shaq out to be a mean genie when we know he's a fun-loving guy. The next problem: the kid. He's obnoxious. . . . The story of *Kazaam* is dreadfully boring with the kid and the genie constantly exchanging tiresome, in-your-face insult humor."

Animated Genies

❋ *Aladdin and His Wonderful Lamp* (1939) Starring Popeye the Sailor, this enormously successful Max Fleischer Technicolor two-reeler has the spinach-chomping sailor releasing a genie from a little golden lamp. The genie, which appears in the form of blue smoke topped with a fez, laughs a lot, but ends up an insignificant character in the 22-minute featurette.

❋ *A-Lad-In His Lamp* (Warner Bros. Looney Tunes; 1948) Bugs Bunny (voice of Mel Blanc) digs a new rabbit hole, unearthing an Aladdin's lamp with a genie nicknamed Smokey (voice of Jim Backus). They fly to Bagdad via "Hare Plane." Bugs drops in on the Royal Palace of Caliph Hassan Pheffer and asks the caliph, "What's up, Beaver puss?" The chase is on, but every time Bugs summons the genie for help, the genie is busy taking a bath. Directed by Robert McKimson.

95

Dreaming of **Jeannie**

❋ *Ali Baba Bunny* (Warner Bros. Merrie Melodies; 1957) "Hassan Chop!" Bugs Bunny and Daffy Duck make a wrong turn while headin' to Pismo Beach. They end up in ancient Bagdad and discover an Arabian treasure cave filled with jewels, coins, and other riches. Hassan, the ogre guard, bursts in on a gluttonous Daffy looting the cave. Bugs remains cool and pretends to be a genie of

Interview with a Genie

Actress Billie Hayes has exercised her thespian abilities in a range of roles throughout her career—from Mammy Yokum in the Broadway and film renditions of Li'l Abner to the wildly wicked Witchiepoo on TV's H. R. Pufnstuf. In the popular Sid and Marty Krofft Saturday morning musical fantasy Lidsville,

she was a resourceful genie named Weenie—a sympathetic force who occasionally bumbled magical incantations.

Where did Weenie the Genie come from . . . a lamp? A bottle?

I really don't know. I'm not sure it was ever known how she materialized in the beginning. I know there was a magic ring involved.

I always thought Weenie the Geenie was written as sort of asexual; even the costume is ambiguous. How did you approach it?

I don't know what the situation was. Middle of the road, I guess. The story line never approached anything romantic or like that. Actually that particular role was intended for Billy Barty. There was a health problem involved at the time and he had to step out of the show before they

Billie Hayes and Sid Krofft in 1997. (Courtesy of Tim Neeley.)

started production. . . . Finally they thought of me. At first the director, Tony Charmoli, had never thought about it—you know, from Witchiepoo to Weenie Genie? I'm little, but not that little. Hense the name Weenie, I guess.

Was this genie difficult to play at all?

To me, it was like a piece of cake. Compared to Witchiepoo, it was a snap. The makeup wasn't extensive and my costume wasn't heavy. We had a few songs to do in the shows. I enjoyed Pufnstuf *far better because of the creative process involved. We did one segment on* Lidsville *where Witchiepoo meets Hoo Doo. I loved that one. It was nuts.*

Did you enjoy working with your costars on Lidsville?

I knew Charlie [Nelson Reilly] from some summer stock things years ago and when we did Lidsville *we got along beautifully. I always thought he was so funny. Butch Patrick was very nice to work with. And I had worked with a lot of little people on* Pufnstuf *the show and then we did the movie. It was sort of like a family. A lot of the same little people worked on both shows. Some called them midgets, but I think "little people" is preferred. But I just fell in love with them. They gave me a lot to think about. I have a tremendous admiration for little people.*

Dreaming of
Jeannie

the lamp to distract Hassan. Bugs is helpless when Daffy "desecrates the spirit of the lamp" and a real genie appears to punish Daffy. Directed by Chuck Jones.

❋ *1001 Arabian Nights* (1959) Feature film starring the nearsighted elder Mr. Magoo. Jim Backus is the voice of Uncle Abdul Azziz Magoo in this musical adaptation of the ancient tales of the Arabian Nights. Costarring the voices of Kathryn Grant (as Princess Yasminda), Dwayne Hickman (as Magoo's nephew, Aladdin), Hans Conried (as the Wicked Wazir), Herschel Bernardi (as the Jinni of the Lamp), Daws Butler (as Omar the rug maker), and Alan Reed (as the Sultan). Columbia Pictures release. Screenplay by Czenzi Ormonde. Produced by Stephen Busustow. Directed by Jack Kinney.

❋ *Shazzaan!* (CBS-TV; 1967—1969) Saturday morning animated action-adventure show about an all-powerful sixty-foot genie named Shazzaan (voice of Barney Phillips). The show's opening narrative explains it all: "Inside a cave, off the coast of Maine, Chuck and Nancy find a mysterious chest containing the halves of a strange ring. When joined, the ring forms the word Shazzan! With this magical

TOP LEFT: *The animated superhero genie Shazzan. (Courtesy of Hanna-Barbera Productions, Inc.)* TOP RIGHT: *Mr. Magoo (voice of Jim Backus) discovers the Jinni of the Lamp (voice of Herschel Bernardi) in the animated feature* 1001 Arabian Nights *(1959).* BOTTOM RIGHT: *Jim Backus and Kathryn Grant Crosby record the voices of Mr. Magoo and Princess Yasminda for the animated motion picture* 1001 Arabian Nights.

JEANNIE

PROD.#64
"JEANNIE"
Hanna-Barbera Prod. 3/15/73

BABU
(close-up size)

"JEANNIE"
PROD.#64
Hanna-Barbera Prod. 3/9/73

command, they are transported back to the fabled land of the Arabian Nights. . . ." Here Nancy and Chuck (voices of Janet Waldo and Jerry Dexter) meet their genie, who also presents them with Kaboobi, a magical flying camel (vocals by Don Messick). Shazzan serves them whenever they call, but cannot return them home until they deliver the ring to its rightful owner. Each half-hour program is divided into two separate adventures. Produced by Hanna-Barbera Studios.

✳ *Jeannie* (CBS-TV; September 1973–August 1975) This Saturday morning animated adaptation of *I Dream of Jeannie* was produced by Hanna-Barbera in connection with Screen Gems Television. While surfing at a California beach, teenager Corry Anders (voice of Mark Hamill—yes, of *Star Wars*) discovers a bottle exposed in the sand and removes the stopper. Imprisoned in the bottle are not one, but two ancient entities: Jeannie (voice of Julie McWhirter) and her bubble-brained apprentice, Babu (voice of Joe Besser). This shapely female genie activates her

Veteran comedian Joe Besser was the voice of Jeannie's bumbling sidekick, Babu. The rotund cartoon genie conjured his powers with the inimitable phrase "Yapple Dapple!"

A Little Off Kiel

Actor Richard Keil—quite literally, one of the giants of the business—is probably most recognized for his menacing portrayal of the steel-toothed Jaws in the James Bond flicks The Spy Who Loved Me *(1977) and* Moonraker *(1979). Before the Bond movies, Kiel made his mark in television during the 1960s with memorable guest appearances on* Honey West, The Twilight Zone, The Barbary Coast, The Wild Wild West, Gilligan's Island,

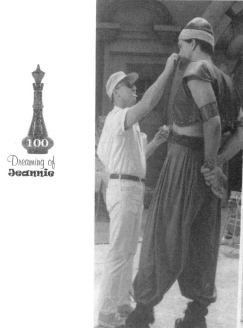

The Monkees, *and, yes,* I Dream of Jeannie, *on which he portrayed Ali, a violent man from Jeannie's past.*

Kiel worked in one of the first episodes, shot while Barbara Eden was "quite a bit pregnant," recalls the seven-foot-plus actor. Kiel's most vivid recollection of I Dream of Jeannie *stems not from any occurrence that took place during filming, but from a little incident afterward.*

"My uncle had come out to California with his wife and kids and they wanted to visit a studio," Kiel says. "I wasn't working right at that time, but I called and spoke to Larry Hagman and asked about bringing them out to the studio. I was friendly enough with him to be able to do that.

"He said, 'Yeah, come on out . . . we're not actually filming, we've got one day of pickup scenes for several shows and we'll be rehearsing, so we're not in costume.'"

Kiel thought he'd impress his kin, drive them through the studio gates, escort them around an actual movie and television studio, maybe take some snapshots.

"I remember my uncle and everybody was there and we watched Larry Hagman and Barbara Eden working," he says, "and they were rehearsing just in slacks and sweaters and things. At the right time, I introduced them all. My aunt, bless her heart, says in front of everybody, 'When are we gonna meet some stars?'"

OPPOSITE PAGE: **Actor Richard Kiel gets prepared for his role and clowns on the set with Barbara Eden in May 1965. Notice the drapes of material on Eden's costume, concealing her six-month pregnancy.**

101

Dreaming of
Jeannie

magic with a swish or a snap of her long red ponytail, while Babu commands power (usually with disastrous results) by crying out "Yapple Dapple!" Only sixteen episodes of this half-hour show were produced. Additional voice talent: Bob Hastings, Ginny Tyler, Janet Waldo, John Stephenson, Hal Smith, Sherry Jackson, Vic Perrin. Some of the characters from this animated *Jeannie* also appeared in *The New Scooby-Doo Movies* in 1973 ("Scooby-Doo Meets Jeannie") as well as Hanna-Barbera's Saturday morning show *Scooby Doo's All Star Laff-A-Lympics* (1977–1978). Babu, on the team "The Scooby Doobys," competes for the gold against other cartoon characters in Hanna-Barbera's stable.

✳ *DuckTales: The Movie—Treasure of the Lost Lamp* (1990) Featuring the voices of Alan Young, June Foray, Christopher Lloyd, Chuck McCann, Russi Taylor, and others. The genie is voiced by Rip Taylor. Critic Leonard Maltin comments: "Disney's premier 'Movietoon' feature falls somewhere between traditional studio standards and Saturday morning gruel. Story centers on an archeological trek for a genie's lamp that can, among other things, make ice cream fall from the sky, pitting Uncle Scrooge McDuck against the evil Merlock." Rated G.

✴ *Aladdin* (1992) Disney's animated feature bottled the bursting talent of Robin Williams as the voice of the big blue genie. This enchanting film turned to pure gold in movie theaters, conjuring up more than $500 million. The character of Aladdin was drawn to resemble actor Tom Cruise, and the film's art and style are lavish—for both the big screen and small. The film took home Academy Awards for Best Score and Best Original Song.

　　TV Guide described *Aladdin* perfectly when the film debuted on cable television in 1995: "The three-star film follows a resourceful 'street rat' named Aladdin (voiced by both Scott Weinger and Brad Kane) who flies by the seat of his harem pants when it comes to his day-to-day survival in a mythical kingdom. A whole new world opens up to the innovative urchin when he unwittingly becomes an Arabian knight in shining armor to the feisty Princess Jasmine (voice of Linda Larkin), and gains possession of a magical lamp. . . . Provides a perfect showcase for Disney's superlative animation, the outstanding soundtrack by Alan Menken, Howard Ashman, and Tim Rice, and Williams's comic 'genie-us' (complete with hilarious imitations and his trademark off-the-cuff humor)." Two successful direct-to-video sequels followed: *The Return of Jafar* (1994) with voice artist Dan Castellaneta (voice of Homer Simpson) stepping in as voice of the blue genie. For *Aladdin and the King of Thieves* (1996), Robin Williams was coaxed to return and provide the genie's vocal schtick.

Dreaming of
Jeannie

Television Genies

✴ *The Twilight Zone* (Episode: "I Dream of Genie"; original broadcast, March 21, 1963; CBS-TV) George P. Handley (played by Howard Morris) purchases a tarnished Arabian lamp, shines it, and discovers a genie (Jack Albertson) who grants one, carefully pondered wish. When Handley realizes that love, wealth, and power would be unsatisfying, he decides upon the ultimate—to become a genie himself. Host Rod Serling concludes: "George P. Handley, a most ordinary man whom life treated without deference, honor or success, but a man wise enough to decide on a most extraordinary wish that makes him the contented, permanent master of his own altruistic Twilight Zone."

A maquette of the spastic genie from Disney's hit animated feature film Aladdin. *The three-dimensional maquette, or statue, is used as a visual guide by the animators when drawing the character. (Photo by Steve Cox.)*

✳ *Lost in Space* (Episode: "The Thief of Outer Space"; original broadcast, November 9, 1966; CBS-TV) Guest star Ted Cassidy (Lurch on TV's *The Addams Family*) portrays a genie enslaved to a futuristic Arab chieftain know as the Thief of Outer Space. Will Robinson, Penny, and Dr. Smith are cornered by The Thief and his genie—a titan who appears in a puff of smoke by the magic of a powerful ring. The Thief is not interested in acquiring riches or causing harm to the Robinsons, but searches for a map to locate his lovely Princess, who was stolen from him 200 years ago by an evil vizier. In the end, the genie thinks Dr. Smith (dressed as a vizier) is his former master, and Dr. Smith sics the genie on The Thief.

✳ *Magic Mongo* (Installments on *The Krofft Supershow,* ABC-TV, 1977–1978) These fifteen-minute episodes appeared as a serial on the second season of Sid and

Marty Krofft's Saturday morning *Supershow* involved a silly genie named Mongo (Lennie Weinrib) who is discovered by three friends (Helaine Lembeck, Robin Dearden, and Paul Hinckley). Somewhat like TV's *Three's Company*—add a genie and subtract the sex—these brief segments involved inept Mongo performing magic and ruining whatever situation was at hand. To exercise his powers Mongo tweaked his ears and rippled his tongue.

❋ *Lidsville* (ABC-TV; 1971–1973) Sid and Marty Krofft's Saturday morning fantasy show starring Charles Nelson Reilly (as Hoo Doo, the evil magician) and Billie Hayes (as Weenie the Genie). Costarring teen actor Butch Patrick (of *The Munsters* fame) as

Ted Cassidy as a genie in Lost in Space.

Dreaming of
Jeannie

Mark, a curious kid who falls into a magician's enormous top hat and detours in a wacked-out land inhabited by giant hat characters.

❋ *Sigmund and the Sea Monsters* (NBC-TV; 1973–1975) Sigmund Ooz, an ostracized leafy-green sea creature with giant rolling eyes, befriends two kids (Johnny Whitaker,

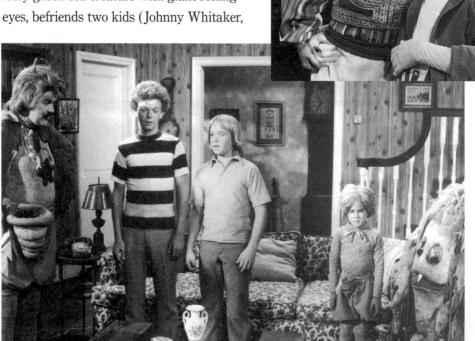

Scott Kolden) who protect him from a menacing clan of sea monsters. Sigmund (voice of Walker Edmiston; enacted by Billy Barty) is aided in the show's second season by Sheldon the Sea Genie (Rip Taylor). Saturday morning sitcom with laugh track; produced by Sid and Marty Krofft.

✳ *Just Our Luck* (situation comedy, ABC-TV, September 1983–December 1983) A genie named Shabu—in the form of a hip black man—is disgusted at becoming a sevant to a young television reporter, Keith Barrow (played by Richard Gilliland). Shabu (played by T. K. Carter) conjures up lots of surprises on the show including some interesting cameos, like Roy Orbison and Wink Martindale. Unfortunately, his magic didn't work against *The A-Team,* the show's competition on another network. Poof! *Just Our Luck* vanished in a matter of weeks.

✳ *Pee-wee's Playhouse* (CBS-TV; 1986–1991) One of Pee-wee's visiting pals to pop into the Playhouse was in the form of a genie—a disembodied, turban-topped talking head named Jambi. Always a jokester, Jambi swiveled his head and worked his magic much to Pee-wee's rapture; he granted wishes if Pee-wee chanted along with him ("mecca-lecka-hi, mecca-hiney-ho"). Occasionally tacked up on the open doors of the jewel-encrusted box which encased Jambi was a small pinup photo of Barbara Eden. (Jambi was played by actor John Paragon.)

✳ *You Wish* (ABC-TV situation comedy: premiered September 1997) Extremely short-lived sitcom produced by the Disney Company about a single mother (Harley Jane Kozak) who unfurls a purple rug and discovers a genie (John Ales) who has been rolled up in the carpet for 2,000 years as punishment. The outrageous, incorrigible genie is in search of a modern master in order to remain free. Actor Jerry Van Dyke joined the cast as the genie's equally powerful grandfather.

OPPOSITE RIGHT: *Actress Billie Hayes is the androgynous Weenie the Genie and Charles Nelson Reilly is the evil magician Hoo Doo in Sid & Marty Krofft's* Lidsville *(1971–73).* OPPOSITE LEFT: *Sheldon the Sea Genie (Rip Taylor, left) assists the kids and Sigmund the sea monster. (Courtesy of Johnny Whitaker.)* ABOVE: *Jambi from the wildly successful* Pee-wee's Playhouse. *(Courtesy of Paul Reubens/Michael McLean & Associates.)*

Say the Secret Word: "Clicker"

The legendary Groucho Marx was lured out of retirement to go before the TV cameras for a rare sitcom cameo on I Dream of Jeannie. It was Marx's neighbor Sidney Sheldon who coaxed him. According to the show's special effects designer, Dick Albain, the comedian preferred not to be paid in cash for his brief appearance, "because he didn't want to pay taxes on it."

As compensation, Sidney Sheldon's office arranged to have Albain install a state-of-the-art RCA color television in Groucho's home. Albain went to Groucho's, discussed placement, and removed a closet door and customized a complete console for the elaborate television system (which also included stereophonic speakers and a phonograph table). "Groucho even had an electric bed that went up and down, the whole bit," Albain recalls.

Upon completion, a proud Albain invited Marx to come in the room to test out the equipment. Groucho entered and seemed impressed with the setup. He said, "Hey, that's a good picture. Give me the clicker."

"There is no clicker," Albain said.

"What do you mean there's no clicker?" Groucho asked.

"There is no remote with this."

Groucho asked if a remote (a rare luxury in those days) could be installed. Albain attempted to explain that he was not authorized to order extra parts. "That's the way it came from the factory," he said.

"Then get it out of here."

Albain talked his way out of the comedian's house, assuming the problem would rest in the hands of the Screen Gems offices. After all, he wasn't about to destroy his own handiwork just hours after construction.

Two days later, Seymour Friedman, head of production for Jeannie, called Albain on the phone and frantically pleaded for him to return to the comedian's home. "Dick . . . you gotta get back over to Groucho's house and pick up that television," Friedman said. "If you don't get out there soon, he's gonna leave *the damned thing in the front lawn. He's not kidding. Go get it. The son of a bitch is giving us a hard time!"*

Albain removed the television unit, took it home, and returned to the studio the next day and purchased the set for himself.

The incomparable Groucho Marx makes a rare sitcom appearance in 1969. Groucho made the cameo as a favor to his friend and Beverly Hills neighbor Sidney Sheldon.

10

No "Laugh-In" Matter

✦

"Gee, *knee?"*

That's right, we said "knee." In the puritanical United States as recently as the early twentieth century, the feminine knee was largely considered so "private" that it was unfit for public presentation. In the days when "real ladies" wore bloomers to the beach, a glimpse of any woman's naked kneecap was considered scandalous indeed.

But Mack Sennett, Hollywood's pioneering comedy filmmaker, helped abolish such Victorian values when he introduced his "Bathing Beauties" to the big screen in the midteens. None of his gals wore bloomers. All of them showed bare knees. And the word "cheesecake" acquired a whole new meaning for most male Americans.

As the century progressed, bathing suits shrank and grew skimpier and skimpier, both on-screen and off. The general disrobing of the American female culminated with the introduction of the bikini in the early 1960s. Never had so much been seen by so many.

In keeping with then-contemporary trends, Barbara Eden's Jeannie costume did show plenty of midriff. What it didn't expose was her navel, and

Mystery Bojangles

Bob Palmer, a veteran film and TV publicist who worked for
Screen Gems during the sixties, vividly recalls the Sammy Davis,
Jr., episode:

Sidney Sheldon had some very good friends who appeared on the
show as a favor. I remember Sammy Davis did a show, and he brought
his dad and his uncle and his entourage, and he was great. He had
this enormous energy, and he was very gregarious. He just
brought a lot of energy to the set. I liked him instantly, and we hit
it off beautifully. I wasn't camped on the set; I would come and go. I'd
been on the set in the morning and everything was fine. We'd taken pictures.

Sammy had done his usual
self-deprecation. Like, when
I said, "Okay, we've finished
with black-and-white, now
let's do some color," Sammy
said, "All right, are you gonna
start with the racial stuff?"
He'd always do a racial put-
on or setups for a laugh.

But when I came back in
the afternoon, you could cut
the tension with a knife. I
said, "What's happened?"
Evidently Sammy was ready
to walk. Something had really

gotten him mad. It turned out to be Larry, and to this day, I'm not sure what it
was. Sammy is a really easygoing guy, but Larry must've said something. I was
told that Barbara got Sammy into her dressing room, closed the door, and really
had a talk with him. And when he came out, he said, "Okay, I'll stick around, let's
finish the job." So Barbara smoothed things over.

Larry was weird. He'd say things that weren't too appropriate, you know? I
think he's a very intelligent man, very bright, but very outspoken. He was wonderful on the show and I think he's one of the most talented guys in the business,
and one of the least appreciated actors around. If you ever saw him in a picture
called *The Group*, in a dramatic role . . . He was brilliant.

*Sammy Davis, Jr.'s anticipated guest spot on the show was personally orchestrated by
Sidney Sheldon, an admirer of the entertainer.*

A tongue-in-cheek episode with cast members from the popular TV show Laugh-In.

that's what provided *Laugh-In* producers George Schlatter and Ed Friendly what might be called the Idea of a Lifetime.

In the late 1960s, Schlatter and Friendly hatched a promotion in which *Laugh-In* stars Dan Rowan and Dick Martin would appear on *I Dream of Jeannie,* while Barbara Eden, in turn, would perform in costume on Rowan and Martin's program and expose, for the first time anywhere, Jeannie's navel. As the *Laugh-In* producers envisioned it, both NBC comedy programs would air on the same evening, thus packing a considerable cross-promotional whallop. But network censor Herminio Traviesas—later to achieve immortality for his run-ins with writers and producers of *Saturday Night Live*—nixed the navel. Sidney Sheldon concurred.

Reflecting on the episode, Sheldon points out that there really was never any great "Jeannie navel controversy" at all, despite the fact that the trivial topic surfaces often in

Entertainment Weekly's pun-filled July 30, 1993, issue listed the editor's choices (all subjective, of course) for the "Greatest Shows on Earth . . . from Get Smart to Gunsmoke—See How They Rerun." Naturally, no one wound up happy with this opinionated compilation—except the Mary Tyler Moore fanatics who found her at the top of the list. Ranking 101 classic programs in order of timelessness, nostalgia value, and television significance, the periodical placed I Dream of Jeannie at Number 35. Although Jeannie trailed behind shows like The Odd Couple, Perry Mason, and The Partridge Family, it led Green Acres, Columbo, and Sanford and Son. Finishing last: Cannon. Go figure.

Dreaming of
Jeannie

interviews to this day. "The *Laugh-In* script called for the shot to open on a closeup of Jeannie's navel, and I didn't think it was in the best of taste, and I said no." Although there was an exchange of cameos with stars of the programs, the navel never slipped out.

"I've been fighting this until it's a joke around the set," Eden told *L.A. Herald-Examiner* columnist Morton Moss back in 1969. "It's the demarcation line. They told me it had something to do with the television code. . . . 'Laugh-In' has shown navels. They paint flowers around them. Does that make any difference? Maybe the navel gets lost in the flowers. But it's all ridiculous. On TV, I've worn dresses cut low on the sides and hips and with décolletage. Nobody has objected. What's there about a navel?"

Apparently plenty, for *Jeannie* viewers never got so much as a glimpse of Eden's forbidden belly button. And this in spite of the fact that several bikini-clad actresses had appeared on the sitcom during the course of its network run. Sidney Sheldon apparently felt that much of the character's mystique would be lost once viewers discovered whether Jeannie had an innie or an outie. Sheldon's no-nonsense no-navel edict effectively killed the idea.

But even her esteemed boss's opinion didn't change Barbara Eden's attitude about the controversy. "People come up to me," Eden told the *Herald-Examiner* at the time, "and ask me, 'Have you really got one?' I answer, 'Yes, you can see it for five cents.'" Eden added that because of inflation, her agent had urged her to "raise the fee to a dime."

OPPOSITE PAGE: *For Art's Sake: NBC artist Art Trugman stylized and applied much of the body painting on* Laugh-In, *with no navel restrictions, he said.*

Void Where Prohibited

TV contests were a big thing in the sixties. How many remember the highly rated birth of Pebbles Flintstone? (Sorry, no prizes awarded here.) To promote the arrival of Fred and Wilma's "chip off the ol' rock," in 1963 Screen Gems sponsored a competition whereby the person who correctly guessed the little cartoon tyke's birth weight could claim a trip around the world. (The winner was a butcher from Florida. He guessed 6 pounds, 12 ounces.) Batman and The Beverly Hillbillies *also sponsored giveaways, the latter promoting a televised walk-on appearance with Granny and Uncle Jed.*

I Dream of Jeannie also pulled out all the stops with a contest to perk sweeps week ratings.

In an unprecedented four-part cliffhanger, which aired in January and February 1968, Jeannie was accidentally locked in a safe that was to be shot to the moon by NASA. In special promos aired during the "miniseries," viewers were asked to guess the safe's combination; the

Jeannie helps out with some sponsor advertising in this rare promotional photo.

winner would receive a trip around the world. *(The answer, by the way, was 4-9-7.)*

Another promotion kicked off the celebration of the hundredth episode of I Dream of Jeannie *to air. The hoopla involved the Jeannie World Sweepstakes, which ran the very next season during a two-parter titled "The Case of My Vanishing Master." The promotion was introduced on television with specially filmed spots. One segment had Barbara Eden, dressed as Jeannie, spinning a large globe.*

"Hello! I am Jeannie," she said, "and I cannot find my master. On what island in the Mediterranean can Major Nelson be? Send your guess on a post-card, here . . ."

Jeannie blinked and a giant postcard with the mailing address appeared on the screen. The first correct entry drawn would win "a jet tourist [translation: coach] trip for two around the world." These crafty contests worked, drawing some respectable numbers. A Screen Gems memo dated February 25, 1969, found in Sidney Sheldon's production files, informed the producer that the recent Jeannie contest prompted more than a million homes to watch and received approximately 225,000 entries.

A third contest promotion spanned a full month, late in 1969. Promos aired during the episodes broadcast on December 2, 9, 16, and 23; a winner was announced on the December 30 show. A twenty-second spot was filmed for the event, this one with the camera's eye discovering Jeannie on her knees, searching for pearls.

"Hello," she said, looking up. "I broke the string of pearls my master gave me as a wedding gift. Before I blink them back, will you help me guess how many remain on the string?" Another tourist trip for two, aimed at jetting around the world, was dangled in front of viewers. Employees and their fami-lies of Screen Gems, NBC, RCA, and their subsidiaries were not eligible, of course. And . . . void where prohibited.

Dreaming of
Jeannie

master of the Game: About Sidney Sheldon

I had no intention of going into television. We looked down on television. People in television were in because they couldn't make it in pictures. That was the philosophy.

Before he was born, Sidney Sheldon's mother, Natalie, was quietly given a prophecy by a fortune-teller. She was told her son would be "world famous" one day.

"That is a true story," he says.

It's doubtful the fortune-teller predicted that fifty years later, Natalie herself would be standing on a set at a major Hollywood studio, preparing to film an appearance on her son's popular network television show. Yes, Sidney Sheldon's mother, a little old lady who sold dresses in Chicago, actually made her prime-time TV debut on *I Dream of Jeannie.* Her famous son stood behind the camera in the dark, watched the scene being filmed and grinned with pride.

Sidney Sheldon, writer, director, and bestselling author, in recent years.

Perhaps the best word to describe *Jeannie* creator Sidney Sheldon is "prolific." His lengthy career has included directing and writing assignments for motion pictures, television, the Broadway stage, and, most important, the publishing industry. Through it all, Sheldon has created an empire of his own, proving to be something of an industry himself, cranking out novels that routinely top the *New York Times* bestseller list. The versatile genius is regarded today as one of the most commercially successful novelists in American history.

Although his name should be cemented in the minds of those players in every communications medium he's conquered over the decades, still people jumble the identity. No, it's not Sidney Shore. Or Sheldon Leonard. Or Leonard Sidney. It's Sidney Sheldon. After all, that Gypsy said he'd be famous—she didn't say it would be perfect.

Sidney Sheldon was born in Chicago on February 11, 1917. Because his father was a contractor and a salesman who traveled frequently, young Sidney attended eight different elementary schools throughout the United States. "I think that made me shy and somewhat of a loner," says the famed writer today. Most likely, it instilled in the lad a sense of professional drive at a tender age. While attending Marshall Field School in Chicago at age twelve, he wrote, produced, directed, and even starred in his first production, which he describes as a "mystery-thriller." His knack for storytelling was blossoming. He no longer remembers the name of that play, but comments that the experience was enough to convince him his future lay in writing.

His college days were spent at Northwestern University, a few miles north of Chicago. During his tenure at Northwestern he joined the debate team, and was the first freshman permitted to participate in the school's intercollege debates. (No doubt this experience, a lesson in verbal artistry you might say, came in quite handy later when Sheldon was dealing with agents, publishers, movie moguls, actors, and network television executives.)

After completing his education at Northwestern, Sheldon, age twenty-two, made the move to Hollywood with hopes of entering the motion picture business. He wrote a sample synopsis of John Steinbeck's novel *Of Mice and Men* as a movie story treatment, and mailed a copy to each of Hollywood's major studios. Within a couple of days, all but one of the studios had responded. The legendary producer David O. Selznick

OPPOSITE PAGE: *Cary Grant entertains his costar, Deborah Kerr, and director Sidney Sheldon between setups while making the MGM motion picture* Dream Wife *(1953).*

(*Gone With the Wind*) hired Sheldon for his first movie-studio assignment, which consisted of reading a screenplay and providing a written analysis, both of which he accomplished within three hours' time. He received a grand total of $3 for his efforts—actually a decent wage for three hours' work in 1939.

Eventually, Sheldon landed at another major studio, 20th Century–Fox, where he read and analyzed screenplays for studio chief Darryl F. Zanuck. The studio boss was duly impressed with the young writer's work, and Sheldon was quickly promoted to screenwriter.

When the United States entered World War II, Sheldon joined the War Training Service, awaiting induction in New York. During that time he collaborated on a number of scripts for Broadway shows. But it was his original screenplay for the Cary Grant vehicle *The Bachelor and the Bobby-Soxer* that put Sheldon on the Hollywood map.

Cary Grant and Sidney Sheldon became friends from that point on. The suave leading man handed Sheldon a book about self-hypnosis, a skill and means of concentration that Sheldon has utilized in his work ever since. "I learned it from a book Cary Grant recommended when I was directing him in the film, *Dream Wife*. He mastered it, even used it at a few parties as a trick. I found it very interesting. Meditating might be a better word for it."

Cary Grant may have been a good-luck charm for his writer friend. *Bobby-Soxer* earned Sheldon a coveted Academy Award for Best Original Screenplay at the ripe old age of thirty. Sheldon's other big-screen writing credits include such classics as *Easter Parade, Song of Norway, Annie Get Your Gun* (all 1948) and *Anything Goes* and the Dean Martin–Jerry Lewis comedy *Pardners* (both 1956). Additional screenplays by Sheldon, or cowritten by him, include *Three Guys Named Mike* (1951), *No Questions Asked* (1951), *Rich, Young and Pretty* (1951), *Just This Once* (1952), *Remains to Be Seen* (1953), *You're Never Too Young* (1955), *The Birds and the Bees* (1956), *The Buster Keaton Story* (1957), *All in a Night's Work* (1961), and *Billy Rose's Jumbo* (1962).

"I once wrote a movie (*Annie Get Your Gun*) with Irving Berlin," Sheldon told the *L.A. Times* in 1982. "Irving told me a story. Someone had said to him, 'Irving, you don't really write all those songs yourself. You must have a little man in the attic writing them.' Irving answered, 'True—but you gotta have the right little man!' "

In television, six-foot Sidney Sheldon became that right man. It wasn't until he created and produced *The Patty Duke Show* in 1963 that he developed the reputation he now enjoys as one of Tinseltown's most prolific scripters.

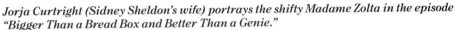

Jorja Curtright (Sidney Sheldon's wife) portrays the shifty Madame Zolta in the episode "Bigger Than a Bread Box and Better Than a Genie."

One day, out of the blue, a William Morris agent called and asked if Sheldon could create and produce a television series for the agency's young performer Patty Duke. She was fresh from an Academy Award–winning performance in the film *The Miracle Worker.*

"I had lunch at the Brown Derby with Patty and twelve little William Morris agents," Sheldon says, recalling how he was instantly enchanted by the smiling young actress, "who was maybe fourteen at the time. I was very touched by her. She was lovely. I brought her home to my wife."

Sheldon's dippy bubblegum sitcom about identical teen cousins Patty and Cathy Lane became a popular show with teenagers and lasted three years on ABC. During its network run, Sheldon insisted upon great control of the series, penning the majority of its scripts. This gave him the confidence and experience he needed to create, produce, and write *I Dream of Jeannie,* perhaps his most lasting legacy in the field of television. (In addition, Sheldon created the short-lived sitcom *Nancy,* starring Celeste Holm, in

1970. His 1980s mystery series *Hart to Hart,* starring Robert Wagner and Stefanie Powers, became quite popular.)

Besides *Jeannie,* Sheldon's most-known works are probably his bestselling novels, published in many languages and distributed throughout the world.

On a recent cable TV show, *On the Inside* (broadcast on the Learning Channel), Sheldon admitted that while he wrote teleplays—or scripts for television—he had no thoughts of writing novels; he didn't even think he had the ability to write one. In fact, he said, there was no desire in his mind to tackle a novel. But he got itchy during what would become the final season of *Jeannie,* and inspiration jabbed his imagination sharply.

"I got an idea," he told interviewer Renee Poussaint. "It was about a psychiatrist who someone was trying to murder. And he had no enemies and he had to figure out who was trying to murder him. The idea kept coming back to me." While still producing *Jeannie,* he gave his secretary strict orders to hold all calls, and divided his days in half—mornings for writing this novel, and afternoons for the TV biz. The concept that kept haunting him was finally being put on paper.

Dreaming of
Jeannie

His finished manuscript, believe it or not, was rejected by several literary agents before a publisher picked it up and paid Sheldon—by this time a highly successful television producer—a mere $1,000 advance. Titled *The Naked Face,* this, his first book, was published just before the end of *Jeannie* in 1969. It was a small printing, a mere 15,000 hardcover copies. He calls it his "deficit book," because he personally covered the costs of all promotion, a book tour, and a kickoff party at the famous Twenty-One Club. Needless to say, the publishers were stunned when *The Naked Face* ended up selling more than 3.1 million paperbacks. (In 1985 the story was made into a major motion picture starring Roger Moore, Rod Steiger, and Art Carney.)

Many literary endeavors were to follow: *The Other Side of Midnight* (1974; over 7.1 million copies sold), *Bloodline* (1977; over 6.4 million copies sold), *Rage of Angels* (1980; over 4.7 million copies sold), and ten others.

L.A. Times writer Paul Rosenfield chronicled Sheldon's novel-writing work habits: "Each weekday morning he paces a second-story office in Holmby Hills, dictating arresting plots into a tape recorder. The next morning, a secretary transcribes the tapes. After 75 days, he has produced a novel. The novel is usually 1,500 pages long; during the next 18 months it will go through twelve rewrites. The result: in five out of six tries, Sheldon has hit No. 1 on every important bestseller list."

Sheldon himself described how he works. "I tell the publisher an idea only in a sen-

Books by Sidney Sheldon

The Naked Face	*Windmills of the Gods*
The Other Side of Midnight	*The Sands of Time*
A Stranger in the Mirror	*Memories of Midnight*
Bloodline	*The Doomsday Conspiracy*
Rage of Angels	*The Stars Shine Down*
Master of the Game	*Nothing Lasts Forever*
If Tomorrow Comes	*Tell Me Your Dreams*

tence or two. That's not ego," he explained, "it's all I happen to know at that point." From that point forward, the novel begins to take shape, and Sheldon's focus narrows and strengthens.

In 1990, film critic Charles Champlin wrote about Sheldon's flourishing book-writing career, stating that Sheldon "was just tidying up the 10th revision of the novel when we talked, and he showed me some yellow markers, presumably to give heart to his valiant secretaries. 'Absolutely Positively Final Draft #2,' one of them read. It followed the unnumbered 'Absolutely Positively Final Draft,' which followed 'Final Draft,' which fooled no one. . . . The plot comes out as he talks his way through as many as 50 pages a day. Then the long revisions begin."

Sidney Sheldon says he loves writing novels because there are no collaborators. Discussing his career recently at a Museum of Television and Radio seminar, he told the small audience: "With television you have people who produce the music. People who are in charge of the art, the look, the sound, the makeup. Many, many collaborators on a production. With a book, it's *you*. You can put this character in any setting. You can make him as rich as you want, have him live in a villa somewhere. . . . When you know the characters, they tend to speak by themselves and take you where they want to. It's a very exciting thing when that takes hold.

"Nobody knows where inspiration comes from," he added. "I feel the work I've done has been given to me. I feel creativity is a gift. We should work hard at developing it. It's been given to us and we should not take credit for it. Really, my life has been a series of miracles."

123
Dreaming of
Jeannie

Jim Backus on Cue

Was actor Jim Backus (a k a shipwrecked Thurston Howell III) a nut for playing pool, or did he just chalk it up to superior acting ability? On Gilligan's Island, *you'll recall he challenged Skipper to a friendly game on the regulation Howell bamboo table. In the film* It's a Mad, Mad, Mad, Mad World, *he was a plastered airline pilot asleep on a pool table. Remember the* Brady Bunch *episode where Backus was Mike Brady's boss, Mr. Matthews, who gets slaughtered in a game of pool by none other than Bobby Brady? In the* Jeannie *episode "Help, Help, a Shark," it's really Jeannie behind the eight-ball when she assists Tony with his shots during a billiards match with General Fitzhugh (Backus).*

"He really didn't play much," says Henny Backus, widow of the late actor. "We didn't own a pool table."

So, Backus wasn't really a pool shark . . . he just played one on TV.

Sheldon may have pegged it. And so did the fortune-teller. After all, only a writer of his caliber could've dreamed up a life-script full of achievements to equal Sidney Sheldon's true history. In addition to taking home an Oscar for *The Bachelor and the Bobby-Soxer,* he received an Emmy Award nomination in 1967 for writing *I Dream of Jeannie.* He also shared a Tony Award for the 1959 Broadway musical *Redhead.* Eight of his Number One bestsellers have been made into highly successful television miniseries. (In one film, *Memories of Midnight,* Sidney Sheldon and his wife can be spotted in a hotel scene.)

Today, Sidney Sheldon and his third wife, the former Alexandra Kostoff, reside primarily in Southern California and London (in a flat they purchased from Andrew Lloyd Webber). His first marriage, to Jane Harding Kaufman in 1945, ended in divorce two years later. Sheldon has one daughter, Mary, from his second marriage, to actress Jorja Curtright. (Curtright died in May 1985.)

His motto, his attitude, his credo, is simple. "People are usually negative and discouraged. Remember this: Nothing can stop you when you set a goal. Nobody can stop you, except yourself. I believe that very firmly."

OPPOSITE PAGE: *Jim Backus plays General Fitzhugh, a small-time hustler who meets his match at the pool table.*

12

Barbara Eden

Officer: You know this is a one-way street?
Jeannie: I was only going one way.

Barbara Jean Moorhead—better known as Barbara "Jeannie" Eden—was born in Tuscon, Arizona, on August 23, 1934. When she was young, her parents divorced and she moved to California with her mother. Her mother then married Harrison Huffman, a telephone lineman; young Barbara took his name.

The all-American cheerleader grew up in the San Francisco Bay area; nurturing her ambition to become a vocalist all along. "For as long as I can remember, I wanted to sing—that was my first love," said Eden in an interview with writer Dinah Marie Kulzer. "I studied at the Conservatory in San Francisco. . . . What actually led to my acting career was something my mother said to me once while I was singing one day. She said, 'Barbara, you're singing all the

Barbara Eden parlayed her sitcom role into a popular nightclub act. One of her Las Vegas skits had her emerge and dramatically disappear into a king-sized replica of the Jeannie bottle.

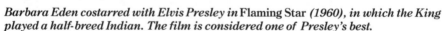

Barbara Eden costarred with Elvis Presley in Flaming Star *(1960), in which the King played a half-breed Indian. The film is considered one of Presley's best.*

notes perfectly, but you don't mean a word of what you're singing. I think you should study acting.' So I auditioned for and received a scholarship to an acting school my mom had heard about on the radio. I began to get parts in plays. I remember thinking, 'Gosh, I like this a lot!' and by the way, learning to act did improve my singing."

As far back as she can remember, Eden wanted to be a star. "I would fantasize when I was a little girl," she told *TV Digest* in 1976. "I'd go see a movie and then go home and play it out in the backyard. I was anyone who was pretty and was in a good movie.

I did have an actress I admired. She's gone now—Vivien Leigh. She and Agnes Moorehead were two ladies I really liked most."

The aspiring performer changed her name (she met a woman named Barbara Eden who was not in show business, and adopted the name because she loved its sound) and left the San Francisco area in the 1950s to pursue her dream of success in big-time show business. "I really wanted to go to New York, but I was scared to death to tackle the big city so I went to Hollywood," Eden said in a 1961 interview with the *St. Louis Post-Dispatch.* "I thought I could earn enough singing to take care of myself while trying to break into the movies. But I soon found out that I needed something steadier in the employment line, so I took a part-time job in a bank operating an IBM machine and spent the rest of my time haunting the offices of casting directors."

When she was discovered, by a producer from 20th Century Fox, she signed a nonexclusive contract with the studio and began work on a new television series, *How to Marry a Millionaire,* in the role Marilyn Monroe covered in the movie musical. Eden

Barbara Eden, Joan Fontaine, Peter Lorre, and Walter Pidgeon in a scene from the campy science fiction flick Voyage to the Bottom of the Sea *(1961). Eden's real-life husband, Michael Ansara, costarred.*

put a different spin on the role, inspired by another stunning blonde: "My idol is Carole Lombard. There never was anyone like her when it came to handling a comedy role, real comedy with just a little tear near the surface all the time. When you come to think of it, there's not too much of a line dividing comedy and tragedy."

Her TV stint as Loco Jones lasted two seasons and led to roles in feature films such as *A Private's Affair* (1959), *Twelve Hours to Kill* (1960), *From the Terrace* (1960), *The Wonderful World of the Brothers Grimm* (1962), and *The 7 Faces of Dr. Lao* (1964). Eden costarred opposite

A NEW STAR IN THE FAMILY 9-8-65
Actress Barbara Eden and husband Michael Ansara show off Matthew. Michael Ansara, 9 days old. Their first child, Matthew, was born Aug. 29. Miss Eden stars in title role of TV comedy, "I Dream of Jeannie."

Jeannie Baby: Barbara Eden plays with her son, Matthew, born in late 1965 during the show's run. (Photo: June, 1966.)

Elvis Presley in 1960's *Flaming Star,* describing him in 1961 as "a terrific actor to work with and lots of fun." Her role in Irwin Allen's all-star *Voyage to the Bottom of the Sea* allowed her to share the screen with such legendary performers as Walter Pidgeon, Joan Fontaine, Frankie Avalon, Peter Lorre, and Barbara's then-husband, Michael Ansara. Eden and Ansara (who played Cochise on ABC-TV's *Broken Arrow* series in the 1950s) were married in 1958; the two had a son in 1965, just after filming of *Jeannie's* first season.

Halloween was a special holiday in the Ansara-Eden house. In a 1965 *TV Week* interview, Barbara Eden explained how she and Ansara had their first, reluctant date on Halloween evening, 1957. "It was all a publicity man's idea," she recalled. "He said that a certain film party on Halloween would be widely covered by magazine photographers and that I should attend with Mike who was starring in the *Broken Arrow* series." Hardly knowing each other, both stalled, but finally agreed to the blind date.

Ansara asked Eden to have dinner with him before the party. Yadda yadda yadda, the two had a wonderful evening, missed the party, and two months later were madly in love. They married on January 17, 1958. The marriage lasted fifteen years. During the *Jeannie* years, Ansara made a few guest-starring appearances on the sitcom, once portraying the evil Blue Djinn, Jeannie's original master, who permanently encased her in the bottle eons ago.

John Lupton (right) was Indian Agent Tom Jeffords and Michael Ansara costarred as Apache chief Cochise in the 1950s television series, Broken Arrow. *Ansara was married to Barbara Eden and portrayed the Blue Djinn on* I Dream of Jeannie.

Post-*Jeannie,* Eden married twice; today, she lives in Beverly Hills, California, with her husband, real estate executive Jon Eicholtz. Barbara's career went in several directions after 1970: TV specials, motion pictures, including *Harper Valley P.T.A.* (she also starred in the TV version), and a string of highly rated TV movies (*Opposites Attract, Your Mother Wears Combat Boots, The Stepford Children, Howling in the Woods, Visions of Murder, Eyes of Terror*).

Reunited: After the cancellation of Jeannie, *Hagman and Eden costarred in an NBC-TV movie drama,* A Howling in the Woods *(1971). The modern horror story set in a small mountain community, had Eden portraying a fashion designer whose husband (Hagman) follows her to her hometown where she has fled to figure out her failing marriage.*

Somehow in that whirl of activity over the decades, Eden has made time to advertise wigs for the Paula Young company.

Over the years Eden has headlined in Las Vegas at the MGM Grand, the Riviera, and the Sahara with a successful live stage show, which she has also taken on the road. In the early 1990s, she starred with Don Knotts in an eleven-city tour of Neil Simon's *Last of the Red Hot Lovers,* and has appeared in national tours of such popular musicals as *South Pacific, Woman of the Year,* and *The Best Little Whorehouse in Texas.*

In addition to her busy performing and personal-appearance schedule, Barbara works tirelessly on behalf of a number of national and local charities, including the Make-a-Wish Foundation, the March of Dimes, the American Cancer Society, and the American Heart Association, among others.

Today, at sixty-five (yes, can you believe it?) Barbara Eden has been bitten by the nostalgia bug. *Jeannie* has never been more popular; Eden has been reprising her blinking alter ego and making appearances in the pink pantaloons again for several popular national advertising campaigns (Old Navy apparel; Lexus sport-utility vehicles).

Eden readily admits that when she received the news, some thirty-five years ago, that she would be starring as a genie in a television series, she had no idea the series would forever alter her life, her public image, and her star status. "Sometimes I'll see myself on screen, and I'm rather taken aback," she says today. "It's like looking in the mirror. I don't like watching myself on the screen. But I can watch *I Dream of Jeannie* now. Enough time has passed that it's almost like watching someone else."

ABOVE TOP: *Fresh from the Bottle: Barbara Eden and Dean Martin sing a duet on his popular NBC variety show.* ABOVE BOTTOM: *Barbara Eden joins host Ed McMahon as a celebrity guest on* Star Search *in the 1980s.*

13

Larry Hagman

✦

This is Nelson—squire to the moons in space.
                                                    —Jeannie

orn in Weatherford, Texas, on September 21, 1931, Larry Hagman was the son of a small-town lawyer and an aspiring teenage singer who eventually became a Broadway star: Mary Martin. After his parents divorced, young Larry was raised by his father, Ben, in Texas. Eventually moving to California, he lived with his grandmother while traveling back and forth to New York to spend more time with his mother. He attended several different schools in his youth and teenage years, in New York, Vermont, Los Angeles, and Texas, where he graduated from high school. It's interesting to note that a major slice of Hagman's life was conducted in military attire: He spent five years in the Black Fox Military Academy when he was a youngster; four years in the U.S.

An early publicity portrait of Larry Hagman, circa 1960.

Air Force as an enlisted man; five years as an Air Force pilot and astronaut on *I Dream of Jeannie.*

While Larry grew up, his mother's career skyrocketed and this petite lady became recognized as a major talent of the American musical stage, starring in original Broadway smash-hit productions such as *South Pacific, The Sound of Music,* and *Peter Pan.* Larry Hagman realized at a very early age how talented his mother was, and the knowledge intimidated him. "Talk about charisma!" he said of her, "she really had it, man. I mean, it was bleeping magic!" He also realized how difficult a life in show business can be. "Even that one year I actually lived with her, I never saw much of her. She had her career; when I went off to school she was still asleep." Undoubtedly, Larry was influenced by his mother's stage success. He tried his hand at acting and found his experience both challenging and enjoyable. During the 1940s and 1950s, Larry appeared in more than fifty plays and musicals; he accepted a part in a London production of *South Pacific*—a role his mother offered him.

In 1952, while in London, Hagman joined the U.S. Air Force, where he was assigned to Special Services until 1956. A year into his military career, he met and (in 1954) married a Swedish dress designer named Maj (pronounced "My") Axelsson. Upon returning stateside, he concentrated more seriously on his acting career and began to appear both on and off Broadway. By 1957, he was working on television as well, and within a few years he was becoming recognized by the public. He had already begun a three-year run as a regular on the CBS daytime soap opera *The Edge of Night.*

Larry proved from the start of *Jeannie* that he had the right stuff as both an actor and a physical comedian. His pre-

Young Larry Hagman, already in uniform at age ten, while enrolled in the Black Fox Military Institute, circa 1941. (Courtesy of Phil Potempa.)

Larry Hagman demonstrates his "Stop Smokin' Wrist Snappin' Red Rubber Band,"
which was widely distributed in the 1980s as part of a campaign sponsored by the
American Cancer Society.

cisely timed falls, slaps, and tumbles proved he had a little bit of the Buster Keaton blessing on him. His sudden jolts of energy and the pratfalls he took when being blinked in or out of a situation were, on many occasions, simply masterful.

Ben Hagman, Larry's father, never did get to see his son star in the network television series. Shortly after the pilot was produced, Larry attempted to have a print made available for the rugged trial lawyer to see, but he died before it arrived. Mary Martin, though, was quite excited at her son's success. In fact, the stage actress was seriously considered to play the mother of Tony Nelson in some episodes—it would have been unique casting, to say the least. "Those cheap fuckers didn't want to pay her enough, I think," Hagman recalls. "You get what you pay for."

Although mother and son had had a prickly relationship—even being estranged for more than a year—Mary Martin knew her son "would only do things that interested him."

"I think that in many ways we are quite alike," Martin said in 1967, while *Jeannie* was running in prime time. "And anyway, we've never, in all our ups and downs, had the usual parent-and-son relationship . . . but it has been fabulous watching him make his own way. He sure has been determined to do it that way. . . . I'm thrilled to watch him coming through so marvelously as an adult. I can't remember anything that has been so satisfying. And I must say, I think being a grandmother is considerably less

Larry Hagman joins his mother, Mary Martin, on her PBS television talk show Over Easy *(with cohost Jim Hartz) in 1981.*

worrisome and frustrating than being a mother ever was."

In that same 1967 Associated Press profile of Larry Hagman, the actor commented: "You should never just take your job for granted. After all, beyond *Jeannie* there is a lot more for me in show business." Wow, did he hit the nail on the head. But did he realize what kind of ride his career was in store for? Was he prepared for success? Absolutely. "For me," Hagman said, "television's for money, exposure, and training." He was nearly broke when he landed the role of Tony Nelson, but the series made him quite comfortable financially, with a beautiful house in an exclusive area of Malibu to show for it.

After *Jeannie,* Hagman continued to work at his own pace throughout the 1970s, even reuniting with Barbara Eden for a TV movie, *A Howling in the Woods,* in 1971. He finally hit stride—and struck oil—in 1978, when he landed the role of the infamous oil, land, and insurance swindler J. R. Ewing on TV's *Dallas.* It became one of the most successful prime-time soaps in television history, and the character was quite a departure for Hagman. As J. R., he was America's favorite TV villain—a despicable heavy with a sly grin whom audiences simply loved to hate. This couldn't have been more evident than during the 1980–81 season, when 80 percent of all television viewers in the country tuned in to the program's season opener. The previous season's finale had ended with J. R. Ewing being gunned down by an unknown assailant and hospitalized, where he remained in critical condition until the fall season premiere resolved the cliffhanger.

It gave the world an entire summer to debate the question, "Who Shot J. R.?" (Not even the cast of the show knew exactly who had perpetrated the crime, since several alternative endings were filmed.) The whole suspenseful affair became a national frenzy, building to a climax as the fall TV season approached. About a dozen characters on the program had motives to kill J. R. Ewing. Bookies around the country loved the drama and took in millions in personal wagers.

Finally, on November 21, 1980, the world found out that Kristin Shepard (played by Mary Crosby) had pulled the trigger. Viewers who tuned in to find out the answer added up to the biggest audience for any show in the history of television up to that time. As the hit show went on, Hagman tagged along, enjoying a remarkable thirteen-year run as J. R. from 1978 to 1991.

Hagman continued to work in films and television throughout the 1980s and 1990s, while advocating Zen and Taoist philosophy—not to mention plenty of Dom Pérignon champagne—to provide his own peculiar brand of comic relief both on and off the set. *Dallas* producer Leonard

Larry Hagman sipping a little of the bubbly in St. Louis, 1984. (Photo by Steve Cox.)

Katzman recalled: "Larry doesn't conform. Every day this week he's come in as someone different. One day he was dressed up as a Chinese coolie, the next day he was a Foreign Legionnaire, then he wore a Japanese wrestler's outfit. He keeps a memento of every day. It might be a rock, a flower, a ballpoint pen, even an old button." There have been lengthy spans of time during which Hagman chooses one day a week to abstain from speech and remain perfectly silent—no talking whatsoever. Certainly, it can be said that Larry Hagman has made a lasting impression on virtually every person with whom he has ever worked.

By the mid-1990s, Hagman's health began to fail noticeably. In 1995 he was diagnosed as having a malignant tumor on his liver—a condition complicated by cirrhosis, the result of his abundant alcohol consumption over the past four decades. Hagman kiddingly told a reporter that he was going to treat his cancer by "injecting alcohol into it—I've been doing that for forty years."

But Hagman's seriously declining health didn't improve until August 1995, when a successful liver transplant was performed on him after he'd spent months on the waiting list for a donor organ. After witnessing his own mother deteriorate and die of cancer, he knew the transplant was his only hope.

The press, naturally, jumped on the story. *The National Enquirer,* which originally broke the story ("Larry Hagman Hospital Drama: 'Dallas' Star in Life & Death Battle with Booze") had him on the next cover. His "race against time" finally came to the finish line on the night of August 22, 1995 at 10:40 P.M. Unbelievably, news stations in Los Angeles actually broke through regular programming with live remotes on hand to cover the landing of a helicopter at Cedars-Sinai Medical Center. All cameras were focused on the attendants wheeling into the hospital a blue Igloo cooler carrying the new liver for Hagman. The organ had been just harvested from an automobile accident victim and a match had been made. The reporters noted that the actor has been reached by beeper and was on his way. Even Hagman was momentarily stunned by the immediate media coverage.

Later, in an exclusive cover story titled "Back from the Brink," Larry Hagman revealed to *People* magazine that for fifteen or twenty years before to his diagnosis, he had been "a pretty heavy drinker." He drank champagne the way schoolkids gulp frosty Coca-Cola on a blasting hot afternoon. He was never out of control, shaking from the DTs, throwing up, or blacking out. Alcohol was a way of life, which began in the *Jeannie* era and took him well into the *Dallas* heyday and beyond; he was consuming up to three bottles of—only the very best—bubbly a day. "The drinking sometimes made it harder to remember lines, but I liked that constant feeling of being mildly loaded," he admitted.

After recovering nicely from the transplant, receiving a megadose of chemotherapy, and quitting the sauce for good, a grateful Larry Hagman seems to be back to his

Dreaming of
Jeannie

Sergeant Larry Hagman, age 23, scooting around London with his fiancée, Swedish-born dress designer Maj Irene Axelsson. Hagman was stationed with the U.S. Air Force in England, where he directed and produced touring shows for airmen in Europe (October 1954).

old charismatic self. He resurrected J. R. Ewing for a couple of TV "reunion" movies and took on the small role of a Texas millionaire in Oliver Stone's controversial film *Nixon*.

Now nearing age seventy and a lot healthier, Hagman is happier than ever; he and his wife, Maj, have relocated to their own private Shangri-La—a dream house in Ojai, California. The return address on their letterhead reads: Heaven.

14

Bill Daily

Only one person besides Major Nelson was wise to Jeannie's existence as a supernatural entity. The character actor who played Tony Nelson's confidant and sidekick, Roger Healey, began life on August 30, 1928, in Des Moines, Iowa. Bill Daily's father died when Bill was very young; his mother worked, and he was raised mostly by aunts and uncles. When he was eleven, he and his mother moved to Chicago and lived in a "rotten" neighborhood—"very low middle class," he says. Music became his friend; he learned to push the bellows and play a mean accordion, later switching to the bass.

Bill Daily started his career after his years in the Army. He began playing string bass and messing around on the piano in various Midwestern clubs. "If I had a choice to live anywhere in the United States, I'd be in Kansas City," says Daily today. "I spent a lot of my summers there growing up. I like the culture, the size, the people." He later joined a group called Jack and the Beanstalks, which Daily himself describes as being "a little far-out."

By the 1950s, Daily was working as a writer-director at Chicago's NBC television station. He performed in nightclubs as a musician, primarily in Chicago and the outlying areas. He also moonlighted, playing music and doing stand-up comedy, in Chicago's Small World club. During this early period of struggle, Daily and his wife, Patricia, tried to adopt a baby. But in those days, according to Daily, adoption agencies looked down upon "itinerant entertainers."

"They don't care about the money you make, as long as you have a secure spot in the community. I was making nine thousand dollars a year and spending sixteen thousand to exist. I was caught in the credit card trap where I had to go out to an expensive restaurant for lunch because I could charge it. You can't have a thirty-five-cent hamburger and give the man a credit card." Despite Bill's status as a performer, he and Patricia were able to adopt two children, Patrick (born 1957) and Kimberly (born 1959).

In addition to his work behind the camera at the local NBC station, Daily performed his own comedy routines on the air. Eventually, he found himself flying regularly between Chicago and Cleveland. Cleveland was the home of *The Mike Douglas Show,* and Daily made more than 200 comedy appearances on the program. Douglas and Daily had previously worked together in Chicago on a TV show called *Club 60.* As Douglas himself remembers it, "He was always doing crazy things at meetings, and finally somebody got the bright idea of putting him on the air. That was the start of it."

Comedian Steve Allen also spotted the talent in Daily and arranged for him to relocate to Hollywood and appear on his national TV show. Allen remarked, "[Bill Daily] wasn't Ed McMahon with Johnny Carson. He was always primarily a comedian with the facility to be funny extemporaneously. He doesn't need writers or a prepared routine."

Daily's work with Allen gave him the exposure he needed to land acting gigs on television. He appeared in guest roles on ABC's *Bewitched* and *The Farmer's Daughter,* and was signed for a small role in the pilot for *I Dream of Jeannie.* Over time, Daily's regular role was built up until he had achieved true second-banana status. Undoubtedly, his beautiful sense of comic timing stems from his years as a jazz musician.

"The rhythm," he told *TV Guide* in 1975, "it's everything, man. Comedy is rhythm. Comedy is time. Look at the top comics. Either they're musicians or they have some kind of musical background. Sid Caesar played fine saxophone in bands. Nobody ever had better timing than Jack Benny and he paid his dues with the violin. Look at all the comics who play instruments—Woody Allen, Bill Cosby, Johnny Carson, Andy Griffith, Morey Amsterdam, Steve Allen, Jackie Vernon, Phyllis Diller. Look at the Marx Brother—Groucho the guitar. Harpo the harp, Chico the piano. People don't know it but Bob Newhart plays fine drums. . . . Music, man, it's the key."

OPPOSITE PAGE: *Bill Daily has* Bewitched *to thank for his debut. He played an adoptive father ("Which was easy for me because my kids are adopted," he says) and Sidney Sheldon saw the episode and kept him in mind for Roger Healey.* ABOVE: *Bill Daily was a quirky fixture as airline navigator Howard Borden on* The Bob Newhart Show *in the 1970s.*

But acting, not music, has sustained Daily in his career as a performer. After *Jeannie,* he directed the game show *It's Your Bet* and wrote radio spots. He's performed many guest spots on television shows and in a handful of TV movies, and in 1987 he starred as a veterinarian in the short-lived syndicated TV series *Starting from Scratch.*

Unfortunately, typecasting will probably plague him forever. To television viewers, Bill Daily will seemingly always have two personas: Major Healey and Howard Borden. Both characters were men in uniform—Healy in green as an officer in the Army Engineer Corps, Borden in his official airline. The personalities were never very distinguishable. Neighbor from hell Howard Borden—the airplane navigator with permanent jet lag and a habit of borrowing things—constantly barged in on the 1970s *Bob Newhart Show* and created a lot of extra laughs on the immensely popular sitcom.

In Joey Green's book *Hi Bob!,* actor Jack Riley ("Mr. Carlin") describes the costar: "I love Bill Daily. Howard was an extension of Bill. Bill is on a very different wavelength than everybody else. Without taking drugs, he's always speeding. He gets ahead of himself. You can hardly understand what he says because he says it so fast. Before he went onstage, he'd exclaim, 'Energy! Energy! Energy!' with these crazy finger movements of his. So we all used to do that. That's how Bill is, and that's how Howard was."

In the 1980s, Daily grew disgusted with Hollywood and made a home for himself and his second wife, Becky, in Albuquerque, New Mexico, where he directs and acts in local theater productions.

OPPOSITE PAGE: *Bill Daily starred as a small-town veterinarian in the short-lived syndicated sitcom,* Starting from Scratch, *1988. (Christopher Barr Photo.)*

LEFT: *Majors Nelson and Healey are the subjects of a documentary about astronauts, in the episode "Everybody's a Movie Star."*

OPPOSITE PAGE: *A rare glimpse of Barbara Eden and her stand-in and double, Evelyn Moriarty.*

BELOW: *Paul Lynde, hilarious as usual, guest-starred as a temperamental film director.*

ABOVE: I Dream of Jeannie was a TV standout, uniquely capitalizing on NASA's budding space program in a contemporary context.

RIGHT: Rehearsing a scene in Tony's driveway. In the background is the house seen prominently on The Donna Reed Show.

OPPOSITE PAGE: Bottle Babe: Jeannie in her glistening abode.

OPPOSITE PAGE: Tony attempts to outsmart the omnipotent Blue Djinn (portrayed by Michael Ansara).

JEANNIE
AT WORK

OPPOSITE: Filming the discovery on Southern California's Zuma Beach, December 1964.

ABOVE: Construction Sight: I Dream of Jeannie switched nights and timeslots five times in five years. The constant wavering did more to dislodge an audience than to cement a foundation.

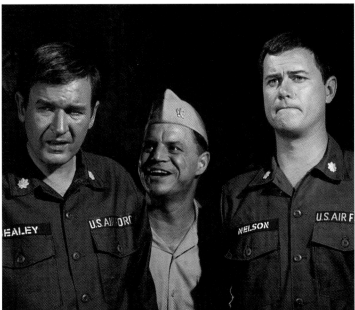

ABOVE: *The Beginning
of the End: The wedding
of Tony and Jeannie,
December 2, 1969. Some
say the marriage ruined
the show.*

LEFT: *Don Rickles,
making the rounds of
sitcoms in the 1960s, guest-
starred in the episode
"My Master, the Weakling."
It was highly irregular to
see Major Healey in Air
Force attire, considering
he was Army Air Corps.*

RIGHT: Bewitched, *TV's supernatural sister-sitcom to* I Dream of Jeannie, *starred Elizabeth Montgomery, Agnes Moorehead, and Dick York.*

OPPOSITE PAGE: *Smoke Gets in Your Eyes: Larry Hagman holds the first season "gold leaf" bottle.*

OPPOSITE: *Not bad for a 2,000-year-old genie.*

LEFT: *Sidney Sheldon, in 1998, marveled at this statue of Jeannie—looked it in the eye and said, "Hi, Barbara." (Photo by Steve Cox)*

RIGHT: *Barbara Eden today, posing with an original bottle she saved from the show. Over the years, the precious glass prop miraculously survived even a couple of major earthquakes. (Courtesy of TV Guide)*

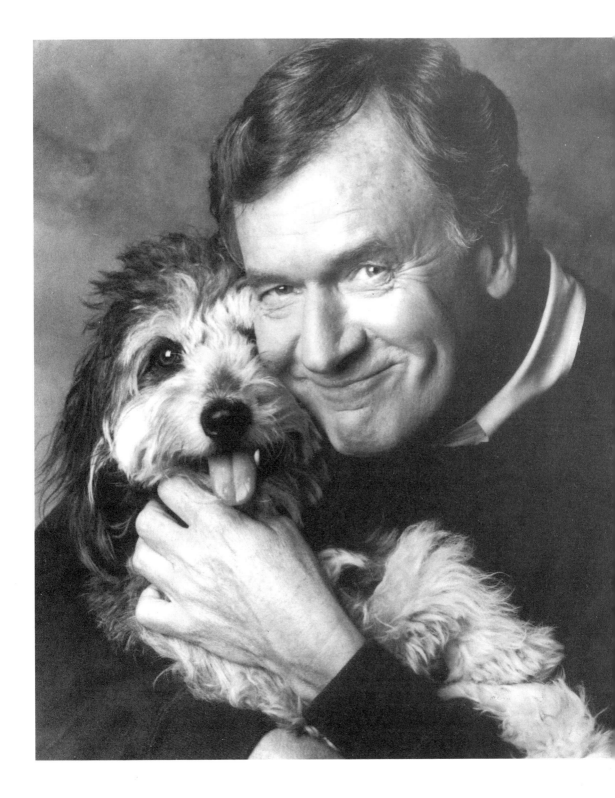

15

Hayden Rorke

♦

Fine. I'll accept that. It's no more ridiculous than any of your other explanations.

—Dr. Bellows

he man who served as full-time foil to the antics of Tony Nelson, Roger Healey, and the irrepressible Jeannie began his career as an actor in the legitimate theater. Hayden Rorke, who enacted the role of NASA's suspicious house shrink, Dr. Alfred Bellows, was born William Henry Rorke in Brooklyn on October 23, 1910.

Bill and his brothers, James and Edward, attended St. Clair's Academy boarding school during their elementary school years. Bill Rorke changed his name after high school, when he began studying at the American Academy of Dramatic Arts and subsequently joined Walter Hampton's repertory company. There he appeared in the classics.

Hayden Rorke regularly received mail from fans who really thought he was a psychiatrist.

THRILLS COME ROCKETING TO THE
SCREEN AS SCIENCE SMASHES
A NEW FRONTIER!

PROJECT
MOONBASE

with
ROSS FORD · DONNA MARTELL
HAYDEN RORKE

Produced by
JACK SEAMAN

Directed by
RICHARD TALMADGE

Story and Screenplay by
ROBERT HEINLEIN and
JACK SEAMAN

A GALAXY PICTURES, INC.
PRODUCTION

A Lippert Pictures
Presentation

...UP
UP
UP!..

TO
A NEW
WORLD
OF
ADVENTURE

...ee man-piloted rocket
...aunched from gigantic
...ce ship!

*Hayden Rorke was obviously no stranger to
spaceship camp. Rorke costarred in this
1953 Lippert film,* Project Moonbase.

"I would always kid Bill about the use of my name. . . ." says his surviving brother, eighty-nine-year-old James Hayden Rorke. "He was the second son, I'm the first. He wound up with my father's name, Henry Rorke. When he went into theater, he took on my mother's maiden name, Hayden, to perpetuate the theatrical tradition in the family." But his family still called him Bill.

My mother's father, William Richardson Hayden, was a producer and a well-known figure in the theater around 1900 in New York," explains James Rorke. "His daughter—my mother—became an actress, an ingénue, only onstage. She was in several plays with Chauncey Alcott. She married my father in 1907, I think."

The Rorke matriarch, Margaret Hayden Rorke, later became a long-time textile industry figure, who created colors used in the inaugural ball gowns of both Eleanor Roosevelt and Mamie Eisenhower. She also standardized the red, white, and blue shades of the American flag during the administration of Herbert Hoover and coordinated colors for the movie industry during the early days of color filming. (She died in 1969 at age eighty-four.)

During World War II, Hayden Rorke joined the U.S. Army and attained the rank of sergeant, touring with its road-show, *This Is the Army.* He also appeared in the show's film version, produced by Warner Bros. in 1943.

Actor and director Gene Nelson first met Hayden Rorke when they served in the

Barbara Eden, Ringo Starr, and Hayden Rorke come together at a party in 1970.

U.S. Army at the same time, both attached to the War Department. They traveled and entertained troops for two years. (Later, Nelson would direct his friend Rorke in the first season of *Jeannie*.) "We stayed in touch over the years," said the late Gene Nelson in a 1996 interview. "He had this pseudo-sophistication that I just loved. Hayden was homosexual. He and Jus [Justus] Addiss lived together for over twenty years. They were a pair. Jus was very straight acting. Never in a million years would you know he wasn't straight."

"Hayden could slip into it," Nelson said, referring to the actor's slightly effeminate demeanor. "He was in so many English plays he had adopted this marvelous English manner, so he could get away with a little fey gesture. I don't think most people knew he was gay."

Rorke gained a reputation as a respected actor and loved working on the stage. He appeared in a number of major Broadway productions including *The Philadelphia Story, Three Men on a Horse, The Iceman Cometh, The Country Wife, A Moon for the Misbegotten,* and *Dream Girl.*

"I would say he was a very professional actor," James Rorke says describing his famous brother. "He was referred to by many of his friends as an actor's actor. Directors and producer could rely upon his performance."

In motion pictures, Rorke played character roles in such films as *Spencer's Mountain* (with Henry Fonda); *The Unsinkable Molly Brown* (with Debbie Reynolds); *The Night Walker* (with Barbara Stanwyck); *The Thrill of It All* (with Doris Day); *An American in Paris* (with Gene Kelly); and *Pillow Talk* (with Doris Day and his longtime pal Rock Hudson).

But it was in television that Rorke achieved his greatest fame, specifically as the confounded psychologist on *I Dream of Jeannie*. He also appeared as a regular on two prior television series: *Mr. Adams and Eve* (CBS, 1957–58) and *No Time for Sergeants* (ABC, 1964–65). In addition, Rorke turned in guest appearances on such hugely popular programs as *The Red Skelton Show, December Bride, The George Burns and Gracie Allen Show, I Love Lucy, Perry Mason, Dr. Kildare, Bonanza, The Jack Benny Program, The Beverly Hillbillies, The Twilight Zone, The Andy Griffith Show, Mannix, Here's Lucy, Barnaby Jones,* and innumerable others.

Rorke and his partner, Jus Addiss, lived a quiet life together in Studio City, California, during the *Jeannie* tenure and they remained in that home for years, along with a number of basset hounds and beagles. In the dog-show circuit, Rorke became a well-known breeder of champion bassets.

Rorke diligently attended press parties, gave interviews, and assisted in publicity for *Jeannie* during the show's run. According to a memo in Sidney Sheldon's personal files, the producer was able to reward the actor by having some of the studio carpenters remodel and paint Rorke's home. (Studio contracts prohibited any type of cash bonus, hence Sidney Sheldon's finagling.)

In 1986, Rorke was diagnosed with stomach cancer. *The National Enquirer* (of course) broke the story about the actor's terminal illness not long after he entered a hospital to undergo tests. Many of Rorke's friends from show business—including both Larry Hagman and Barbara Eden—visited him to lift his spirits.

"His partner, Jus, died before him," said Nelson. "I was never really clear on it. I went to spend the day with Hayden when he was sick at home. I was at his bedside before he died. I had to help him in and out of bed, help him walk. He had an IV with him. He was very pale, his hair was white. It was a sad day for me."

Hayden Rorke died at his home on August 19, 1987, at age seventy-six, and was buried next to his mother at Holy Cross Cemetery in Culver City, California.

Dreaming of
Jeannie

Hayden Rorke relaxes between takes while filming in Honolulu. Crowds routinely gathered to watch the show being made, catch a glimpse of the cast, get an autograph, or take a snapshot.

16

Emmaline Henry

*Amanda Bellows: Oh, you're camping in your living room. How
marvelous. Oh Alfred, why don't we do things like this?
Dr. Bellows: Amanda, I spend my days curing people who do things
like this.*

not long before taking on the role of Amanda Bellows, actress Emmaline
Henry costarred briefly with John Astin and Marty Ingels in a peculiar sitcom
called *I'm Dickens . . . He's Fenster.* At the time, *TV Guide* described her as a
"tall, pleasant, rather good-looking blonde with an alarmingly low-key temperament. . . . But looks are deceptive. Emmaline, a lace-curtain Irisher from
Philadelphia, is the kind who sneaks up on you. Her comedic talents, which half
the time seem to be lying dormant, can suddenly develop a kick like a mule."

Born in 1930, Emmaline Henry aspired to be a singer. At the tender age of

Marty Ingels, Emmaline Henry, and John Astin in the short-lived TV series I'm
Dickens . . . He's Fenster *(1962).*

Mad About Amanda

BY MARK HUGHES

Every hall of fame has members who are not known by the masses, but who are definitely included because of the contributions they made to their profession. If there were a TV Style Hall of Fame, one actress would be at the top of the list: Emmaline Henry. Yes . . . Amanda Bellows.

On I Dream of Jeannie, *Emmaline Henry played the zany, nosy, albeit fabulously classy wife of Dr. Alfred Bellows, portrayed by Hayden Rorke. Surely you're not still saying "Amanda who?"*

As a kid, when all my friends were at school talking about Samantha Stephens's cool powers or Jeannie's kooky schemes, I was mesmerized by this wonderful chameleon. Her ability to hop from charity ball collections of garage refuse to Major Nelson's shower while never faltering made me want more . . . MORE AMANDA!

Weekly, I prayed she'd cross the screen. When Jeannie's invisible, uniform-wrecking dog Djinn-Djinn was on the loose, an unsuspecting Amanda headed into her husband's office sporting the latest in the "military look" only to emerge seconds later shrieking hysterically, in an outfit shredded like a Cobb salad. I actually think this was one of the best moments in TV sitcoms.

Á la Lucy, Amanda was able to combine her talent for comic timing with her flawless figure and fashion strength. As far as I was concerned, Mary Tyler Moore had nothing on her. I remember distinctly an episode where Amanda was perched—not sitting, but perched—atop Dr. Bellows's desk reading confidential files. When her husband queried, "Amanda, what makes you think you can do that?" She replied: "I'm a colonel's wife, daaarling." I saw my soul mate before me on the small screen and was hooked.

I always dreamed that I would one day wed Amanda. Mary Tyler Moore was too cutesy for me, and as far as Jeannie was concerned, my mom and dad would never let me hook up with a girl who lived in a bottle. But they would have definitely welcomed Amanda home for the holidays. I hoped when she came to

meet my parents, she'd wear the same black-and-white sequined gown that she wore to a dinner party with Alfred the night Major Nelson broke into their house to retrieve Jeannie's bottle. Opera gloves, perfectly coiffed hair, and peau-de-soie mules completed this housebreaking ensemble. People today don't look that great when treading out for a night on the town.

I've spent the rest of my years praising Amanda's fierceness to all who would listen. Many have said, "You know, Mark, I see what you mean!" I knew she'd be proud of me.

Last year, I was struck with the notion to track down Emmaline Henry and tell her how much she enriched and influenced my life. Unfortunately, I was too late. She had lost a courageous battle with cancer in 1979. I was crushed. A chapter of my life would be closed forever.

Certainly, I will always have Amanda in my life through video, but I wanted her to know she gave me the style sense to move effortlessly through the vicious circles of the entertainment industry while still being a bit of a madcap, zany nut. The next time you catch yourself watching one of the many style shows on the air, pop in an episode of I Dream of Jeannie that includes Amanda. I promise, you'll discover Elsa Klench has nothing on her!

Sign of the Times

The transportation department in Cocoa Beach, Florida, soon realized it would need to produce extra street signs after dedicating a new I Dream of Jeannie Lane in 1996. "We have a spare of the same street sign here in the office," says Rob Varley, director of tourism in Brevard County (also known as the Space Coast). "They had to install the sign on an extra-tall pole because it was stolen twice."

The half-mile residential street in Cocoa Beach, located off the A1A (Beach Coast Highway), was dedicated with no less than Barbara Eden in attendance at the ceremony. Can't you just imagine the address labels for the residents in the local condominiums: "72 I Dream of Jeannie Lane, Cocoa Beach, FL."

158

Dreaming of
Jeannie

twelve, she "possessed a traffic-stopping coloratura soprano voice" and performed on radio shows locally. In her twenties, she moved to Hollywood and began singing in the chorus of musicals, landing a role in *Little Boy Blue* at the El Capitan Theater in 1950. Producer Max Showalter was less impressed by her voice than by her "zany warmth that flooded the stage." Eventually she toured in other musicals, such as *Top Banana,* in which she was understudy to Kaye Ballard. She kicked around other shows and even took over for Carol Channing in the road company of *Gentlemen Prefer Blondes.*

Her television debut on *The Red Skelton Show* in 1961 led to many guest shots in the 1960s, on shows including *The Munsters; The Farmer's Daughter; Petticoat Junction; The Don Knotts Show;* and *Green Acres.* Her motion picture appearances include *Divorce American Style* (1967); *Rosemary's Baby* (1968); and *Harrad Summer* (1974). She also appeared on TV in *Mickey; Love, American Style; The Bob Newhart Show; The Streets of San Francisco; Three's Company; Eight Is Enough;* and *Backstairs at the White House* (a 1979 miniseries).

According to a news article, Emmaline Henry remained unmarried; she died on October 8, 1979.

OPPOSITE PAGE: *Emmaline Henry in the early 1970s.*

159

Dreaming of
Jeannie

17

Barton MacLane

General Peterson was portrayed by talented character actor Barton MacLane, born on Christmas Day, 1902 in Columbia, South Carolina. (A few sources list his birth year as 1900.)

MacLane was usually a supporting actor in B films, although he was occasionally cast as a leading man. A veteran of more than 200 motion pictures, he started out in the late 1920s as a contract player for Paramount Pictures, acted on radio for a few years, and later spent most of his time in movies at Warner Bros. playing gangsters, cops, and thugs. In his career, MacLane landed roles in such classics as *Dr. Jekyll and Mr. Hyde* (1941), *The Maltese Falcon* (1941) in which he played the cynical police detective, and another Bogie favorite, *The Treasure of the Sierra Madre* (1948). MacLane's television work was more limited, however. Besides his semiregular role as the stuffy general on *I Dream of Jeannie,* he starred in one prior TV series, *The Outlaws* (1961–62).

MacLane was a graduate of Wesleyan University and attended the

Veteran character actor Barton MacLane portrayed General Martin Peterson.

American Academy of Dramatic Arts. It's little known that he was also an avid card player. In the mid-1950s he invented a card holder mainly used for canasta. According to a news article, "the gadget is made of folded sheet plastic bound with alligator-patterned plastic, with a wire support adjustable to fit any kind of table. It holds as many as 75 cards." MacLane called it the Westwood Card Holder; he made it for himself and constructed several for friends before deciding it had commercial possibilities.

MacLane died on New Year's Day, 1969, of double pneumonia, at St. John's Hospital in Santa Monica, California. He was sixty-six years old at the time and was still working semiregularly on *I Dream of Jeannie.*

Among MacLane's additional film credits are *The Cocoanuts* (1929); *His Woman* (1931); *Big Executive* (1933); *Hell and High Water* (1933); *Tillie and Gus* (1933); *Lone Cowboy* (1934); *Black Fury* (1935); *Frisco Kid* (1935); *Man of Iron* (1935); *Stranded* (1935); *Bengal Tiger* (1936); *The Walking Dead* (1936); *The Adventurous Blonde* (1937); *Born Reckless* (1937); *The Prince and the Pauper* (1937); *San Quentin* (1937); *Gold Is Where You Find It* (1938); *Prison Break* (1938); *You and Me* (1938); *Mutiny in the Big House* (1939); *Stand Up and Fight* (1939); *Gangs of Chicago* (1940); *Melody Ranch* (1940); *The Secret Seven* (1940); *High Sierra* (1941); *All Through the Night* (1942); *Highways by Night* (1942); *Bombardier* (1943); *Song of Texas* (1943); *The Cry of the Werewolf* (1944); *The Mummy's Ghost* (1944); *Secret Command* (1944); *Scared Stiff* (1945); *The Spanish Main* (1945); *Tarzan and the Amazons* (1945); *Santa Fe Uprising* (1946); *Cheyenne* (1947); *Tarzan and the Huntress* (1947); *Walls of Jericho* (1948); *Red Light* (1949); *Bandit Queen* (1950); *Kiss Tomorrow Goodbye* (1950); *Rookie Fireman* (1950); *The Half-Breed* (1952); *Sea of Lost Ships* (1953); *The Glenn Miller Story* (1954); *Blacklash* (1956); *Last of the Desperadoes* (1956); *The Naked Gun* (1956); *Naked in the Sun* (1957); *The Geisha Boy* (1958); *Noose for a Gunman* (1960); *Pocketful of Miracles* (1961); *The Rounders* (1965); *Town Tamer* (1965); *Arizona Bushwhackers* (1968); *Bucksin* (1968).

Dreaming of
Jeannie

Character actor Barton MacLane.

18

Vinton Hayworth

♦

Vinton J. Hayworth's final work in show business was his television portrayal of fairminded General Winfield Schaeffer in the last two seasons of *I Dream of Jeannie*. Born on June 4, 1906, in Washington, D.C., Hayworth began his acting career in Washington around 1925. He pioneered in his hometown on WRC radio and later moved to New York, broadcasting on WOR. Eventually, in Chicago, Hayworth became one of the original radio news broadcasters. He might be best remembered for the popular radio program *Myrt and Marge,* in which he portrayed the character of Jack Arnold.

Hayworth spent two years on Broadway in a 1942 production of *Doughgirls* and later moved to Southern California to make films. His niece was dancer Ginger Rogers; his wife (Jean Owens Hayworth) and Lela Rogers (Ginger's mother) were sisters. Hayworth was a founding member of the American Federation of Radio Artists (later AFTRA—to

Actor Vinton Hayworth as General Winfield Schaeffer.

"Guzman, We Have a Problem."

Shooting episodes in Honolulu posed many logistical difficulties, all of which had to be thoroughly worked out before the cast and crew left Southern California. One little surprise caught director Claudio Guzman off guard.

Both Hal Cooper and Claudio Guzman were to direct episodes in the islands, relieving each other of duties and allowing some time for fun in paradise. One morning, when filming was about to begin, word spread that the actor who was to play guest star Milton Berle's chauffeur was stuck back in L.A. on another shoot. "We were faced with immediately trying to get somebody," says Hal Cooper. "Not everybody knows how to be a good foil for Milton Berle and how to handle him. He's a tough guy, a professional, and he knows what he wants."

Cooper volunteered. He put on the dark overcoat and driver's cap and performed the role of Eddie the chauffeur himself.

include Television *and* Radio Artists). He was the president of AFTRA (1951–54) and for eleven years served on AFTRA's national board of directors.

In the 1940s, the actor worked in many feature films at 20th Century Fox. His film credits include *The Girl He Left Behind; The Great Man; Police Dog Story; Chamber of Horrors;* and *The Confession.* In Walt Disney's television series, *Zorro* (1957–59), Hayworth portrayed Magistrate Galindo. Additional episodic TV appearances include: *Gunsmoke; Perry Mason; Alfred Hitchcock Presents; Philco Television Playhouse; The Beverly Hillbillies; Dennis the Menace; Hazel; The Munsters;* and *Petticoat Junction.*

Hayworth died on May 21, 1970, just a few months after filming his last episode of *I Dream of Jeannie.*

OPPOSITE PAGE: *Director Hal Cooper goes over a scene with the actors.*

19

The Maid Did It:
The Unsolved Murder
of Herb Wallerstein

◆

It's unsolved as far as the family is concerned, because we know more. For legal purposes, the case is closed. It's over . . . but there are questions.

—Alexandria Wallerstein

hen the story hit the local evening news on September 29, 1985, the Hollywood entertainment industry was shocked to hear about the brutal murder of Herb Wallerstein, a well-known director and studio executive. The bludgeoned body of the fifty-nine-year-old man had been discovered by detectives that morning after it had been removed from the murder site, placed in an automobile, and torched only a few blocks from his home in a quiet Woodland Hills, California, neighborhood.

TOP: *Herb Wallerstein, circa 1950s.* BOTTOM: *Brothers Rowe and Herb Wallerstein just starting their careers in television. (Both photos courtesy of Alexandra Craig.)*

In some ways the illogic apparent in the outcome of this case is more maddening than the result of the O. J. Simpson trial. The obvious miscarriage of justice in the California court system remains simply mystifying. Mind-boggling. So if you don't wish to jump into a riddle to which there is no answer—advance to another chapter.

Naturally, the murder of this Hollywood director caused a media uproar in Los Angeles, and the funeral was a circus. Following the services, family and friends mourned at the Wallerstein home. "At the funeral, nobody knew who did it," says the victim's niece, Alex Wallerstein. "At the time, the maid was running around the house taking care of everybody. We kept thanking her for all the work she was doing. She was hovering over my aunt, taking care of her, cleaning the house, making food, consoling her."

Those from the *I Dream of Jeannie* days remembered Herb Wallerstein as a tall, nice-looking man who worked in different capacities such as assistant director, director, and associate producer during the first couple of seasons. Herb also worked on many other TV shows: *Rin Tin Tin; Father Knows Best; Hazel; Mission: Impossible; Star Trek; Bewitched; Gunsmoke; The Partridge Family; The Wild Wild West; The Six Million Dollar Man; Wonder Woman; Quincy.* Wallerstein and his two brothers, Rowe and Norman, began in the Columbia Pictures mailroom in the 1940s and later were among the new pool of assistant directors being passed around the Columbia Pictures/Screen Gems lot in the 1950s and into the 1960s. Each brother successfully worked his way up the film or television ladder, and developed a respectable, prominent career. Herb had freelanced for about twenty years until 1978, when he became senior vice president of studio production at 20th Century Fox. He stayed until 1985. During his tenure, he supervised such film productions such as *Alien, The Rose, 9 to 5, Breaking Away,* and *Porky's.*

The violent death of this man, who was described as "well-liked, outgoing, genteel," sadly went unsolved—though there was a suspect. Wallerstein's live-in housekeeper, a short, heavyset Salvadoran woman named Mayra Melendez Lopez, twenty-five, was charged with the murder of her employer two months after it occurred; the case quickly made it to trial. Lopez had been the prime suspect from the outset, said Los Angeles police detective Joseph Diglio at the time.

After confessing—on audiotape—to the beating and murder of Herb Wallerstein,

Lopez was later acquitted of all criminal charges by a Van Nuys, California, Superior Court jury and set free.

Unbelievable.

Imagine the family's horror: While initial news of the murder was shocking, the eventual arrest of the culprit was even more astonishing. And after the trial, the acquittal of the confessed killer in July 1986 overwhelmed everybody. The phrase "getting away with murder" took on a grievous new meaning in this family.

And of course, the mystery remains: What went through the minds of the jurors when they deliberated for two days and rendered a not guilty verdict on the charges of voluntary manslaughter and arson? And why wasn't the perpetrator charged with *involuntary* manslaughter or, at the very least, obstruction of justice? The system somehow failed deplorably.

"It was such a violent, tragic death," says Alex Wallerstein. "It was so unfair. And it saturated the news. I sat there and every news channel had it on, and they would show the drawings of the suspect—her—and then they'd show a picture of Uncle Herb."

Lopez, who had worked for the Wallerstein family for a little over six years, claimed self-defense. Although she did not testify during her trial, the tape recording of her sobbing admission was played for the jury. She confessed to bludgeoning Wallerstein with a baseball bat while other family members were vacationing in Mexico, but claimed that she acted in self-defense only after her employer inexplicably kicked the family dog, threw ice cream in her face, and hit her repeatedly, blackening her eye.

"He threw the tray and ice cream in my face," Lopez said in her confession. "I went to pick up the tray, he hit me. . . . When I fall down, he hit me in the eyes. . . . I took the bat . . . and hit him." The Associated Press reported additional details from the tape: "Asked why she didn't telephone police, Lopez said Wallerstein disconnected the telephone. She also said she was scared."

The *L.A. Times* reported: "In an effort to conceal the killing, she said she dragged Wallerstein's body out of the house and put it in the backseat of his car. She said her boyfriend then drove the car two blocks away and parked it. Two days later, the boyfriend, who has not been located, grew concerned that his fingerprints might be discovered on the vehicle, so he set it afire, Lopez said."

The prosecution presented a witness who identified Lopez as the individual she saw fleeing from the car minutes before it burst into flames. There were undeniable similarities between the police sketch (based on the witness's memory) and the maid, Lopez.

171

Dreaming of
Jeannie

Alex Wallerstein, who was thirty years old when her uncle was murdered, fumes about it still today. She can't erase the memory of her father, who was "always the strong one," breaking down at his brother's funeral—the only time she ever saw him weep.

"My uncle Herb was a diabetic," she points out. "And my uncle was sick that weekend with the flu while the rest of his family went to Mexico. You give a diabetic the flu and they're *really* down. The fact that he was in bed when she bludgeoned him. She was so little and fat. What on earth could he have threatened? What could have possessed her to do this in self-defense?

"She didn't just hit him. She bludgeoned him with a baseball bat. The woman redressed him, took his body out of the house, and put it in his son Danny's car, torched the car, and took his belongings and hid the murder.

"And the self-defense thing," Alex continues, "well, she had no black eyes at the funeral. No signs of abuse. Uncle Herb had a temper, but never a physical temper. Uncle Herb lived rather modestly. He didn't dress lavishly. Very conservative. What on earth could he have done to make her kill him while he was lying in bed, sick?"

The maid's initial statements eventually led police to the murder weapon, which was buried on a hillside about half a mile from the Wallerstein home.

Dreaming of
Jeannie

The *L.A. Herald-Examiner* reported on the trial: "Lopez said she went on a cleaning binge to eradicate blood and other evidence of the crime, then buried the murder weapon, the bloody sheet, a blond wig she wore to avoid detection and the victim's wallet at a nearby school." The wallet and other valuables were found and the police also discovered bloody sheets, which were used as evidence. The house had been scrubbed clean by the maid in an effort to cover up the incident. She remained in the employ of Wallerstein's widow and no one knew the truth until police assembled evidence and charged her two months after the death.

The tragedy and its sequel were a blow to the entire Wallerstein clan in Southern California. The Wallerstein brothers and their families were never active in the Hollywood "scene," explains Alex Wallerstein, so the attention the case received was alarming. "We went to public schools, we had the normal weekend barbecues, the family plays Monopoly on Saturday nights. . . . Our families were not in the Hollywood thing. Not big on that, and there weren't a lot of stars running in and out of our home. But were we exposed to it? Yes."

Because most of the Wallerstein brothers worked for many years in the entertainment industry—including Alex, who worked as a stand-in for a few years—the whole

In the fall of 1990, Barbara Eden became a semiregular on Larry Hagman's hit prime-time soap, Dallas. (According to news reports, the reunion was the brainchild of Hagman's mother, actress Mary Martin.) But wait . . . Eden played billionaire femme fatale LeAnn De La Vega, the owner of a Venezuelan oil empire, who becomes a rival to J. R. Ewing (Hagman). In one episode, empress De La Vega mentions that her maiden name was Nelson.

family was well-known. Says Alex: "Whenever I'd run into Larry Hagman over on the lot when he was doing *Dallas,* he'd look at me and joke, 'Uh-oh, it's a Wallerstein.'"

The kicker in the whole drama, however, came from within the family. Alex still finds it ironic that her uncle's wife, Emmita, and their adopted son, Danny, happened to be in Mazatlán, Mexico, when the crime occurred. "It was really weird that Danny went to Mexico during school time," she adds. "I have often wondered many times if that maid just took the rap for somebody else."

Stranger yet, widow Emmita testified on behalf of her killer-housekeeper at the trial. The Wallersteins were stunned and confused. "I remember talking to the detectives during the case," Alex says. "They were really upset the way it turned out."

Norman Montrose, a deputy district attorney at the time, labeled Lopez's account of the killing "a fairy tale" and attempted to argue to the jury that she used "excessive force" by striking Wallerstein at least three times with the baseball bat—once in the groin and twice in the head. Montrose told the *L.A. Times:* "The problem with the prosecution is that there are only two people who really know what happened—one is dead and the other gave a self-serving statement to police. I can't cross-examine a tape." (Lopez's public defender, Mark Lessem, chose not to put his client on the stand in her own defense, so cross-examination was not possible.)

To complicate matters, Alex Wallerstein now reveals there were additional, unsubstantiated family concerns that did not surface during the trial. These details and speculations are not to be scoffed at; they may or may not have led to other motives and accomplices. The police were satisfied then that they had the killer, confession in hand. But much time has passed, and the case has never been reopened for further investigation. Lopez, the acquitted maid, has since "either been deported, or she left the country," she says.

Dreaming of
Jeannie

20

Feminism and the Jeannie

By Susan J. Douglas

I Dream of Jeannie ran from 1965 to 1970 and featured a woman with magical powers; the show was predicated on a flagrant sexual display of Jeannie's body and her desires, even if the network censors made sure Barbara Eden's belly button was discreetly hidden. The premise rested on a male fantasy of a regular guy discovering a beautiful, naive, unworldly woman who will do anything for him and calls him Master, or, more formally, addresses him by his military rank. (That the "regular guy" was an astronaut played into another male fantasy, for good measure.) But the implied power and availability of Jeannie's sexuality were always a threat to her master, Captain (later Major) Tony Nelson, and sometimes he was most relieved and happiest when she was "in her bottle." Jeannie was always more amorous and sexualized than her master, and this, of course, is what got them into so much trouble. Captain Nelson tried in vain to contain Jeannie both physically and sexually, and in those episodes where Jeannie's bottle was lost, there was considerable tension until it was found and Jeannie could get back inside it again.

    I Dream of Jeannie differed from *Bewitched* in crucial ways that already suggested a backlash against the earlier show's discourse of empowerment. Jeannie did not intervene in community affairs the way Samantha did; in fact, she cared little for the public sphere. She was not the ideal 1960s wife who happened to have magical powers. In her pink chiffon harem pants, red bra, pom-pom-trimmed bolero jacket, and chiffon-draped headpiece, Jeannie was from another place and time, an anachronism in 1960s suburban America. She was the dumb, shapely, ditzy blonde with too much power, which she often used impetuously. Hyperfeminized, Jeannie was unreasonably jealous and possessive, giggled a lot, and was overly enthusiastic about whatever her master did; in fact, she often behaved and was treated like a child. Although she got her master into embarrassing situations, unlike Samantha she left him to explain his own way out. She was not seen as shrewder or more creative than Captain Nelson; after all, he was an astronaut, embedded in a world of science and technology, in the military-industrial complex women allegedly couldn't master. Jeannie's main goal was to serve Captain Nelson obsequiously, to get him to pay more attention to her and, she hoped, marry her. Although Captain Nelson kept insisting that he was the master of the house, Jeannie's magic constantly undermined that assertion. Yet the balance of power always tilted toward him, because Jeannie was more devoted to him and more emotionally dependent on him than he was on her.

Dreaming of
Jeannie

The fact that Jeannie didn't know how to behave like a "normal" woman was the basis for a number of plots in the show. In one telling episode, we see how *Jeannie,* despite its reliance on many of the same visual gags and tricks as *Bewitched* differed ideologically from its predecessor. In a 1965 episode, "The Americanization of Jeannie," Jeannie comes to feel that Captain Nelson devotes too much time and attention to his work and not enough to her. She reads a women's magazine and finds an article titled "The Emancipation of Modern Women." She asks, "What does emancipation mean?" and he answers, "You don't have to worry about anything like that." "Oh yes I do," she insists. "I want to understand your way of life so I can please you." She continues reading the article. "Are you a loser in the battle between the sexes? Is the man in your life aloof, indifferent, difficult to please? Does he fail to appreciate what you have to offer as a female? Answer: Challenge his masculine arrogance. Be

OPPOSITE PAGE: *Eden and Hagman filming the episode "The Americanization of Jeannie."*

independent, self-reliant, unpredictable. You must learn to cope with him on his own grounds. In short, you must become a modern American woman."

The next day, Nelson comes home to find the house a mess and no dinner on the table. Jeannie walks into the living room in a bathrobe and curlers and says "Hiya, old boy," instead of her usual, more fawning greeting. Nelson accuses her of not doing any housework, but Jeannie responds by citing part of her magazine article, "How Not to Be a Drudge." "Share the work with him," reads Jeannie as she reaches for a box of chocolates. "I'm an astronaut, not a house-keeper," explodes Nelson. "You must broaden your horizons," retorts Jeannie as she hands him a broom.

"She is ever-present, all-powerful; and single-mindedly devoted to doing good deeds for her Master. . . . No, Jeannie isn't perfect, but she's close enough to it that she reminds most American men of absolutely no one they know."
—TV Week, *1966.*

Needless to say, Nelson tells Jeannie that a real woman doesn't behave this way; his reactions, as well as the narrative, repudiate the role reversal she proposes. At the end of the episode, their original relationship is restored, and Nelson advises her, "You need an outlet for your affection. You need a pet." Advice from a magazine about female emancipation turns out to be very bad advice because it undermines the woman's femininity, makes her appear ridiculous, and alienates the man's affections. The advice, of course, is a parody of feminism, for it urges women to be deliberately unattractive and completely self-indulgent, and to make men do the housework while women do nothing at all.

Bewitched never took such a head-on approach to role reversal, so it didn't draw such stark boundaries between male and female spheres. *Bewitched* blurred gender roles; *I Dream of Jeannie* accentuated them. Yet both shows anticipated feminism and hailed the prefeminist viewer. Samantha was clearly a role model, while Jeannie was an extreme version of femininity that girls ought not to model themselves after. When women like that got power, look out.

Out and About

Actress Ellen Degeneres had this to say when presenting at the 50th Annual Emmy Awards telecast in 1998:

"I love television. I really, really do. Television can entertain us. It can inspire us. It can educate us. It's a way for us to look at other people's lives that we might not be accustomed to and learn something from. It's a way to feel represented, to feel validated, to look at someone on television and say, 'That's me! There's someone else like me out there!' Before *Mr. Ed*, anyone who heard a horse talking to them thought they were crazy. People said it was unnatural, that horses didn't talk. Growing up as a little girl, I felt isolated and I know I wasn't alone. I, like many other young girls, would fantasize about dressing a little slutty, pleasing my man—even calling him master. And if I was naughty, I'd be put in a bottle with a cork on it . . . till my master thought it was time to come out."

179

Dreaming of **Jeannie**

Thus, *I Dream of Jeannie* was more of a warning. In *Betwitched,* Darrin's work in an advertising agency was repeatedly compromised by the inappropriate exercise of female power. In *I Dream of Jeannie,* the ante was upped: Now magic inspired by female desire, jealousy, and possessiveness threatened to disrupt one of the crowning achievements of 1960s male technocracy, the U.S. space program. Even NASA was no match for female power and sexuality run amok. In *Bewitched,* female power could be accommodated; in *Jeannie,* it could not. Because of these differences, the central mixed message remains: Female power, when let loose in the public sphere, is often disruptive to male authority, but sometimes it also bolsters that authority. These colliding messages made *Bewitched* and *I Dream of Jeannie* simultaneously cautionary and liberatory. The schizophrenic female persona such shows helped constitute saw female obsequiousness amply rewarded. But the viewer also saw empowering images of a woman physically zapping things—including men—into their proper place.

SUSAN J. DOUGLAS is the author of *Where the Girls Are: Growing Up Female with the Mass Media,* an engaging, insightful, and often irreverent analysis of our popular culture and how it helped shape female psyches.

21

Bill Daily on Almost Everything

◆

Author's note: Discussing his career from his home in Albuquerque, New Mexico, Bill Daily proves to be a reporter's delight. His stream of consciousness moves a mile a minute, so if you can catch him and keep up, you end up having a great time. Many interviewers have posed the same question to Daily: "Whom did you prefer working with—Larry Hagman or Bob Newhart?" Daily is eager to expound on this—and nearly any other topic. Candidly, he provided his thoughts about the five years he spent on *I Dream of Jeannie*.

On Bob Newhart vs. Larry Hagman

Newhart was the nicest person I've ever worked with. I mean that. But he didn't like physical comedy, and Newhart is a nightmare to work with because he doesn't want to rehearse because that's the best for his comedy timing. We just did it and that's it. When you don't rehearse anything, everything's a nightmare.

A family of hillbillies mistakes Tony and Roger for a couple of Martians in the episode "U.F.Ohhhh Jeannie!"

Larry, he's crazy. But Larry and I would work things out, go over it. Larry loved to do that. I not only love Larry, but I loved working with him.

Larry was very professional. He always knew his lines, but he didn't like the lines. The scripts would have us standing there for fifteen minutes in a two-shot with nothing else to do. Larry and I would actually direct the movement. If we were on a scaffold, Larry would say, "Okay, you fall down and the paint falls on you. I'll fall down here and you walk there and I'll move over here. This is moving pictures, folks!" We worked out a ballet. I loved that stuff, working out the business. If you tried that today, they'd throw you out of the studio. So without Larry, there wouldn't have been any show.

On Working with Larry Hagman

I noticed in one of those extensive *Playboy* interviews with him—and you know, those things go on for hours, they talk and talk—he talked for eighty thousand pages and never mentioned *Jeannie*. And that was five years of his life. He seemed very unhappy about that period of time. I never understood it. I'd sure like to know. I think with his new liver came a new attitude.

Larry was a little of an egomaniac. I think that made him insecure. He wanted to be the star and everything went to Barbara [Eden]. When someone big would come on the show, like Sammy Davis, Jr., he would tighten up. Larry's personality would change. He'd get weird and clam up and get angry and hide in his trailer. He wanted to be noticed, so he did other things, like a naughty boy. He would do things to get noticed. It all boils down to he wanted to be the star. And he was. Not many people have realized how brilliant he was in that. People who don't do comedy don't know the importance of

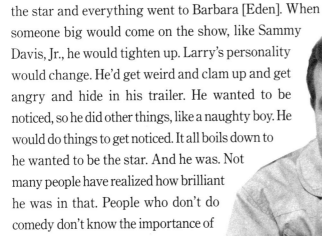

OPPOSITE PAGE: *Bill Daily, a fresh face in sitcoms, ready for the long haul in TV Land.*
RIGHT: *Major Healey with Sam the chimpanzee.*

a pivot man, which makes the jokes work. But when someone wanted a cover for *TV Guide,* they didn't want us, they went with Barbara with the tits. So I think it had a lot to do with his ego. When he was the star of *Dallas,* he was a different person.

Toward the end, Larry wouldn't talk to anyone, he just hid in his room. He wouldn't do off-camera lines. He was unhappy with everybody. Here, I'm the third or fourth banana and it's my first show. I'm just trying to struggle through it. I didn't know any different. I don't know why Larry was so damned upset. I don't know if he was upset because I got a lot of the jokes and Barbara got all the star billing, but he slowly pulled away from that show. I just would love to know, somehow, someday, what really pissed him off. I hope it wasn't me. I hope I had nothing to do with it. As tough as he was to work with and his temperament, I liked the work and I liked him. I learned a lot. I wish we could do another one before we both have strokes. I would have given him my liver, but I was gone.

On Working with Barbara Eden

Barbara was very cool, calm, very easygoing. She was the star, a gracious star. She never complained, she never bitched, she never pulled any "star" shit. She was a dynamite lady throughout the whole thing.

Something that Barbara and I should have never done and it was unfair to Larry . . . we let him be the heavy. We should have come in sometimes when the scripts got so awful. Larry got upset. He didn't know how to handle it and we let him take the blame. He never wanted more money, he just wanted better scripts. Without Barbara, so sweet and kind, we wouldn't have gone on as long as we did. Because I'm crazy and Larry's crazy. Hayden Rorke, he was beyond a gentleman, and between those two, they held it together.

On Hayden Rorke

I didn't know he was gay. No one ever brought it up. I know he lived with a guy for years. I don't remember him ever having a girlfriend, but I never thought of it. He was such an incredible entertainer and such a nifty guy. Hayden was never effeminate, always played it straight on the set. He was always a complete gentleman. But hey, that was great for me because I'm a womanizer. I got all the girls. I'm oversexed anyway. I

OPPOSITE PAGE: *Hayden Rorke laughs at a real pisser of a gag with Bill Daily at a party.*

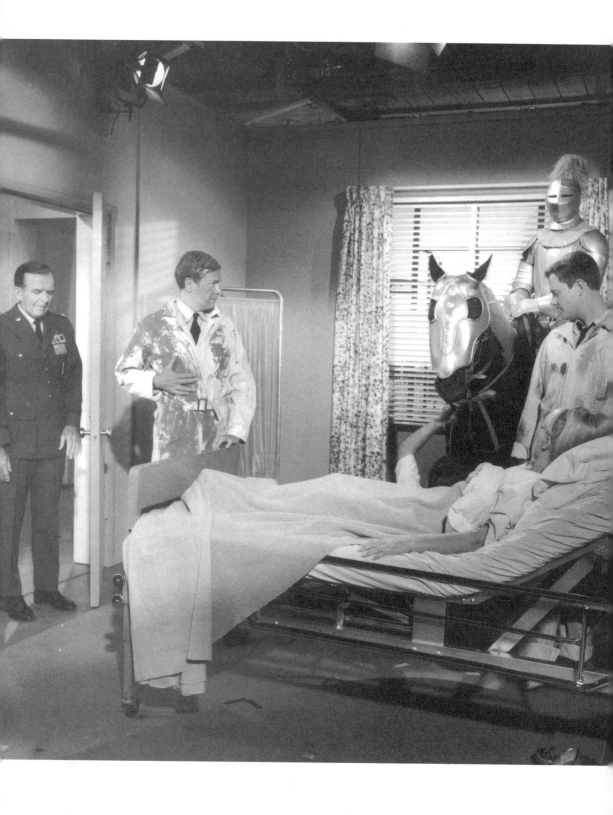

dig women. Let me tell you, when Farrah Fawcett played my girlfriend in a few episodes, oh my God, I get a hard-on just thinking about it.

On Sidney Sheldon

Very often during the show, my wife and I went to sit-down, intimate dinners on Monday nights with Sidney Sheldon at his home. Lots of celebrity guests, Groucho Marx, Cary Grant. We'd have drinks and maybe watch a movie. I was very "in" with Sidney at that time because of his fall[ing] out with Larry. I became his "star." I was lucky to be a part of it, there at those dinners with all those superstars.

In person, Sidney is beyond brilliant. But I wonder why he couldn't write some of that down. He is one of the quickest, wittiest men I've ever known, but when he wrote *Jeannie,* I sometimes wondered what happened to all that wit.

On Comedy

My favorite, all-time comedian is Jack Benny. I copied my style and mannerisms from the funniest man alive, Harry Ritz. We all copied him, ask any comic. I flunked second grade because of him—I was out watching his movies. Jerry Lewis did him as well.

ABOVE: *Seventies portrait of Bill Daily.* OPPOSITE PAGE: *Suffering from amnesia, Jeannie is finally convinced by Tony that she possesses special powers and she blinks up a knight in shining armor.*

22

Barbara Eden "Jeannie"

Sidney Sheldon

The End

What can you say about a 2,000-year-old genie who doesn't die?

That she was beautiful. And resilient. That she knew Mozart and Bach. And the Beatles. And Tony.

Consider, for a moment, the basic premise of *I Dream of Jeannie*—in case you've forgotten. As created by Sidney Sheldon, this story is about a stranded astronaut who uncorks a beautiful blonde in diaphanous finery who declares she is now his slave. "What really comes out of the bottle," Sheldon said at the time, "is a lot of trouble."

Writer Edgar Penton assessed the relationship of Tony Nelson and Jeannie: "Trouble arises from the fact that Jeannie, however supernatural she may be, is also a woman . . . feminine, jealous, and capricious. Although she insists on calling Tony 'master' and proclaims that her only desire is to grant his every wish and obey his every whim, more often than not, she is the one who controls *him*."

No escape hatch for this astronaut. The fateful wedding of Tony Nelson and Jeannie during the show's fifth and final season.

Larry Hagman insists it wasn't a sexist show. "The question is, *who* was the slave and *who* was the master? We weren't trying to send out any messages in those days. We were just trying to get a laugh."

"Actually," Sidney Sheldon pointed out even in the beginning, "it is in some ways symbolic of the relationship between masterful man and his supposedly servile woman that exists in real life. They may both claim that he's the boss, but in practice it doesn't usually work that way."

It was the sexual tension, some believe, that carried the relationship between Tony Nelson and Jeannie. It also held viewers' attention and kept the audiences returning each week. Marriage seemed out of the question, even midway through the series.

Said Barbara Eden at the start of the show's third season: "I've been chasing [Tony Nelson] for years and can't catch him because that would be the end of the show. If we got married, I think it would ruin the series.

"Besides," she added, "who can marry a genie? She's a wisp."

Yes, the tale of Tony and Jeannie is a love story, reflecting the wide range of subtleties, nuances, and complexities of any human partnership. In reality, marriage—or any official union—is supposed to be the healthy outcome of a loving relationship. An apogee, a ripening, a zenith. A blossoming in a relationship, when two set off together to face the world and exist in each other's love.

But what did love and marriage have to do with this sitcom? Some speculate that it might have been wiser to continue the live-in arrangements as they were. It was the chase in Tony and Jeannie's relationship that fueled viewers and when it was time to marry off the two, it meant the end, not a new beginning.

No Deposit, No Return

Undeniably, the most miserable thing in Sidney Sheldon's personal production files is a memo on Screen Gems stationery, dated 1970, from production head Seymour Friedman.

It says, in part:

"This is to confirm that since we have no further use for the large Jeannie bottle set, it will be removed from Stage #1 and destroyed."

Jeannie 0, Apollo 13

The final original episode of I Dream of Jeannie ("My Master, the Chili King") aired May 26, 1970, and from that moment on, we've skated on reruns forever. This particular humorless episode about Tony's Texas cousin Arvel was slated to air six weeks prior, on April 14, 1970, but something happened.

While it's true a record number of viewers were riveted to the TV screen at 7:30 that night, Eden's near-navel had nothing to do with it. Jeannie *had vanished, preempted by continuous breaking-news coverage of the terror that forced NASA into its finest hour. There were no comedic astronauts in this broadcast.*

The entire nation held its breath as teams of technicians here on earth scrambled and sweated to secure the safe return of NASA's Apollo 13 crew members, James A. Lovell, John L. Swigert, and Fred W. Haise. The astronauts, who nearly drifted into space, pushed themselves to the brink as they attempted to repair the command module, which had suffered a major malfunction, placing their lives in jeopardy. The dramatic story was told by filmmaker Ron Howard in the 1995 mega-hit motion picture, Apollo 13.

191

Dreaming of
Jeannie

"They never should have gotten married," says Larry Hagman of the characters. "It was downhill from then on."

Bill Daily compared the wedding on *Jeannie* with the union of Max and 99 on *Get Smart* following several successful seasons of their own. "Marriage killed both of us," Daily says. "You know what happened? Sidney Sheldon didn't want to do it or lose the show. We were never great in the ratings, always iffy. If we were number one we would have still gone on.

"What happened," Daily explains, "was the network came in and told us, 'She's got to get married.' And that was the end of the show. Sidney fought it. Once Jeannie was married, it was down the toilet. The focus of the show changed. We all knew it was going to happen."

Love means never having to say you're sorry about bad ratings.

23

Reentry

◆

When NBC announced plans to resurrect Jeannie *for a TV movie, Johnny Carson joked, "She now appears when you rub a bottle of Geritol."*

 had no intention of playing Jeannie again," insisted Barbara Eden to a *L.A. Times* reporter in 1985.

Something swayed Eden. Maybe the time was right, and she decided it would be fun to blink again in a TV movie, *I Dream of Jeannie: 15 Years Later*. "It's like being in a time warp," she told one writer. "I said to Bill Daily, 'This is crazy—nothing's changed since 1965!'"

There were a few modifications. The two-hour NBC movie update involved Eden, then fifty-one, once again pulling on the pink pantaloons—only this time, her navel would see the light of day. Eden was startlingly well-preserved, hav-

Wayne Rogers replaced Larry Hagman in the dreadful television "reunion" movie, I Dream of Jeannie: 15 Years Later *(1985).*

"Jeannie's Diner"

*U*nlike other classic sitcoms, I Dream of Jeannie *has inspired only a handful of comedy parody songs, and that's a generous estimate. One of the most popular and timely is "Jeannie's Diner," cleverly conceived by Mark Davis, who has contributed many a jingle to NBC-TV's prime-time promos.*

The chanty, mantralike parody has been aired on radio and released on CD and was featured in an exquisite I Dream of Jeannie *promotional campaign on Nick at Nite. The parody's impact reached further than composer Davis ever imagined when he devised the piece, he says.*

"Jeannie's Diner" is actually a twist on a twist. It began as a Suzanne Vega single "Tom's Diner," an a cappella song about a New York coffee shop which was released on her album Solitude Standing *in 1987. Later in 1990, a British band called D.N.A. sampled the original "Tom's Diner," adding a funky instrumental track and Vega's vocal. The song reached Number 5 on a Billboard chart in November 1990.*

Mark Davis, a producer at Premier Radio Networks, took the concept one step further and wrote the "Jeannie's Diner" parody—a tribute to one of his favorite sitcoms—and it became a popular novelty song on morning radio shows throughout the country. The next year, it wound up on an album released by Vega—a compilation of "Tom's Diner" parodies. The CD, released by A&M records, sold throughout the world and Dr. Demento featured the "Jeannie's Diner" theme on his nationally syndicated radio program in 1992.

When cable TV's Nick at Nite began airing I Dream of Jeannie *in prime time in 1993, the parody was noticed by the network's vice president of On-Air Promotions, Scott Webb. "Diner" became a flashy feast of nostalgia in a music video produced as a promo for the sitcom on Nick at Nite. The music video was produced by Agi Fodor and directed by Barney Miller, with a set designed by Steve Thomas; it included a gorgeous, blond Barbara Eden look-alike in a harem costume. It has aired on MTV as well, and won an award at the Broadcast Design Awards competition. In 1996, Nick at Nite received a Gold World Medal for Entertainment Program Promotion at the International Film and Television Festival.*

194
Dreaming of
Jeannie

ing remained curvaceous and trim since the last time male audiences lusted after "Jeannie" in prime time.

People magazine noted, "Jeannie's beltline may have been lowered, but her consciousness has been raised. Barbara Corday, cocreator of 'Cagney and Lacey,' produced this sequel and tries to give its frothy heroine a NOW twist." Unfortunately, the feel and the overall tone of the movie lacked the frantic pace of the original series, and was nearly devoid of the physical comedy vital to the sitcom's appeal. Ironically, the movie was directed by longtime *Bewitched* veteran William Asher.

There was a twist in this TV movie plot: This "now" Jeannie was more assertive and independent; the mother of one son (played by Mackenzie Astin), she is sick of being taken for granted by her "master," and she moves out. The ad line for highly publicized two-hour movie: "Jeannie Shows Her Master Who's Boss."

Weeks before its broadcast, Eden, Bill Daily, and Hayden Rorke were all busily pro-

I Dream of Jeannie: 15 Years Later

Broadcast: NBC-TV, October 20, 1985
Production Company: Can't Sing, Can't Dance Productions/Columbia Pictures Television
Executive Producer: Barbara Corday
Producer: Hugh Benson
Director: William Asher
Written by Irma Kalish, from a story by Dinah Kirgo, Julie Kirgo, and Irma Kalish
Music: Mark Snow
    Cast: Barbara Eden, Wayne Rogers, Mackenzie Astin, Bill Daily, Hayden Rorke, John Bennett Perry, Dody Goodman, Lee Taylor Allan, Dori Brenner, Ronalda Douglas, André De Shields, Michael Fairman, Dierk Torsek, Belita Moreno, Nicole Eggert, Niall Gartlan, Hettie Lynne Hurtes, Helen J. Siff, Brandon Call, Bill Shick

moting the reunion of *I Dream of Jeannie's* original cast. Most of the cast. Larry Hagman was the maverick.

Hagman pauses for a moment. "I'm trying to think what happened there," he said in a recent interview, a dozen years after the fact. "Bill Asher was producing it. I got a call one day while I was doing *Dallas.* The person asked if I would come in for costume fittings. I said, 'For what?' They said, 'The reunion film of *I Dream of Jeannie.*'

"This was somebody from NBC," Hagman points out. "They said, 'We understand you're going to be in it, a cameo or something.'

"I hadn't been approached. Then they told me they were starting on Wednesday and they needed me by Monday for costume fittings. I asked who was producing. So I called Bill Asher and I said, 'I don't understand. What's happening?'"

According to Hagman, he relayed his surprise at all of this to Asher, who was equally shocked, only for a different reason. "Then I heard this noise on the other end of the line," Hagman said, making a painful choking sound. "Bill said, 'NBC assured me . . .'

"I told Bill, 'Hey, I don't want to throw a curve, but honest to God, I don't know anything about it.'"

TOP: *Still magical, Jeannie became a contemporary woman fighting to save her marriage in the TV movie* I Dream of Jeannie: 15 Years Later. RIGHT: *Barbara Eden, Bill Daily, and Hayden Rorke reprise their* I Dream of Jeannie *roles along with Wayne Rogers as astronaut Tony Nelson in the NBC-TV movie,* I Dream of Jeannie: 15 Years Later *(1985).*

Fill in the Blink

Test your knowledge, oh great one. If you think you are a master of I Dream of Jeannie *trivia*, take a stab at these teasers:

1. Jeannie's birthdate is _____.
2. Which star of TV's Charlie's Angels *made two guest appearances on* I Dream of Jeannie?
3. Identify the most powerful and most feared of all genies: _____.
4. _____ was Tony Nelson's romantic interest prior to Jeannie.
5. In what episode does Roger Healey find out about Jeannie's special qualities?
6. Which stars of TV's M*A*S*H *appeared in* I Dream of Jeannie?
7. What member of TV's Addams Family *cast portrayed Jeannie's uncle, Suleiman of Bensengi?*
8. _____ is the name of Jeannie's candy, which executes hidden fantasies in those who eat it.
9. Jeannie's mischievous dog is named _____.
10 Tony Nelson was sometimes called _____ in his youth.

Answers

1. April 1, 64 B.C. 2. Farrah Fawcett 3. The Blue Djinn (portrayed by Michael Ansara)(4. Melissa Stone (portrayed by Karen Sharpe) 5. Episode #17: "The Richest Astronaut in the Whole World." 6. Mike Farrell and Jamie Farr 7. Jackie Coogan (Uncle Fester on The Addams Family) 8. Pip Chicks 9. Djinn-Djinn 10. "Bunky" Nelson

LEFT: *Djinn in Tunic: Michael Ansara is the menacing Blue Djinn.*

Hagman says there was never any discussion between himself and any of the other cast members or Sidney Sheldon. No preproduction lunches, no reminiscing on the telephone, no "Hey, this will be fun. . . . It'll be great to get together again. . . . We're gonna have a good time." None of that.

Following a day of burning up the phone lines back and forth, production associates for the TV movie made one last call and delivered to Hagman a late, but formal invitation.

"I said, 'Okay, sure, what are you paying?'" Hagman recalls, "and they said five thousand."

That was when *Hagman* began choking. "I said to them, 'God, somehow that doesn't. . . .' Well, I told them, 'Why don't you just pay me what Barbara's getting?' and of course that became out of the question. So I didn't do it.

"And to tell you the truth, I didn't watch it. I've got the movie on tape, but I've just never gotten around to it."

Hagman is definitely a man who has mellowed over the years. He added: "I loved doing [*I Dream of Jeannie*] when we did it. I hate going home again. Revisiting. Except for *Dallas,* which has paid a hell of a lot more than [the *Jeannie* movie] offered."

Bill Daily says he was "charged" about reuniting with his old friends and freezing for the camera just for old times' sake. He remembers the sinking feeling in his stomach the first day of production. "I was incredibly disappointed," he says. "When we did the first *Jeannie* movie, they said [Larry Hagman] was going to be in there. I'm in my dressing room getting ready and Wayne Rogers walks in. . . . That just killed me."

As military roles go, Wayne Rogers was exceptionally funny in *M*A*S*H,* but the cast of *I Dream of Jeannie* had been expecting Larry Hagman, and frankly, fans were hoping to see him next to his TV wife, too. If anything, viewers wanted some comic relief from the years of cultivated loathing that they expended on J. R. Ewing.

Despite the casting substitution, the movie aired and NBC couldn't have been more pleased with the results. As for ratings, it placed a close second to a World Series game that night and ended up as the eleventh-highest rated TV movie that year. In 1991, NBC decided to go to the well again and scheduled another TV movie, *I Still Dream of Jeannie,* with Eden—now fifty-seven—donning the harem outfit.

During the flurry of press hype, Eden told *TV Guide:* "To reprise something you did like that 25 years ago is pretty scary," she said. "I'm human, and of course, I thought about it more than twice. If I were playing any other part, I think I would have to grapple with its appropriateness, but Jeannie is different. She's a classical character. The costume isn't a beach bunny costume, after all. I would never do that. What really concerned me about my age was, I didn't want to disappoint the audience who is used to seeing me as Jeannie looked 25 years ago. But I just decided to go ahead and do it."

No one stood in for Larry Hagman or Wayne Rogers this time. The character of Tony Nelson was written out of the script, something about an extended secret mission in space. Bill Daily joined Eden for the second sequel, but even he couldn't provide the humorous or nostalgic kick-start this script desperately needed. (Hayden Rorke had died of cancer a few years earlier.) The character who did return was Jeannie's jealous sister, the brunette terror of equal power who decides to make life miserable for her sprite sister with the astronaut master.

Any curiosity that had swelled within fans over the years was probably quenched by the first TV reunion. This second go was not well received by casual viewers or even by die-hard *Jeannie* fans. It struck out in the ratings, demolished by the World Series and a rival revival, *Dynasty: The Reunion.* To make matters worse, the country watched much of the San Francisco Bay area burn in a tragic fire on that day. Needless to say, the big news that evening was not about a lady named Jeannie—no matter how good she still looked.

A reunion for the two stars of *I Dream of Jeannie* finally transpired one morning in March 1995. Larry Hagman and Barbara Eden sat down for a chat on NBC's *Today* show, when Katie Couric paid tribute to a handful of TV comedy classics. The *I Dream of Jeannie* installment was the first of the five-part pretaped series, which explored a handful of television's most popular sitcoms. It was an ode to those eternal reruns, which have miraculously taken on a life of their own.

Hagman, in an extraordinary pretransplant interview, appeared thin and slightly jaundiced, although his obvious deterioration was not broached. Nonetheless, his attitude was warm, upbeat, and surprisingly nostalgic. Eden's and Hagman's mutual fondness and affection had never been more evident than in this rare moment in television history.

"Here was a guy," Hagman said of his character, "with the most beautiful girl in the world. He could do anything, go any place. It was really fantasy and real fun."

At the right time, the perky host asked her guest to do her "thing," Eden obliged: She folded her arms and blinked them all off the set.

One of Mickey Rooney's most brilliant performances, one which earned him an Emmy Award, was that of a lonely, dependent mentally retarded man named William Sackter ("Bill for short"). The true story was made into a now classic TV movie in 1981. Bill is about the friendship between young filmmaker Barry Morrow (portrayed by Dennis Quaid) and a simple-minded adult man who has spent forty-six years in a state mental institution and suddenly must cope with the outside world. Poor Bill didn't seem to get much satisfaction out of life, but he perks up when his favorite television show is on . . . yep, it's I Dream of Jeannie.

Bill is hooked on Jeannie. *Several times in the movie, he refers to the program. "Television . . . oh boy," he says with wide eyes, "I Dream of Jeannie, that's . . . a cutie." His new friend Barry decides to point the camera at him and film a documentary about his life. "Is this going to be like the* Dream of Jeannie *show?" Bill asks shyly. "That's a good one."*

Bottled Products

Compared to the rest of that swarm of wacky sixties sitcoms, I Dream of Jeannie *was accompanied by a surprisingly scant line of merchandise during its original run. If you throw it in a pile, original Jeannieana basically amounts to this: a few dolls, a paperback book, two issues of a Dell comic book, a board game, Halloween costumes . . . and not much else.*

Hungry fans of the show, however, are known to collect these vintage items and virtually anything bearing the image of Barbara Eden or the bottle (whether it was officially marketed or not). If you really went hunting, maybe scanning the multitudes of Jeannie *websites on the Internet, you might locate additional items for sale or trade: original NBC press releases,* TV Guide *issues featuring Hagman and Eden on the cover, a Barbara Eden record album, Jim Beam bottles, animation cels, life-sized standees of Eden as Jeannie, color and black-and-white publicity photographs, scripts from the original productions, 16 mm films of the episodes . . . the list goes on.*

In the mid-1990s, Trendmasters, a St. Louis–based toy company, released a line of kiddie toys based on the series' characters. Rather than featuring an image of Barbara Eden on their colorful packaging, Trendmasters employed a generic blond cartoon of a curvaceous genie (highly reminiscent of Disney's Little Mermaid) along with the TV show's recognizable title logo. Trendmasters developed and marketed an array of Jeannie items: play sets, lockets, miniature "Magic Wish Bottles," and a Jeannie Magic Palace.

The upscale dollmaker Madame Alexander marketed a collectible set of Jeannie and Major Nelson dolls (in the form of costumed babies) in 1996. The price tag: $195. In addition, the Nickelodeon cable network produced a collector's wristwatch (with a pink wristband) featuring the animated Jeannie from the show's cartoon opening. The Columbia House Video Library has released many episodes of I Dream of Jeannie *on videocassette (by subscription) and a line of Screen Gems TV Classics has been marketed in video stores, including volumes of* I Dream of Jeannie.

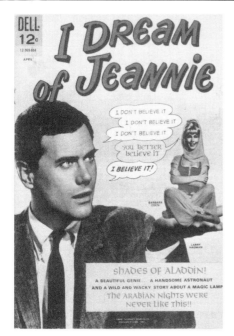

TOP LEFT: TV Guide *(February 1966) described Barbara Eden: "beautifully chic, poised, well-coiffed actress. . . . She is also emotional, sentimental, practical and, above all, ambitious." (Reprinted by permission of* TV Guide. *Copyright 1966, News America Publications, Inc.)* ABOVE: *"Miss Barbara Eden" hi-fi and stereo LPs released on Dot Records label, circa 1966, 1967.* TOP RIGHT: Jeannie *paperback book, published by Bantam, circa 1966.* LEFT: *Only two issues of a* Jeannie *comic book (Dell Comics) were released, circa 1966. (Courtesy of Daniel Wachtenheim.)*

BOTTOM: *Milton Bradley's* Jeannie *boardgame, circa 1966. (Courtesy of Darren Dill.)* TOP LEFT: *Current* Jeannie *play set produced by Trendmasters.* RIGHT: *Vintage 18-inch Jeannie doll featuring sleep-eyes and rooted blond hair; made by Libby-Marjorette in 1966. One of these dolls is featured in the episode "My Master, the Author." (Courtesy of Daniel Wachtenheim.)* OPPOSITE PAGE TOP: *Larger than life: Roseanne and Tom Arnold posed for the cover of* Esquire, *March 1993. Soon after, Roseanne was dreaming of divorce. (Reprinted courtesy of* Esquire *magazine and the Hearst Corporation.)* OPPOSITE PAGE BOTTOM: *A Halloween party on the popular Fox TV show* Beverly Hills 90210 *has Steve (Ian Zierling, left) and Clare (Kathleen Robertson, right) going as Major Nelson and Jeannie in the episode "Gypsies, Cramps & Fleas."*

Changing Times at *The New York Times*
By ROBERT SAM ANSON

JIM HARRISON'S
New Novella

Esquire

THE MAGAZINE FOR MEN

Shakespeare's Dead!
Roseanne's in Syndication!

The Final Victory of the American Sitcom!

Roseanne and
Tom Arnold
as the bad
dream of
Jeannie

PLUS: The Twenty-five Most
Important People in TV Comedy
AND: How
You Too Can
Get Rich!

0 748515 2   03

March 1993 · $2.50

205

Dreaming of
Jeannie

LEFT: *One of Barbara Eden's original costumes on display at Planet Hollywood, Beverly Hills, circa 1990s. The bottle is a reproduction. (Photo by Dan Thome.)*
BOTTOM: *The new Jeannie Halloween costume made by Rubie's (1997). Jodie Marhanka, model. (Photo by Salvador Pequeño.)*

206
Dreaming of
Jeannie

Crazy for Jeannie

While working in the programming department of a small—but mighty—Los Angeles television station in the mid-1980s, Elizabeth Moran faced a demented *Jeannie* fan. True story. Keep in mind, one of Moran's work responsibilities was to field calls from viewers. Unfortunately, the station's security was minimal, and gaining access to any office at the station was strangely easy. On this particular day, Moran wished she had taken leave.

All morning, I kept getting these calls from this woman and she was wacko. She kept asking where she could purchase the original I Dream of Jeannie *costume. I kept telling her it was either in a broadcasting museum or it's not in existence or maybe Barbara Eden had it. I had no idea. I told her repeatedly, "We just air the show, ma'am." She kept calling. Finally, the switchboard began questioning and complaining because this woman would not go away.*

I stayed in the building for lunch that day, which was unusual, and I went around to reception to pick up my messages. There was this woman in the lobby who was like, well, she was a bag-lady version of Jeannie. She had the whole hair thing with the big ponytail that Barbara Eden had . . . the whole flowing pink costume and she had a long Arabian sword. You know, like a machete. I thought, "Oh, my God."

This lady was in our lobby demanding to see someone about purchasing the I Dream of Jeannie *costume, and remember, there was no protective wall or glass-enclosed area for the receptionist.*

I called the security desk and they arrived and hauled her out. I'll never forget it. What's so weird, is that a couple of days later, our crack security force really blew it. We had a life-size cutout figure of Adam West as Batman standing in the lobby. This same security officer thought it was an intruder one night and shot at it. Later, the management took away the bullets and the gun.

Epilogue: Elizabeth Moran no longer works at the small—but mighty—Los Angeles television station, and says she is glad of it.

Dreaming of
Jeannie

24

Episode Guide

✦

Cast

Maharani Jeannie I (a k a Jeannie)..Barbara Eden

Anthony (Tony) Nelson*...Larry Hagman

Roger Healey*..Bill Daily

Dr. (Colonel) Alfred Bellows..Hayden Rorke

Amanda Bellows (1966–70)..Emmaline Henry

General Wingard Stone (1965–66)..Philip Ober

General Martin Peterson (1965–69)..Barton MacLane

General Winfield Schaeffer (1969–70)...Vinton Hayworth

Captains Tony Nelson and Roger Healey were eventually promoted to major.

Network: NBC

First Prime-time Telecast: September 18, 1965

Last Prime-time Telecast: September 1, 1970

Syndication: Screen Gems/Columbia Pictures Television

Jeannie assists her master in the desert of Skull Flats, Utah, on a NASA survival mission in "Guess What Happened on the Way to the Moon?"

Facts about the Pilot

✳ *Filming for the pilot concluded on December 4, 1964.*

✳ *Emerging from her bottle, Barbara Eden actually spoke Persian. The script originally called for her to utter Arabic, but a tutor for that language could not readily be found in Hollywood.*

✳ *The bird digging its claws in Larry Hagman's arm was Jimmy, a young red-tailed hawk. Jimmy had appeared in other motion pictures, including* Bikini Beach *(1964),* John Goldfarb, Please Come Home *(1965), and* The War Lord *(1965). When working opposite Charlton Heston in* The War Lord, *the bird was found to suffer from a sight defect. Jimmy was fitted for contact lenses by an optometrist rather than being replaced.*

✳ *The beach scene was filmed at Southern California's Zuma Beach, the same location used in some early episodes of* Gilligan's Island.

✳ *A* Variety *critic lambasted the pilot two days after it aired: "Screen Gems, having scored strongly with 'Bewitched' last season, makes an attempt to emulate its own success with this new entry . . . only this time the doll is a genie instead of a witch. Unoriginal in execution, 'Jeannie' is also unimaginative and unfortunate. It is one of the weaker entries of this new season."*

✳ *The end credits list Larry Hagman as portraying Captain Anthony Wilson.*

Actor Phil Ober plays General Wingard Stone in the first season. Ober was married to actress Vivian Vance—you know, Ethel on I Love Lucy. **Phil Ober died in 1982.**

The following is a complete list of episodes (30 filmed in black and white, 109 in color), in order of their air date.

First Season

1. "The Lady in the Bottle" (Pilot)
Air Date: September 18, 1965
Written by Sidney Sheldon
Directed by Gene Nelson
Guest Cast: Philip Ober, Karen Sharpe, Baynes Barron, Joe Higgins, Richard Reeves, Warren Kemmerling, Patricia Scott, Don Dubbins

After an emergency with NASA's failed *Stardust I* rocket, astronaut Tony Nelson's capsule lands on a remote island in the Pacific Ocean. There he stumbles upon a bottle and uncorks a 2,000-year-old voluptuous, blonde genie. Tony attempts to leave the genie behind after he is rescued, but he has unwittingly become her master—for life. The genie, known as Jeannie, appears at Tony Nelson's house in Cocoa Beach, Florida, and the astronaut frantically tries to keep her existence a secret from his coworkers as well as his fiancée, Melissa.

2. "My Hero?"
Air Date: September 25, 1965
Written by Sidney Sheldon
Directed by Gene Nelson
Guest Cast: Richard Kiel, Henry Corden, Florence Sundstrom, Jan Arvan, Peter Brocco, Pamela Curran, Magda Harout, Jeno Mate

Jeannie is reminded of Ali, a man who hit her while she was shopping in Baghdad 2,000 years ago. Tony insists on avenging the callous act, unaware it occurred centuries ago.

Note: Beginning with this episode, notice the excess netting and material around Eden's costume and waistline to conceal her pregnancy. In this episode, Florence Sundstrom portrays Jeannie's mother, but later in the series Jeannie's mother is portrayed by Lurene Tuttle, and eventually Eden assumed the role herself.

Actor Henry Corden commented in 1998 about this episode: "I only did this one episode, which was surprising to me. Since I played Jeannie's father, I suspected they would bring me back, but it didn't happen. They needed some kind of Indian accent of sorts and I was happy to work with all of them—mainly just glad to get the job. I was friends for years with Barbara's husband, Mike Ansara, long before they were mar-

ried." Corden, a longtime character actor in film and television, replaced Alan Reed as the voice of Fred Flintstone in 1977 and has been recording the character ever since.

3. "Guess What Happened on the Way to the Moon?"

Air Date: October 2, 1965

Written by Tom Waldman and Frank Waldman

Directed by Alan Rafkin

Guest Cast: Byron Morrow, Ron Brown, Tom Anthony

Tony Nelson and Roger Healey are ordered to spend a week in Furance Canyon, Nevada, to test their ability to survive on the moon. Except for water, they are to live off the land in 100-degree temperatures during the day, and 10 below freezing at night. Jeannie tags along to ease their suffering during the mission.

4. "Jeannie and the Marriage Caper"

Air Date: October 9, 1965

Written by Tom Waldman and Frank Waldman

Directed by Alan Rafkin

Guest Cast: Karen Sharpe, Philip Ober, John Hudson, Mako, Sal Ponti

Tony forbids Jeannie to accompany him and Melissa on their honeymoon. Jeannie turns herself into a Filipino "houseboy" named Kato, and Melissa—eager to get married—suggests they take the houseboy with them to Europe. As it turns out, an old boyfriend of Melissa's admits he's still in love with her and the engagement with Tony is off.

5. "G.I. Jeannie"

Air Date: October 16, 1965

Written by William Davenport

Directed by Alan Rafkin

Guest Cast: Edmon Ryan, Jane Dulo, Eileen O'Neill, Peg Shirley, Bob DoQui

Jeannie becomes jealous when she discovers that Tony has a sexy new secretary, so she insists on joining the WAAFs and taking over the job. When she is assigned to a base in North Africa, Jeannie decides to resign her post and rejoin civilian life.

6. "The Yacht Murder Case"

Air Date: October 23, 1965

Written by David Braverman and Bob Marcus

Directed by Gene Nelson

Guest Cast: Lindsay Workman, Richard Webb, Sandra Gould, Robert Dorman, Roy Taguchi, David Brian, Sharon Farrell, Victoria Carroll, Ella Edwards

Tony is saddled with the job of taking aerospace tycoon P. J. Ferguson on a tour of the base. Ferguson's beautiful daughter, Nina, has her eye on the astronaut. P. J. Ferguson persuades Tony's superior to order him to have cocktails aboard his yacht. Tony is forced to imprison Jeannie in the vacuum cleaner, but she eventually escapes and joins them. When Jeannie blinks herself off the yacht, the Fergusons assume Tony has pushed her overboard.

Note: Barbara Eden's pregnancy is apparent in the scene where she quietly descends the stairway at home, following Roger Healey.

7. "Anybody Here Seen Jeannie?"

Air Date: October 30, 1965

Written by Arnold Horwitt

Directed by Gene Nelson

Guest Cast: Dabney Coleman, Davis Roberts, Ed Stoddard

Tony must undergo a physical before he and Roger Healey undertake a historic space probe the following week. Worried about the dangers of the space walk, Jeannie forbids her master to go and decides to wreck the physical exam and baffle Dr. Bellows. It works, and Tony is grounded. After changing her mind, Jeannie makes Bellows believe that he is losing his mind.

213

Dreaming of **Jeannie**

8. "The Americanization of Jeannie"

Air Date: November 6, 1965

Written by Arnold Horwitt

Directed by Gene Nelson

Guest Cast: Steven Geray, Del Moore, Jacques Roux, Bobby Johnson, Mittie Lawrence, Jewell Lain, Yvonne White, Tania Lemani

Tony presents Jeannie with a book, *How to Be a Woman.* Jeannie studies the emancipation of the American woman and decides to share her work with her man; she lies around the house, neglects the chores, and allows the place to become a mess. Jeannie takes the author's advice quite literally, purchasing an expensive wardrobe and tackling the job market like other modern females.

Note: Larry Hagman was terrified of "Simm" the lion and extremely hesitant about his scene sitting right next to the roaring beast. Barbara Eden said she loved the creature and felt no uneasiness (even in her pregnant state) petting the lion freely during filming. The full-grown African lion was the same beast seen in *The Addams Family* TV series, owned and "worked" on the set by trainer Steve Martin.

9. "The Moving Finger"

Air Date: November 13, 1965

Written by Harry Essex and Jerry Seelen

Directed by Gene Nelson

Guest Cast: Nancy Kovack, David McLean, Woodrow Parfrey, Dick Balduzzi, Jim Begg, Arthur Romans, Stephen Whittaker, Joe Brooks

When Tony is assigned as a technical expert on a new movie being filmed in Hollywood, Jeannie becomes jealous of the film's female lead, Rita Mitchell. Jeannie decides to become an actress herself, patterning her persona after the tempestuous silent star Pola Negri. Jeannie takes a screen test and realizes that genies do not register on film.

Note: Despite the fact that genies are not supposed to be able to appear on film (as is established in this episode and restated in the "Wedding" episode), her image appears in the newspaper in the episodes "The Second Greatest Con Artist in the World" and "The Biggest Star in Hollywood." In "The Used Car Salesman," Jeannie even appears on television.

10. "Djinn and Water"

Air Date: November 20, 1965

Written by Mary C. McCall, Jr.

Directed by Gene Nelson

Guest Cast: J. Carrol Naish

Jeannie returns to Baghdad and retrieves her ancient great-grandfather, Bilejik, to introduce him to her new master. Bilejik possesses a formula to convert salt water into fresh water utilizing seeds as a filter. Unfortunately, the seeds are extracted from a plant which has been extinct for almost two thousand years.

11. "Whatever Happened to Baby Custer?"

Air Date: November 27, 1965

Written by Austin Kalish and Irma Kalish

Directed by Gene Nelson

Guest Cast: Billy Mumy, Herbert Voland, Grace Albertson, Arthur Adams

A young boy named Custer Jamison witnesses Jeannie's powers at Tony Nelson's house. Dr. Bellows tells Custer he believes his story, and the two spy on Tony and

OPPOSITE PAGE: *Jeannie blinks her former pet, Simm, back into her life.*

Jeannie. Bellows is sure he has stumbled on a top secret aerospace project when he witnesses occurrences of levitation.

Note: This is the final episode Barbara Eden filmed while pregnant. It is interesting to note that cowriters Austin and Irma Kalish later wrote for the animated *Jeannie* series at Hanna-Barbera. In addition, Irma Kalish wrote the 1985 TV movie *I Dream of Jeannie: 15 Years Later.*

12. "Where'd You Go-Go?"

Air Date: December 4, 1965

Written by Bob Fisher and Arthur Alsberg

Directed by E. W. Swackhamer

Guest Cast: Don Mitchell, Bruno Della Santina, Elizabeth MacRae

Tony's former girlfriend Diane drops in for an evening out with her old flame. In an attempt to make her master jealous, Jeannie turns the tables and goes out on a date for the evening—with Roger Healey. Roger falls in love with Jeannie and she must ward off his advances.

13. "Russian Roulette"

Air Date: December 11, 1965

Written by Bob Fisher and Arthur Alsberg

Directed by E. W. Swackhamer

Guest Cast: Richard Gilden, John Beck, David Azar, Lael Jackson, George DeNormand, Arlene Martel, Paul Reed

Tony and Roger are assigned to escort Russian cosmonauts during a goodwill visit. One of them, Major Tionkin, turns out to be a female named Sonya, who wants to marry Tony. By mistake, Roger Healey gives Sonya the bottle in which Jeannie resides.

14. "What House Across the Street?"

Air Date: December 18, 1965

Written by Arthur Alsberg and Bob Fisher

ABOVE: *Tossed in Space: Young Billy Mumy plays curious Custer Jamison, a witness to some odd events in the episode "Whatever Happened to Baby Custer?"*

Directed by Theodore J. Flicker

Guest Cast: Lurene Tuttle, Jack Collins, Avis Scott, Walter Woolf King, Oliver McGowan

Jeannie consults her mother about how to persuade Tony to marry her. Her mother suggests she marry Roger Healey. To undermine the plot, Tony insists that Roger meet Jeannie's parents in their own home. Jeannie whips up a house on a vacant lot across the street and also conjures up a set of all-American folks to impress Healey.

15. "Too Many Tonys"

Air Date: December 25, 1965

Written by Arnold Horwitt

Directed by E. W. Swackhamer

Guest Cast: Henry Hunter

Assuming she is going to marry Tony, Jeannie prepares for the wedding by producing a phony—a twin for Tony who begins to romance her. Dr. Bellows sees the two together and comes to the conclusion that a wedding is to take place the next week. Jeannie nearly goes through with a wedding, but backs out at the last minute.

16. "Get Me to Mecca on Time"

Air Date: January 8, 1966

Written by James Allardice and Tom Adair

Directed by E. W. Swackhamer

Guest Cast: Jamie Farr, Joseph Gillgoff, Foster Brooks, Owen Cunningham, Alice Reinheart, Lael Jackson, Felix Locher, Ray Hastings

217

Dreaming of Jeannie

Jeannie's magic is out of whack due to an astrological juxtaposition—it's the Day of the Ram, on which every genie and master must make a pilgrimage to Mecca where they recite sacred words. (If not, the genie will vanish into limbo forever.) Things have changed in Mecca over the years and the two run into difficulty locating the spot where they must recite the sacred words.

17. "Richest Astronaut in the Whole Wide World"

Air Date: January 15, 1966

Written by William Davenport

Directed by E. W. Swackhamer

Guest Cast: Gerry Lock, Danielle Beausejour, Nadine Nardi, Britt Semand

Finally, Roger Healey discovers the secret of Jeannie's existence when he accidentally releases her from the bottle. He tricks Jeannie back into her bottle and becomes her new master. Roger treats himself to luxurious surroundings courtesy of Jeannie's powers and refuses to return Jeannie to his pal, Tony. In order to rescue Jeannie, Tony must put Roger's position as astronaut in jeopardy.

18. "Is There an Extra Genie in the House?"

Air Date: January 22, 1966

Written by Charles Tannen

Directed by Hal Cooper

Guest Cast: Bernard Fox, Emmaline Henry, Judy Carne

Tony refuses to allow Jeannie to assist Roger with her powers, so Jeannie offers to summon her cousin, Marilla, to help out instead. When Roger returns from an assignment on a remote island, he mistakes a pair of magicians (dressed in Arabian outfits) for relatives of Jeannie, there to help him.

19. "Never Try to Outsmart a Genie"

Air Date: January 29, 1966

Written by Martin A. Ragaway

Directed by Herb Wallerstein

Guest Cast: Peter Brocco, Ila Briton, Orville Sherman, Lenore Kingston

Jeannie nags Tony about accompanying him on an ocean voyage to Italy. Roger is all for Jeannie staying put so he can use her to acquire some things he has always wanted. Dr. Bellows, who hears about the gifts Roger is about to give his friends, decides that Roger is suffering from megalomania. Tony

RIGHT: *From Baghdad to Bombay: Emmaline Henry and Bernard Fox appear in the first-season episode, "Is There an Extra Jeannie in the House?" Emmaline Henry became a show regular as Amanda Bellows the following season, and Bernard Fox disappeared and popped up later as "Dr. Bombay"—the warlock doc on* Bewitched.

finally agrees to let Jeannie travel abroad with him, but she has difficulty obtaining a passport. Alas, she must travel in her bottle.

20. "My Master, the Doctor"

Air Date: February 5, 1966

Written by Sidney Sheldon

Directed by Hal Cooper

Guest Cast: Peter Leeds, Jane Dulo, Don Larson, Maureen McCormick, Julio Medina, Elaine Nelson, Carol O'Leary

Roger Healey is about to undergo an appendectomy. When Tony casually mentions to Jeannie that he once aspired to become a doctor, Jeannie turns her master into a sur-

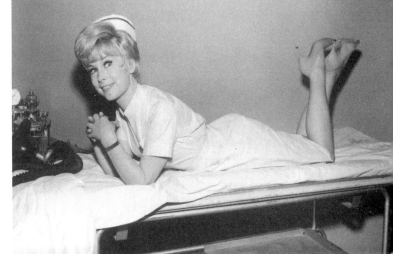

geon—masked, gowned, and ready in the operating room, scalpel in hand. Roger discovers that Tony is his surgeon and insists he no longer needs the operation.

21. "Jeannie and the Kidnap Caper"

Air Date: February 12, 1966

Written by Sidney Sheldon

Directed by Hal Cooper

Guest Cast: Richard Loo, James Hong, Linda Ho.

Tony insists that Jeannie stop catering to his every need, so she takes a sacred oath of the genies and refuses any further request. Trouble occurs when Tony is kidnapped by two Chinese secret agents and Jeannie cannot assist. If she aids her master and breaks the oath, her supernatural powers will vanish. Instead, she alerts Roger Healey, who must become her new master in order to allow her intervention.

22. "How Lucky Can You Get?"

Air Date: February 19, 1966

Written by Sidney Sheldon

Directed by Claudio Guzman

ABOVE: *Taking a Turn for the Nurse: Eden poses for the photographer on the set of the episode "My Master, the Doctor."*

Guest Cast: Ted DeCorsia, Tim Herbert, Buddy Lewis, Paul Hahn, Melinda Fee, Evelyn Dutton, Clifford Guest

To celebrate their promotions, Majors Nelson and Healey are off to Reno for fun and relaxation. The problem: Roger wants to take Jeannie along and Tony wants her to stay at home. Roger stashes Jeannie in his luggage. In Reno, Jeannie fixes the craps games so Tony rolls the dice and wins a fortune while Roger continually loses.

23. "Watch the Birdie"
Air Date: February 26, 1966
Written by Sidney Sheldon
Directed by Hal Cooper
Guest Cast: Ray Teal, Herbert Anderson, Jerry Barber, Gene Boland

Jeannie gives Tony the skill of a professional golfer. General Peterson insists that Tony become his golf partner for an upcoming match against his rival, Admiral Tugwell. Refusing to allow Jeannie to create any more problems, Tony corks her in the bottle—intent on playing his own game of golf.

24. "The Permanent House Guest"

Dreaming of
Jeannie

Air Date: March 5, 1966
Written by Sidney Sheldon
Directed by Hal Cooper
Guest Cast: Martin Ashe, Jack Davis, Romo Vincent, Kate Murtagh

Jeannie is disappointed that her master never asks for anything extravagant—like a yacht. She whips up an elephant for him just as Dr. Bellows arrives. Bellows decides to investigate fully and moves in with Tony. Eventually, Bellows has a series of nerve-racking experiences, which lead him to think the house is haunted.

25. "Bigger Than a Breadbox and Better Than a Genie"
Air Date: March 12, 1966
Written by Sidney Sheldon
Directed by Claudio Guzman
Guest Cast: Joseph Abdullah, Lincoln Demyan, Alice Dudley, Natalie Leeb, Jorja Curtright. Special (uncredited) guest appearance by Colonel Chuck Yeager.

Fortune-teller Madame Zolta impresses Roger Healey. Tony Nelson, skeptical of the medium's methods, decides to investigate by attending a séance. When Madame Zolta produces Tony's nonexistent Uncle Jeff and Aunt Susan, he confirms she is a fraud. Jeannie arrives and creates havoc at the séance, embarrassing con artist Zolta.

Note: Rampant nepotism in this episode. Madame Zolta was portrayed by Sidney Sheldon's wife, Jorja Curtright. Mrs. Bates was portrayed by Sheldon's seventy-year-old mother, Natalie Leeb. Why famed aviator Chuck Yeager, seen briefly at the beginning, was not given screen credit is anyone's guess.

26. "My Master, the Great Rembrandt"

Air Date: March 19, 1966

Written by Sidney Sheldon

Directed by Claudio Guzman

Guest Cast: Booth Colman, Jonathan Hole, E. J. Andre

Jeannie has turned one of Tony's own paintings into an exact copy of a Rembrandt. Tony is accused of stealing the original from the Louvre. A French art expert, Pierre Millay, is called in to examine the masterpiece in question.

27. "My Master, the Thief"

Air Date: April 2, 1966

Teleplay by Sidney Sheldon

Story by Sidney Sheldon and Robert Kaufman

Directed by Claudio Guzman

Guest Cast: Kathee Francis

Jeannie visits a local museum, which is featuring an exhibit from Bukistan, her old homeland. Seeing a pair of ancient slippers that used to belong to her, she takes them. Dr. Bellows naturally gets wind of the theft and attempts to catch Tony red-handed.

28. "This Is Murder"

Air Date: April 9, 1966

Written by Sidney Sheldon

Directed by Hal Cooper

Guest Cast: Ivan Bonar, Vic Tayback, Gila Golan

Tony is assigned as escort for Princess Tarji, who is visiting the United States. Jeannie is determined to kill the princess, because her family insulted Jeannie's family three thousand years ago. Desperate, Tony gives Jeannie a series of jobs to keep her occupied—assignments like building a ski chalet in Bermuda and creating a pineapple plantation in Alaska. Jeannie returns, still determined to kill Tarji, but Tony smooths over the dispute.

221
Dreaming of
Jeannie

29. "My Master, the Magician"

Air Date: April 23, 1966

Written by Sidney Sheldon

Directed by Hal Cooper

Guest Cast: Chet Stratton, Don Mitchell, William Benedict, Chester Hayes

Jeannie delivers dinner to Tony in his office. Overhearing them late one night, Dr. Bellows informs General Peterson that Tony is having an orgy. Later, when Bellows catches Tony levitating, Tony attempts to cover it up by explaining he is an amateur magician. Bellows asks Tony to perform his act at a base show and then calls in Nestor the Great (from Cincinnati) to expose Tony as a fraud.

30. "I'll Never Forget What's Her Name"

Air Date: May 7, 1966

Written by Sidney Sheldon

Directed by Hal Cooper

Guest Cast: Greta Lenetska

Tony is supposed to escort his aunt's friend, Miss Gordon, around Cocoa Beach. Accidentally Tony gets hit in the head with a vase in the kitchen, and develops amnesia. He mistakes Jeannie for Miss Gordon, falls in love with her, and proposes marriage. Every time Roger tries to reveal the truth to Tony, Jeannie blinks him elsewhere. It takes another blow to the head to straighten Tony out.

Note: This is the final episode of *Jeannie* produced in black-and-white; it was one of NBC's—and all of television's—last programs broadcast in glorious gray tones. By the fall of 1966, all the networks and almost every program had switched to broadcasting "in living color."

Second Season

31. "Happy Anniversary"

Air Date: September 12, 1966

Written by Sidney Sheldon

Directed by Claudio Guzman

Guest Cast: Arthur C. Romans, Donald Mitchell, Michael Ansara

Jeannie is excited about the first anniversary of her rescue by Tony. Her idea is to celebrate on the deserted island where they met. Tony, however, is scheduled to make a space flight, so Jeannie reroutes his capsule and forces it to drop on the island—just as

it did a year ago. There, Tony accidentally releases another genie, the most powerful of them all—the Blue Djinn. Jeannie, frightened of the angry Blue Djinn, explains that he is the one who imprisoned her in a bottle centuries ago. Tony eventually traps the Blue Djinn in the vacuum cleaner.

Note: Michael Ansara (Blue Djinn) was married to Barbara Eden. Later, he guest-starred in other roles on the series. Although this is the first episode of the series to *air* in color, the episode "The Fastest Gun in the East" was the first shot in color.

32. "Always on Sunday"

Air Date: September 19, 1966

Written by Sidney Sheldon

Directed by Hal Cooper

Guest Cast: Bob Hoffman, Pancho Segura

Thinking Tony is overworked, Jeannie blinks every day Sunday. The calendar is stopped, and every day will be Sunday until he is rested. Tony becomes infuriated and Jeannie decides she has failed her master; she wants to leave. Meanwhile, Tony, who can't ski, is left on top of a Swiss mountain.

Dreaming of **Jeannie**

Note: Pro tennis star Pancho Segura makes a brief cameo appearance on the tennis court with Major Nelson. *Daily Variety* noted of this second of the season openers: *Jeannie,* judging from Monday's episode, looks weak against the ABC western, *Iron Horse* and CBS comedy, *Run, Buddy, Run*" (September 21, 1966).

33. "My Master, the Rich Tycoon"

Air Date: September 26, 1966

Written by Sidney Sheldon

Directed by Claudio Guzman

Guest Cast: Paul Lynde

Harry Huggins, a representative of the IRS, visits the home of Tony Nelson and makes a wisecrack about the house

Bill Daily: *"We did about three shows with Paul Lynde, some funny stuff. I hear that he was mean and bitter and nasty. I never saw it. But I worked with some directors who said he was a nightmare. Well, old fags are like old poodles, they get real feisty when they age. I loved working with Paul Lynde."*

looking tacky. To impress him, Jeannie blinks the house full of luxuries, expensive art-work, and a safe brimming full of cash. Naturally Huggins wants to assess Tony's apparent wealth. Tony's efforts to persuade Jeannie to get rid of the wealth fail. Finally, Jeannie transforms everything into junk (the Michelangelo now has six fingers on one hand).

A scene from "My Master, the Rainmaker."

34. "My Master, the Rainmaker"
Air Date: October 3, 1966
Written by Sidney Sheldon
Directed by Claudio Guzman
Guest Cast: Romo Vincent, Robert F. Lyons, Steve Ihnat

Tony is impressed with Jeannie's ability to control the weather. Dr. Bellows witnesses a snowstorm and spreads word around the base that Tony Nelson can control the atmosphere. This prompts an Air Force sergeant to ask Tony for his help with his brother's farm in Alabama which is suffering from drought.

35. "My Wild-Eyed Master"
Air Date: October 10, 1966
Written by Sidney Sheldon
Directed by Hal Cooper
Guest Cast: Jean Marie, Howard Wendell

Tony strains his eyes while studying for a suborbital flight. When Dr. Bellows orders him to undergo an eye exam, Jeannie helps him pass. Now he possesses X-ray vision, and can see people in their underpants.

36. "What's New, Poodle Dog?"
Air Date: October 17, 1966
Written by Sidney Sheldon
Directed by Hal Cooper
Guest Cast: Dick Wilson, Norm Burton, Hazel Shermet, Kevin Tate

Roger tells Jeannie how he has arranged a double date for Tony and himself with two gorgeous women—on the same night Tony promised to take Jeannie out. In order to prevent Roger from telling Tony about the plans, Jeannie turns Roger into a French

RIGHT: *Major Nelson assumes that Jeannie blinked Major Healey into a great Dane.* ABOVE: *Larry Hagman and the old poodle.* BELOW: *Dressed for a date in the episode "What's New, Poodle Dog?"*

poodle. The dog ends up at the pound, where Tony coughs up five dollars to rescue him—only Tony takes the wrong canine. Eventually, the dog is mistaken for a pooch that is to be flown into space.

37. "Fastest Gun in the East"

Air Date: October 24, 1966
Written by Sidney Sheldon
Directed by Hal Cooper
Guest Cast: Whit Bissell, Eddie Firestone, Fred Krone, Bud Perkins, Richard Reeves, Hoyt Axton, Stephanie Hill

While watching a Western on TV, Tony mentions that he wishes he could have lived during that period of American history. Jeannie immediately blinks them back in time, where Tony is a U.S. marshal confronted by a gang of outlaws. Jeannie, as a dance hall girl, helps Tony face down the mob.

38. "How to Be a Genie in Ten Easy Lessons"

Air Date: October 31, 1966

Written by Sidney Sheldon

Directed by Hal Cooper

Tony is complaining that Jeannie constantly interferes and misuses her powers, and suggests she use the book *The Arabian Nights* as a genie guide. According to the book, Jeannie discovers genies are always searching for ways to torture or destroy their masters. She pleads that she cannot follow the book's advice; however, Tony orders her to follow it to the last detail and he finds himself in an open crocodile pit.

39. "Who Needs a Green-Eyed Genie?"

Air Date: November 7, 1966

Written by Sidney Sheldon

Directed by Hal Cooper

Guest Cast: Ted DeCorsia, Joan Patrick, Orville Sherman

Jeannie catches Tony sneaking out on a date and locks him up in a jail cell in the middle of the living room. Racked with jealousy, she attempts to ruin his date the next night by turning the woman into a chimp. Infuriated by her constant interference in his personal life, Tony threatens to leave home. Jeannie does, however, save Tony's life when he is threatened by an ex-convict.

Dreaming of
Jeannie

40. "The Girl Who Never Had a Birthday" (Part I)

Air Date: November 14, 1966

Written by Sidney Sheldon

Directed by Claudio Guzman

Tony discovers that Jeannie has no birthday. She explains that because she was born more than two thousand years ago, no one in her family recalls the exact date of the blessed event. Tony vows that he will somehow track it down for her, but after his attempts fail, he urges her to forget about it. So depressed over it is Jeannie that she begins to vanish and fade away. Tony must discover Jeannie's birthday before she loses all of her power and vanishes completely.

41. "The Girl Who Never Had a Birthday" (Part II)

Air Date: November 21, 1966

Written by Sidney Sheldon

OPPOSITE PAGE: *Jeannie's idea of a joke?*

Directed by Claudio Guzman

Guest Cast: Larry Gelman, Martin Ashe, Bart Greene, Diane Stanton, Jack Fife, Siri, Kenneth Washington

Tony turns to the NASA computer known as ERIC to hunt down Jeannie's birthdate. He has the result in his hands when Dr. Bellows grabs it, insisting the computer is not a fortune cookie. Roger must now assist Tony in reprogramming the computer while Tony distracts Dr. Bellows. (Although Jeannie's powers are restored, her birthday is not revealed until a few episodes later.)

42. "How Do You Beat Superman?"

Air Date: November 28, 1966

Written by Sidney Sheldon

Directed by Claudio Guzman

Guest Cast: Mike Road, Fred Hessler, Julius Johnsen

Tony is glued to the TV during football season, and Jeannie decides to make him jealous to get his attention. She conjures up a man and claims to be engaged to him. Tony finally realizes that if a stranger could marry a genie, he could, too, and decides to propose to Jeannie.

43. "My Master, the Great Caruso"

Air Date: December 5, 1966

Written by Sidney Sheldon

Directed by Hal Cooper

Guest Cast: Frank DeVol, Arthur Peterson.

Jeannie blinks Tony the powerful voice of opera singer Enrico Caruso so that her master can perform on a TV talent contest. Tony regrets making Jeannie promise not to make him sing like Caruso anymore, because Dr. Bellows has already entered him in the contest. Roger Healey finally reveals Jeannie's birthday: April 1.

ABOVE: *Composer Frank DeVol makes a guest appearance in the episode "My Master, the Great Caruso." DeVol, an accomplished musician and composer, wrote the theme for TV's* My Three Sons *and cocreated* The Brady Bunch *theme with Sherwood Schwartz.*

Note: Balding actor Frank DeVol, who plays Hennessey in this episode, is also the prolific songwriter who wrote the memorable TV themes for *My Three Sons, Family Affair,* and *The Brady Bunch,* among others.

44. "The World's Greatest Lover"

Air Date: December 12, 1966

Written by Sidney Sheldon

Directed by Hal Cooper

Guest Cast: Julie Gregg, John Milford

Jeannie tries to help Major Healey find a date by blinking it so that every woman who lays eyes on him will fall in love with him. The fiancée of a jealous mobster falls under the spell, as does Amanda Bellows.

Note: This episode marks the debut of Emmaline Henry as Amanda Bellows.

45. "Jeannie Breaks the Bank"

Air Date: December 19, 1966

Written by Sidney Sheldon

Directed by Hal Cooper

Guest Cast: John McGiver, Tom Palmer, Lindsay Workman, Queenie Leonard, Torben Meyer

Jeannie has run up a staggering food bill and Tony runs short of funds. To assist, Jeannie enlarges his Christmas Club account at the bank to more than $3 million. Naturally, Dr. Bellows finds out and involves General Peterson in the matter.

46. "My Master, the Author"

Air Date: December 26, 1966

Written by Sidney Sheldon

Directed by Richard Goode

Guest Cast: Butch Patrick, Mary Foran, Kimberly Beck

Jeannie writes a book on how to raise children, but submits it to a publisher under Tony's name. When the book is published, Dr. Bellows challenges Tony to transform his young nephew, Richard. General Peterson brings his granddaughter to Tony for curing of shyness.

Note: The 18-inch Jeannie doll used in this episode was actually licensed merchandise from the show manufactured by Libby-Marjorette in 1966. Today, these dolls, mint in box, can sell for as much as $400 at auction.

47. "The Greatest Invention in the World"

Air Date: January 9, 1967

Written by Sidney Sheldon

Directed by Hal Cooper

Guest Cast: Groucho Marx, William Bakewell

 Tony allows Jeannie to grant Roger one wish. Roger accidentally wishes he hadn't made Tony spill coffee on his clothes. He wastes his wish, and in doing so, convinces Dr. Bellows that Tony has invented an indestructible material.

 Note: Groucho Marx's gag appearance at the tail end of the episode is suspiciously brief. It's too bad the script didn't take full advantage of the comedy legend's leers and sardonic delivery.

48. "My Master, the Spy"

Air Date: January 16, 1967

Written by Sidney Sheldon

Directed by Hal Cooper

Guest Cast: Louis Mercier, Byron Morrow, Noah Keen, Guy DeVestel, Benny Rubin, Davis Roberts, Larry Hall, Fred Krone, Charles Horvath

 Jeannie tricks Tony into having lunch in Paris. Because he is supposed to be at a top-security conference, she produces a duplicate Tony to attend the vital meeting. Dr. Bellows is made aware of Tony's presence in Paris and investigates the possibility that spies are among them.

49. "You Can't Arrest Me . . . I Don't Have a Driver's License"

Air Date: January 23, 1967

Written by Sidney Sheldon

Directed by Hal Cooper

Guest Cast: Herb Vigran, Billy M. Greene, Alan Hewitt

 Trouble starts when Jeannie drives off in Tony's car without his permission, and is pulled over. She tricks Tony into giving her driving lessons. Too late: News of the traffic violations hits the front page and Tony must build a defense in court.

50. "One of Our Bottles Is Missing"

Air Date: January 30, 1967

Written by Sidney Sheldon

Directed by Claudio Guzman

Guest Cast: Frank Puglia, Richard Lapp

Amanda Bellows insists on having Jeannie's bottle for her own living room, but Tony refuses to part with it. Amanda decides to have a replica made and takes Jeannie's bottle anyway. Tony must resort to breaking into the Bellowses' home and retrieve the bottle—claiming to be sleepwalking.

Note: In a final scene, Tony, clutching the bottle, yanks out the stopper and tosses it onto the coffee table. The stopper falls off the front of the table and it breaks—like a popping lightbulb. Listen and you'll hear Bill Daily utter "Be careful" under his breath.

51. "My Poor Master, the Civilian"
Air Date: February 6, 1967
Written by Sidney Sheldon
Directed by Hal Cooper
Guest Cast: Kathleen Hughes, Jane Zachary, Nadia Sanders, Carol Worthington, Kathleen Freeman

Tony is being phased out of the space program and placed at a missile plant in Columbus, Ohio. Jeannie and Roger attempt to make Tony see how dreary his new job will be and discourage him from accepting the position.

52. "There Goes the Best Genie I Ever Had"
Air Date: February 20, 1967
Written by Sidney Sheldon
Directed by Hal Cooper
Guest Cast: Virginia Ann Ford, Willy Kooperman, Ron Brown

Roger wants Tony to double-date with Miss Universe and Miss Galaxy and for a while Tony considers it despite the fact that Jeannie would disapprove. In a series of flashbacks, Tony recalls the predicaments in which Jeannie has entangled him, but finally, he realizes how lost he would be without her.

53. "The Greatest Entertainer in the World"
Air Date: February 27, 1967
Written by Sidney Sheldon
Directed by Claudio Guzman
Guest Cast: Sammy Davis, Jr., James J. Waters, George Rhodes, Bob Melvin, Murphy Bennett

To help Tony organize a celebration for General Peterson's tenth anniversary as a general, Jeannie produces a double for entertainer Sammy Davis, Jr., to accommodate his scheduling conflict. Sammy thinks he's heading for a breakdown in the process.

54. "My Incredible Shrinking Master"

Air Date: March 6, 1967

Written by Sidney Sheldon

Directed by Claudio Guzman

    Jeannie has a nightmare and tells Tony something terrible is about to happen to him, like an attack by a large cat. Accidentally, Jeannie shrinks her master to six inches tall, and Tony desperately tries to escape from a curious cat, which chases him around the house.

55. "My Master, the Pirate"

Air Date: March 13, 1967

Written by Sidney Sheldon

Directed by Claudio Guzman

Guest Cast: Joseph Perry, Elaine Devry, Digby Wolfe, William Bagdad, Al Wyatt

    Jeannie whisks Tony back in time to the deck of Captain Kidd's pirate ship. Tony is immediately attacked, but somehow he wins and is chosen as the new captain by the cutthroat crew. Tony realizes that a beautiful prisoner aboard, Diane Nelson, is actually his great-great-grandmother.

WESTERN UNION
SENDING BLANK

Telefax   *Telefax*

| CALL LETTERS | | CHARGE TO | 4273 | 10-12-66 |

SAMMY DAVIS   STRAIGHT WIRE
AMBASSADOR EAST HOTEL
CHICAGO, ILL.   (Deliver, do not phone)

I JUST WANT YOU TO KNOW HOW EXCITED ALL OF US
ARE THAT YOU'RE GOING TO DO I DREAM OF JEANNIE.
THE WHOLE CAST IS LOOKING FORWARD TO WORKING
WITH YOU.   WARMEST REGARDS.
                   SIDNEY SHELDON

LEFT: *Sammy Davis, Jr., performing in the episode "The Greatest Entertainer in the World."* ABOVE: *Sidney Sheldon's telegram to Sammy Davis, Jr., confirming his guest appearance. (Sidney Sheldon Collection, USC Cinema-Television Library.)*

56. "A Secretary Is Not a Toy"

Air Date: March 20, 1967
Written by Sidney Sheldon
Directed by Claudio Guzman
Guest Cast: Eileen O'Neill, Bing Russell, Ila Briton, Donald Briscoe, Jack Mills, Lincoln Tate, David Loud.

Jeannie decides that her master deserves a promotion and becomes a secretary for General Peterson in order to influence him. Dr. Bellows becomes suspicious and calls the CIA in to investigate. His inquiry reveals that Jeannie does not legally exist.

Note: CIA agent Amos Lincoln is played by actor Bing Russell, father of actor Kurt Russell.

57. "There Goes the Bride"

Air Date: March 27, 1967
Written by Sidney Sheldon
Directed by Larry Hagman
Guest Cast: Abraham Sofaer, Jack Bailey, Charles Irving, Shirley Bonne, Jonathan Hole, Bill Quinn, Larry Hall

Tony is the best man at a wedding and this prompts Jeannie to decide it is time for her to marry. Roger tells Jeannie to play hard-to-get. She resorts, however, to a powerful and dangerous spell which she places on her master—a forbidden thing, according to Haji, chief djinn.

58. "My Master, Napoleon's Buddy"

Air Date: April 3, 1967
Written by Sidney Sheldon
Directed by Claudio Guzman

Top: *Rehearsing a scene with guest star Jack Baily (kneeling next to Hagman, who is lying on the floor mat)*. Bottom: *Larry Hagman directs his first episode, "There Goes the Bride" (1967)*.

Guest Cast: Aram Katcher, Danielle Demetz, Booth Colman

Jeannie blinks Tony back in time to speak with Napoleon so he can change the course of history. Tony astounds Napoleon with his forecast of the future, but Napoleon concludes that he is a Russian spy and orders his execution. Tony is determined, however, to prevent the defeat at Waterloo.

59. "The Birds and the Bees Bit"

Air Date: April 10, 1967

Written by Allan Devon

Directed by Larry Hagman

Guest Cast: Lorette Strome, Jimmy Jarratt, Judy Rockley, Abraham Sofaer

To his delight, Tony discovers that genies lose all their powers if they marry a mortal. He immediately proposes to Jeannie, but Roger thinks it's a big mistake. Haji, the chief djinn, disapproves of the marriage and previews what it will be like in his crystal ball. Jeannie must admit to Tony that their children might be genies.

60. "My Master, the Swinging Bachelor"

Air Date: April 17, 1967

Written by Sidney Sheldon

Directed by Hal Cooper

Guest Cast: Bridget Hanley, Woodrow Parfrey

Amanda Bellows invites herself to dinner at Tony's to satisfy her curiosity. Tony tries to get rid of Jeannie temporarily, but when she sees the pretty women hired to cater the dinner, she decides to stick around and sabotage the event. She whips up a cake that makes everyone revert to childhood.

61. "The Mod Party"

Air Date: April 24, 1967

Teleplay by Peggy Chantler Dick

Story by Peggy Chantler Dick and Douglas M. Dick

Directed by Claudio Guzman

Guest Cast: Dabney Coleman, Hilarie Thompson, Cathleen Cordell, Hollis Morrison, Paul Potash, Mason Cury, Sue Williamson, Laurance Hall, Judy-Ann Jones

Unfortunately, Dr. Bellows schedules a meeting on the night of Roger's cool "mod" party. Tony and Roger tell Bellows they are going hunting, but Alfred and Amanda

OPPOSITE PAGE: *Jeannie goes a little too far reversing the aging process in "My Master, the Swinging Bachelor."*

decide to crash the "mod" party with the intent of catching Tony and Roger in a lie. When the Bellowses enter the party, Tony begs Jeannie to produce hunting attire. She blinks Tony and Roger into Roman togas, carrying bows and arrows.

Third Season

62. "Fly Me to the Moon"
Air Date: September 12, 1967
Written by Robert Marcus
Directed by Hal Cooper
Guest Cast: Larry Storch, Parley Baer, Howard Morton, Judy Pace

Jeannie turns Sam the Space Chimp into a human male. The problem is, Sam the

human does not want to return to chimp form and runs away. Jeannie screws up a blink and accidentally turns Tony into a chimp; Tony nearly gets shot into orbit.

Note: Bill Daily recalls an injury that occurred on the set of this episode. "Larry Storch wanted to do this thing where he'd leap from a tree," says Daily. "He played an ape. I said to him, 'Don't do that.' It was only a few feet from the next branch on this tree. We got a stunt guy to do it and there was a nail in the tree and the stunt guy ripped his arm up. It was ugly. It would have been Larry. Me, I'm a coward. I hate physical stuff."

63. "Jeannie or the Tiger"
Air Date: September 19, 1967
Written by James Henerson
Directed by Hal Cooper
Guest Cast: In case it's not evident, Barbara Eden also portrays Jeannie's sister, a k a Jeannie II. In addition, there are numerous additional cast members who go uncredited.

Jeannie summons her sister, because they haven't seen each other in two hun-

Variety *(September 1967): "The season opener was considerably enhanced by a fine comic portrayal by Larry Storch as a space monkey who was turned into a man through one of Jeannie's mistakes. Always an excellent mugger, Storch found comedic catnip in the wild role."*

dred years. Jealous, the brazen sister tricks Jeannie into her bottle and assumes her identity.

64. "The Second Greatest Con Artist in the World"

Air Date: September 26, 1967

Written by Allan Devon

Directed by Claudio Guzman

Guest Cast: Milton Berle, Hal Cooper, Fred Clark, Herb Jeffries, James Daris, Yankee Chang, Bert Darr, Wayne Harada

In Hawaii, Jeannie promises not to attract attention, but creates a stir when it is revealed she is wearing an ancient scarab pin worth a fortune. Charles, a servant to Mr. Vanderhaven (the richest man in the world) poses as Vanderhaven and attempts to con Jeannie out of her diamond pin. She outsmarts *him* in the end.

Note: Eddie the chauffeur is played by Hal Cooper, a frequent director on *I Dream of Jeannie,* who stepped into the role out of necessity at the last minute.

65. "My Turned-On Master"

Air Date: October 3, 1967

Written by Dennis Whitcomb

Directed by Hal Cooper

Guest Cast: Pedro Gonzales-Gonzales, Bryan O'Byrne.

To avoid trouble at a press banquet, Jeannie switches her powers over to Tony, who unknowingly transfers them to Dr. Bellows. Anyone who wishes for something—gets it!

66. "My Master, the Weakling"

Air Date: October 10, 1967

Written by Ron Friedman

Directed by Claudio Guzman

Guest Cast: Don Rickles, Harry Harvey, Sr., Carl Byrd, Robert Pickering, David Soul

Tony and Roger must undergo an extensive physical fitness program. Commander Kiski wants to make sure the men aren't "softened," the way his Aunt Effie tried to soften him. Jeannie blinks and gives Kiski the personality of his sweet old Aunt Effie, but Tony orders her to restore him to his normal, snarling self.

Note: That's 23-year-old actor-singer David Soul (*Starsky and Hutch*) as the uniformed orderly answering the general's question in the tent scene.

67. "Jeannie, the Hip Hippie"

Air Date: October 17, 1967

Written by Christopher Golato

Directed by Hal Cooper

Guest Cast: Phil Spector, Terry Messina, the Boyce & Hart Group (Tommy Boyce, Bobby Hart, William Lewis, Steve O'Reilly)

Tony is planning a camping trip as a long-overdue vacation, but Dr. Bellows holds him up. Tony must help Mrs. Bellows find a replacement singing group

The Boyce & Hart Group made a guest appearance on the episode "Jeannie, the Hip Hippie" (1967).

for a charity bazaar immediately, so Jeannie assists.

Note: Songwriting team Boyce & Hart, who had many pop hits in the 1960s (especially with the Monkees—"The Monkees Theme," "Last Train to Clarksville," "(I'm Not Your) Steppin' Stone," "Valleri," "She," "I Wanna Be Free"), also appeared on TV's *The Flying Nun* and *Bewitched*. Watch closely for the shot where Jeannie goes to a record store. Although the sitcom takes place in Cocoa Beach, the stock footage shown is actually Hollywood; evident along the sidewalk are the famous stars emblazoned on Hollywood Boulevard. Also notice Bobby Hart, when blinked from the record store into the Nelson home, is holding the Monkees' debut record album. You can spot a pre-Monkees Davy Jones album framed on the recording studio wall in the scene with Phil Spector.

When Jeannie accidentally gets bopped on the head and lands in the hospital with amnesia, attorney Harley Z. Pool (Richard Deacon) quickly attaches himself to the case in "Who Are You Calling a Genie?"

68. "Everybody's a Movie Star"

Air Date: October 31, 1967

Written by Mark Rowane

Directed by Claudio Guzman

Guest Cast: Paul Lynde, Larry Vincent, David Loud

Hollywood director Allan Kerr arrives in Cocoa Beach to film a documentary about the space program and he chooses Tony and Roger to star. Roger hams it up and Tony must find a way to tell him he's overdoing it.

69. "Who Are You Calling a Genie?"

Air Date: November 7, 1967

Written by Marty Roth

Directed by Hal Cooper

Guest Cast: Richard Deacon, Chet Stratton, Corrine Camacho, Arthur Adams

This is the amnesia episode—a standard comedy plot in all sixties sitcoms. Jeannie gets konked on the head at NASA and lands in the hospital with amnesia. Tony and Roger have to convince her who she is—or she abruptly screams! Attorney Harley Z. Pool is most anxious to handle the case against NASA for poor, defenseless "victim" Jeannie.

70. "Meet My Master's Mother"

Air Date: November 14, 1967
Written by Marlene Fanta Shyer
Directed by Claudio Guzman
Guest Cast: Spring Byington

Tony's mother arrives to take care of her son. Mother insults Jeannie and even pours dishwater in her bottle—while Jeannie is in it. Jeannie tries to drive Mother out of the house, but all attempts fail. Mother insists that Tony is in need of an old-fashioned girl and eventually introduces him to Jeannie.

71. "Here Comes Bootsie Nightingale"

Air Date: November 21, 1967
Written by Paul West
Directed by Hal Cooper

Guest Cast: Carol Wayne, Jesse White

Tony has been asked to escort a beautiful movie star named Bootsie Nightingale to a charity ball hosted by Amanda Bellows. How will he keep his date with Bootsie and conceal it from Jeannie? Roger, who is in love with Bootsie, eventually gets the opportunity to escort the movie star but gets a little clumsy as the night progresses.

72. "Tony's Wife"

Air Date: November 28, 1967
Written by Christopher Golato
Directed by Claudio Guzman
Guest Cast: Shannon Farnon

Jeannie's conniving sister tells her that her stars are under the terrible Sign of the Jinx and she will give her master bad luck if she does not leave for fifteen years. Jeannie attempts to set Tony up and get him married off before she departs.

Tony Nelson's mother (guest star Spring Byington) dreams of the ideal wife for her son.

73. "Jeannie and the Great Bank Robbery"

Air Date: December 5, 1967
Written by Seaman Jacobs, Fred Fox and James Henerson

Directed by Larry Hagman

Guest Cast: Severn Darden, Mike Mazurki, Vince Howard, Allen Davis, Geoff Edwards, Sue Taylor

To get Jeannie out of the way, Tony tells her to go "find someone who needs help." Innocently, Jeannie gets caught up with two thieves and she unwittingly assists them in a bank heist. (They tell her she is making a withdrawal on behalf of the Transylvanian Orphan Society.)

74. "My Son, the Genie"

Air Date: December 12, 1967

Written by Bill Richmond

Directed by Claudio Guzman

Guest Cast: Bob Denver, Sheldon Allman, Sal Ponti, Mousie Garner

Harold, an apprentice genie, is sent to Jeannie for a day's training. Coincidentally, the President plans to come by Tony Nelson's home to congratulate him on an impressive orbital flight. Harold, a walking disaster, nearly ruins the executive visit.

75. "Jeannie Goes to Honolulu"

Air Date: December 26, 1967

Written by Mark Rowane

Directed by Claudio Guzman

Guest Cast: Don Ho, Brenda Benet, Natalie Leeb, Frances Gordon, Lee Saltonstall, The Alii's

Tony attempts to divert Jeannie by telling her he is going to the North Pole, where it is 65 below zero. Actually, Tony and Roger are heading to Honolulu. Discovering the truth, Jeannie pops up at Waikiki Beach and causes problems for her master. Tony lies again, telling her he is escorting a princess on the island as part of a secret mission.

Note: Location filming for this episode took place around the Royal Hawaiian Hotel in Honolulu, on the island of Oahu, right in the heart of Waikiki Beach. One of Honolulu's original luxury resorts, built in 1927, it is also called the Pink Palace of the Pacific. Don Ho, Hawaii's most famous entertainer, and his group perform two numbers, "Ain't No Big Thing" and "Days of Our Youth." The segment features a music video with Ho's young son, Dwight. "I named him after Dwight D. Eisenhower," Ho says. The veteran singer is amazed by how many baby-boomers remind him of this episode as well as his momentous appearance on *The Brady Bunch*. "I've done so much more in my career, and this is what they ask about. But it's nice to remember."

ABOVE: *Half Nelson: Funny how censors didn't mind Tony Nelson's exposed navel, or the navels of other beachcombers in the scene, but Jeannie was stuck in a one-piece.* OPPOSITE PAGE: *Don Ho, still a staple of Hawaiian entertainment, made a guest appearance during the show's production in the islands. "Next to* The Brady Bunch, *people ask me most often about the [Jeannie episode] I was in," the singer commented in 1997.*

In the nightclub scene, the first of the older ladies to request Major Nelson's autograph is Natalie Leeb (Sidney Sheldon's mother), making her second appearance on the show.

76. "The Battle of Waikiki"

Air Date: January 2, 1968

Written by Marty Roth

Directed by Hal Cooper

Guest Cast: Michael Ansara, Theodore Nobriga, Marc Towers, Pat Meikle

Tony wishes he had met King Kamehameha, who defended the Islands from invasion 200 years ago. Jeannie blinks up the King, in full regalia. Unimpressed by the changes in the islands, the king decides to mount an invasion, and leads an attack on the general's luau.

Note: King Kamehameha is portrayed by Michael Ansara, married to Barbara Eden at the time.

77. "Genie, Genie, Who's Got the Genie?" (Part I)

Air Date: January 16, 1968

Written by James Henerson

Directed by Claudio Guzman

Guest Cast: Edward Andrews, Lou Antonio, Dennis Cooney, Joseph Perry, Jack Smith, Sidney Coute, Jack Donner

When Tony hears someone approaching, he tells Jeannie to disappear. She pops herself into a safe and is accidentally locked in. Even her smoke can't escape. Tony and Roger work frantically to free her because the safe contains experimental equipment destined for the moon.

78. "Genie, Genie, Who's Got the Genie?" (Part II)

Air Date: January 23, 1968

Written by James Henerson

Directed by Claudio Guzman

Guest Cast: Reta Shaw, Edward Andrews, Lou Antonio, Dennis Cooney, Susan Howard, Joseph Perry, Ned Wertimer, John Harmon

Tony thinks Jeannie is locked in a combination safe bound for the moon, but Roger reveals that the safe is still in the warehouse. The safe eventually gets lost and is nearly destroyed in a junkyard crusher. Meanwhile, Jeannie is still held captive in the safe, and the only one who knows the combination is the President of the United States.

Note: For those who are obsessed with Jeannie's bottle, this episode features a great close-up of the vessel in the scene where Tony and Roger mourn the loss of Jeannie.

79. "Genie, Genie, Who's Got the Genie?" (Part III)

Air Date: January 30, 1968

Written by James Henerson

Directed by Hal Cooper

Guest Cast: Ted Cassidy, Al Dennis, William Bagdad, Mike Farrell, Debbie Wong

While Jeannie is locked in the safe, her sister drops in and uses the opportunity to snare Tony. Jeannie's sister convinces Tony he must go to Baghdad to meet with the chief of genies to rescue Jeannie from the safe. Both Tony and Roger end up being blinked into a birdcage.

Note: Astronaut Arland is played by twenty-eight-year-old Mike Farrell, best known for his role as B. J. Hunnicut on TV's *M*A*S*H*. It was one of Farrell's first TV roles.

80. "Genie, Genie, Who's Got the Genie?" (Part IV)

Air Date: February 6, 1968

Written by James Henerson

Directed by Hal Cooper

Guest Cast: Benny Rubin, Ron Masak, William Fawcett

Tony's in a panic (what else?) when he realizes that a genie locked up for a full moon belongs to the one who frees her. Dr. Bellows reports that Dr. Wedemeyer, a demolitions expert, is coming to open the safe and Tony sends Roger to delay him. In a race against time, Tony ends up having to disarm an explosive being used to open the safe. The combination is finally revealed: 4-9-7.

81. "Please Don't Feed the Astronauts"

Air Date: February 13, 1968

Written by Ron Friedman

Directed by Hal Cooper

Guest Cast: Paul Lynde, Ted Cassidy, Hazel Shermet, Sally Ann Richards

The veteran film, radio, and television comedian Benny Rubin plays Dr. Wedemeyer, who saves Jeannie from captivity in a safe.

Commander Porter puts Roger and Tony through hell in a nutritional experiment at the base hospital. After an intense physical workout, Porter sends them on a rigorous survival mission in the wilderness, where Jeannie comes to their aid. Porter ends up nearly getting killed in what he thinks is a mirage in an Arabian Village.

82. "My Master, the Ghost Breaker"

Air Date: February 20, 1968

Written by Christopher Golato

Directed by Hal Cooper

Guest Cast: Jack Carter, Ronald Long, Leslie Randall

Tony is informed that he has inherited a dilapidated 300-year-old English country manor. Jeannie and Roger are convinced that the estate is haunted, but Tony insists someone is trying to scare them out of ownership.

83. "Divorce, Genie Style"

Air Date: February 27, 1968

Written by James Henerson

Directed by Hal Cooper

Guest Cast: Woodrow Parfrey, Abraham Sofaer

Jeannie resents Tony's praise of Amanda Bellows's cooking and housekeeping.

She asks Haji, the master of genies, to remove her powers so she can prove herself worthy to Tony. For one week she is a mortal. Amanda assumes that Tony and Jeannie are married and that Tony is a rotten husband. Sympathetically, she tries to arrange a divorce for Jeannie.

84. "My Double-crossing Master"

Air Date: March 5, 1968

Written by Mark Rowane

Directed by Hal Cooper

Roger tells Tony that he is through with women, insisting that none of them can be trusted. Tony bets Roger that Jeannie is loyal—and to prove it, Tony disguises himself as a dashing Brit, "Geoffrey Tiffin-Smythe," in order to trick her. Jeannie sees through Tony's gag and plays along.

85. "Have You Ever Had a Genie Hate You?"

Air Date: March 12, 1968

Written by Allan Devon

Directed by Claudio Guzman

Guest Cast: Carole Williams, Jan Sherman

Dreaming of **Jeannie**

Jeannie's wicked brunette sister arrives bearing gifts for Jeannie: two flasks, one with a love potion, the other with a hate potion. Jeannie's sister switches them so Jeannie turns on Tony. Later, Roger samples the love potion and Jeannie falls madly in love with him. For heaven's sake, what to do?

86. "Operation: First Couple on the Moon"

Air Date: March 19, 1968

Written by Arthur Julian

Directed by Claudio Guzman

Guest Cast: Kay Reynolds, William Smith

Tony is scheduled to blast off to the moon and exist in a Lunar House with a female scientist. Jeannie's sister offers to fix it so no other woman goes to the moon with her master. Jeannie II actually gets herself assigned to accompany Tony to the moon.

87. "Haven't I Seen Me Someplace Before?"

Air Date: March 26, 1968

Written by Marty Roth

Directed by Claudio Guzman

Guest Cast: Pat Delaney, B. B. Boland, Steve Vincent

Jeannie presents Roger with one birthday wish. Unwittingly, Roger wishes he could change places with Tony, who is set to fly *Trailblazer I*. From that moment on, Tony and Roger inhabit each other's bodies, although each has his own voice. Only Roger can take back his own wish.

Fourth Season

88. "U.F.Ohhhh Jeannie!"
Air Date: September 16, 1968
Written by Marty Roth
Directed by Hal Cooper
Guest Cast: J. Pat O'Malley, Kathleen Freeman, William Bassett, Lisa Gaye

The *Variety* review (September 18, 1968) of this season opener neatly sums it all up, on-screen and off-screen:

> Jeannie began its fourth season with a witlessly amiable story about hillbillies who mistake Astronaut Major Larry Hagman and his cuddly little genie for Martians when they crash in the mountains in an experimental airplane. And if that weren't enough, Jeannie gets knocked out and they try to revive her by throwing a bucket of water, only it isn't water, it's mountain dew, and you can just imagine what happens when a 2,500-year-old genie gets drunk on moonshine.
>
> Miss Eden is still very pretty and in a highly stylized way, competent to her comedic chores. Larry Hagman has never gotten over a certain starchiness. The production values appear to have declined from last year. It's still basically a show for the kids and the very tired older folk looking for lightweight escapism.

89. "Jeannie and the Wild Pipchicks"
Air Date: September 23, 1968
Written by James Henerson
Directed by Claudio Guzman
Guest Cast: Reta Shaw

Jeannie's mother sends her some homemade candy called "pipchicks," which releases all inhibitions; NASA wants Tony to whip up a fresh batch for testing. General Peterson sends some to the President, and Tony must intercept the mail.

90. "Tomorrow Is Not Another Day"

Air Date: October 7, 1968

Written by Bruce Howard

Directed by Hal Cooper

Guest Cast: Stewart Bradley, Herbie Faye, Johnny Silver, Roosevelt Grier, Xavier Nash

When the newspaper doesn't arrive, Jeannie blinks one up, but Roger has given her the wrong date, so she prematurely summons the following day's edition. Roger grabs the sports section and heads to the racetrack. Tony is alarmed by the headline: "Astronaut Breaks Leg in Accident." Jeannie tries to protect her master in a plastic bubble.

Jeannie becomes alarmed when she finds she's foretold the future with an advance look at the news.

Note: Former L.A. Rams football star Rosey Grier makes a brief appearance. The famed member of the Rams' "Fearsome Foursome" in the sixties, turned to entertainment and had quite a nice little acting career going for him through the 1970s.

91. "Abdullah"

Air Date: October 14, 1968

Written by Marty Roth

Directed by Claudio Guzman

Guest Cast: Jack Riley, Margie Hall, Shyrl Formberg, Ila Britton, Jane Dulo

Tony is shocked when he finds Jeannie holding a baby. Actually, she is baby-sitting her infant nephew, Abdullah. Jeannie leaves to take over her brother's duties and Tony is left with the baby. Tony fakes a cold and stays home, but Dr. Bellows is sure he has developed the Patagonian flu and rushes to examine him.

92. "Have You Heard the One About the Used-Car Salesman?"

Air Date: November 4, 1968

Written by James Henerson

Directed by Hal Cooper

Guest Cast: Carl Ballantine, Bob Hastings, Henry Beckman

Jeannie makes a mistake meeting Carl Tucker, an unscrupulous used-car salesman who wants to sell Tony's car back to her. Eventually, Jeannie catches on to Tucker's scheme and exposes his unethical sales on television.

93. "Djinn-Djinn, Go Home"

Air Date: November 11, 1968

Written by James Henerson

Directed by Hal Cooper

Guest Cast: Terri Messina, Edward Cross

Mrs. Bellows falls in love with the stray dog at Tony's house. Actually, the dog is Jeannie's pet, Djinn-Djinn, from Baghdad, a cute little mutt who can become invisible. The dog has an aversion to uniforms and will attack on sight. Djinn-Djinn makes his way to NASA and wreaks havoc on the uniformed staff.

94. "The Strongest Man in the World"

Air Date: November 18, 1968

Written by Ray Singer

Directed by Claudio Guzman

Guest Cast: Jerry Quarry, Richard X. Slattery, Steve Roberts, Pepper Martin, Hollis Morrison, Slapsy Maxie Rosenbloom, Lee J. Lambert

General Hamilton sees Tony knock out a gang that is pestering Jeannie and decides that "One Punch Nelson" should represent the Air Force in the Armed Forces Boxing Tournament. Tony is unaware, however, that his power punch is assisted by Jeannie.

95. "The Indispensable Jeannie"

Air Date: November 25, 1968

Written by James Henerson

Directed by Claudio Guzman

Guest Cast: Roger Garrett, Bobbi Collins

To test whether Tony and Roger will be able to stomach each other on a trip to the moon, Dr. Bellows orders Roger to move in with Tony. Since they must learn to fend for themselves, Tony sends Jeannie away for a week. In her absence, Jeannie arranges that their every wish be granted.

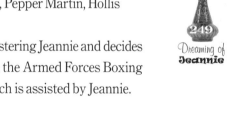

Larry Hagman taking home movies during an outdoor shoot on **I Dream of Jeannie.**

96. "Jeannie and the Top Secret Secret"

Air Date: December 2, 1968

Written by Searle Kramer

Directed by Hal Cooper

Guest Cast: Sabrina Scharf, Vinton Hayworth, Joseph Perry, Valerie Hawkins, Bruce Kirby, Bill Quinn, Tom Palmer

Dr. Bellows orders Tony to deliver some film to the Pentagon; he must wear civilian clothes. The assignment ruins his anniversary plans. Tony asks Roger to take Jeannie out. Jeannie poses as a stewardess to spy on her master and becomes jealous because of seemingly incriminating coincidences on the airplane with a woman and Tony. Consumed by jealousy, Jeannie changes the top-secret NASA film.

Note: Character actor Vinton Hayworth portrays General Watson in this episode. Later in the season Hayworth assumed a semiregular role as General Schaeffer.

97. "How to Marry an Astronaut"

Air Date: December 9, 1968

Written by James Henerson

Directed by Hal Cooper

Guest Cast: Vincent Perry

Jeannie's sister, who has been married forty-seven times, informs Jeannie that she is using the wrong methods to encourage Tony to propose to her. Jeannie II pretends she is after Roger, and urges Jeannie to copy the moves on Tony—by granting his every wish. Tony is leery of Jeannie II and tries to urge Roger not to marry Jeannie's sister. In the end, it's a showdown of the Jeannie siblings.

98. "Dr. Bellows Goes Sane"

Air Date: December 16, 1968

Written by James Henerson

Directed by Richard Kinon

Guest Cast: Joe Flynn, Paul Vaughn

Dr. Bellows sends General Peterson a damning report that could jeopardize Major Nelson's career. Titled, "A Clinical Report on Major Anthony Nelson: A Factual Dossier on Every Unexplained Incident in Which Major Nelson Has Been Involved for the Last Three Years," the document must be destroyed and Tony knows it. General Peterson, in the end, is convinced that it's the base psychiatrist who has lost his mind.

99. "Jeannie My Guru"

Air Date: December 30, 1968

Written by James Henerson

Directed by Claudio Guzman

Guest Cast: Michael Margotta, Hilarie Thompson, The Lewis and Clarke Expedition

General Schaeffer and his hippie daughter, Suzie, are Tony Nelson's new neighbors. Suzie learns Jeannie's secret and decides to blackmail Tony. When Jeannie helps Suzie, she and her hip poet boyfriend hail Jeannie as their guru. Suzie wants Tony to spring the news of her engagement on her father, who will be furious.

100. "The Case of My Vanishing Master" (Part I)

Air Date: January 6, 1969

Written by James Henerson

Directed by Hal Cooper

Guest Cast: Benny Rubin, Joe La Grasso, Jerry Shane

Tony is working on a new plan for *Apollo 12* and is unable to notify Jeannie before Dr. Bellows has him flown to a secret hideout. Jeannie is unaware that Dr. Bellows has planted a double in Tony's house while he is away on the covert mission. Tony's double becomes confused by Jeannie's behavior.

Note: Joe La Grasso (a k a Joe Leitel) was a grip and later a propmaker on *I Dream of Jeannie* and *Bewitched* and took his role in this two-parter for fun. Later, La Grasso became an award-winning professional bodybuilder.

101. "The Case of My Vanishing Master" (Part II)

Air Date: January 13, 1969

Written by James Henerson

Directed by Hal Cooper

Guest Cast: Benny Rubin, Joe La Grasso, Jerry Shane

Tony is still away on a mission, but transmits a message to Roger that his double plans to marry Jeannie. Roger tells Jeannie she is being tricked by

Certainly not Air Force regulation footwear.

an imposter; she is convinced when Tony's double cannot recall how they met. Tony's double proves to be an enemy agent.

102. "Ride 'Em Astronaut"

Air Date: January 27, 1969

Written by James Henerson

Directed by Claudio Guzman

Guest Cast: Mark Miller, John Myhers, Richard Erdman

Jeannie is chosen Queen of the Supermarkets, being the millionth customer at Food City. Meanwhile, Tony brushes off Dr. Bellows's request that he be the Grand Marshal of the Cocoa Beach Rodeo, because he's afraid of horses. Tony is worried the Food City promotion will arouse suspicion about Jeannie. He accidentally enters a bucking-bronco contest at the rodeo.

103. "Invisible House for Sale"

Air Date: February 3, 1969

Written by James Henerson

Directed by Hal Cooper

Guest Cast: Harold Gould, Joan Tompkins, Ed Peck

Thinking that Tony would have more time for her if they lived in an apartment, Jeannie puts his house up for sale. Apartment living is not what Jeannie wants, so they are popped back to the old homestead. Jeannie blinks the house invisible so no one will buy it.

104. "Jeannie, the Governor's Wife"

Air Date: February 10, 1969

Written by Christopher Golato

Directed by Hal Cooper

Guest Cast: Xavier Nash, Mel Gallagher, Tommie Banks, Jack Smith

Jeannie learns that Tony doesn't trust any political candidate, so she decides to run Tony himself for Governor of Florida. Power-hungry Roger urges Tony to run, but Tony refuses—despite the flood of campaign contributions.

Note: This episode (logged as production #4233) was written by Sidney Sheldon (using pseudonym Christopher Golato) and originally titled "The Next President of the United States." The network asked him to change the situation to a gubernatorial race.

253

Dreaming of **Jeannie**

OPPOSITE PAGE: *Larry Hagman caught in a candid snapshot taken while filming on location.*

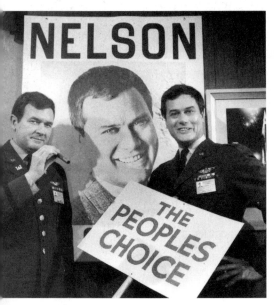

Jeannie insists on running Tony for governor.

105. "Is There a Doctor in the House?"

Air Date: February 17, 1969

Written by Christopher Golato

Directed by Oscar Rudolph

Jeannie's mama has put Tony under a spell; the astronaut falls asleep and wakes at the sound of a whistle. Jeannie has her mama come back with her and remove the spell. Mama ends up falling in love with Dr. Bellows. Tony is given an exotic, highly pungent necklace to ward off sleeping sickness.

106. "The Biggest Star in Hollywood"

Air Date: February 24, 1969.

Written by James Henerson

Directed by Claudio Guzman

Guest Cast: Judy Carne, Arte Johnson, Gary Owens, George Schlatter, Sid Melton, Susan Howard

Tony and Dr. Bellows leave for Hollywood on business. Gary Owens and George Schlatter see Jeannie and ask her to appear on TV's *Laugh-In*. Meanwhile, overzealous Roger becomes Jeannie's agent and convinces her to go along with his plans to make her a huge Hollywood celebrity. In Tinseltown, Roger attempts to keep Jeannie's identity a secret, claiming she is a princess. Determined to get Jeannie back to Cocoa Beach, Tony imprisons her in her bottle; he tells curious Dr. Bellows the unique bottle contains shaving lotion—which Bellows naturally wants to use.

Note: The working title for this episode (production #4229) was "Sock It to Me, Jeannie," but the network requested a change because it was too suggestive.

107. "The Case of the Porcelain Puppy"

Air Date: March 3, 1969

Written by James Henerson

Directed by Claudio Guzman

Guest Cast: Woodrow Parfrey

Jeannie tests out a new method of transforming things into porcelain. When Tony suddenly finds his report for Dr. Bellows has turned to porcelain, he explains that he has taken up ceramics at home as a hobby. Jeannie accidentally turns Djinn-Djinn the dog into porcelain and Amanda Bellows insists on keeping the lovely ceramic doggie.

LEFT: *Cast members from TV's* Laugh-In *(Arte Johnson, Gary Owens, and Judy Carne) guest-star.* RIGHT: *Hayden Rorke was best seen clothed.*

255

Dreaming of
Jeannie

108. "Jeannie for the Defense"

Air Date: March 10, 1969

Written by Bruce Howard

Directed by Hal Cooper

Guest Cast: Dick Sargent, J. Pat O'Malley, William Bassett, William Bramley, Ann Morgan Guilbert, Kay E. Kuter, Elsie Baker, Bruce Howard

In the small town of Clarkston—a trap for motorists—Tony gets a ticket and brushes a man's car. He is arrested and put in jail with a drunk, but he won't allow Roger to call Jeannie for help. Tony takes over his own defense in court and Jeannie assists in proving that he has been railroaded.

Note: Bruce Howard, who wrote this episode, also plays the drunk.

109. "Nobody Loves a Fat Astronaut"

Air Date: March 17, 1969

Written by Christopher Golato

Directed by Claudio Guzman

Jeannie II decides to try to get between Tony and her sister by illustrating how dangerous a trip to the moon would be. Jeannie is concerned and urges her master to resign from NASA. Jeannie II terrifies Tony and he is sure it is Jeannie's doing. When Jeannie II turns Tony into a 300-pound astronaut, Jeannie must blink him back to normal.

110. "Around the World in 80 Blinks"

Air Date: March 24, 1969

Written by James Henerson

Directed by Claudio Guzman

Guest Cast: Richard Mulligan, Jerry Shane, Xavier Nash, Sandy Harbin

Jeannie kisses Tony good-bye before he goes into lunar orbit with Roger and Commander Wingate. Realizing she might have passed her cold on to her master, Jeannie brings him back to care for him. The illness affects her blink and instead she accidentally retrieves Wingate from the orbital mission.

111. "Black–Mail Order Bride"

Air Date: March 31, 1969

Written by James Henerson

Directed by Claudio Guzman

Guest Cast: George Furth, Barbara Bostock, Teddy Quinn, Kerry MacLane, Damian London, Arthur Adams, Syl Lamont

A reporter named Charlie Farnum wants to get an exclusive story on Tony. Posing as a plumber, he plants audio recorders and a camera in Tony's house while Jeannie is decorating. Jeannie catches the reporter in the act, but he vows revenge and creates a long-lost wife and son whom Tony has purportedly abandoned.

112. "Jeannie-Go-Round"

Air Date: April 7, 1969

Written by James Henerson

ABOVE: *In the episode "Nobody Loves a Fat Astronaut," Barbara Eden debuted the new U.S. Air Force WAF (Women in the Air Force) uniform and accessory beret. The apparel, including the innovative new headgear, was designed by Harry Gilbert of the M. Born Company of Chicago, and was to project a "forward look." The entire new WAF outfit was authorized for wear in the spring of 1969, according to NBC press releases distributed at the time.*

Directed by Claudio Guzman

Guest Cast: Dave Barry, Lainie Nelson, Karen Carlson

Jeannie II poses as a press agent in order to interrupt her sister's date with Tony. Tony becomes confused and thinks Jeannie II is *his* genie, just driving him crazy. Finally, the two Jeannies become invisible and have it out and Tony explains away the destruction as an earthquake.

113. "Jeannie and the Secret Weapon"

Air Date: April 14, 1969

Written by Larry Markes

Directed by Leo Garen

Guest Cast: Ron Masak, Dick Schaal, Sheldon Collins, Jeff DeBenning, Ed Prentiss

Jeannie gets involved in Tony's business by making a small model of a space vehicle (called Agnes) able to fly. Tony orders Jeannie to get rid of the model, so she gives the "toy" to a young kid in the park—the son of an unsuccessful inventor. Tony is accused of selling the model of a secret weapon and faces court-martial. At the NASA hearing, Jeannie helps Tony prove that Agnes cannot fly.

Note: The scenes in the park, filmed around a large water fountain, were shot on the Columbia Ranch facility—now the Warner Ranch, in Burbank, California. The tiered fountain (seen many times in location shots on *Jeannie* and *Bewitched*) is a permanent structure located near the entrance of the facility; it is the same fountain prominently used in the opening of the hit sitcom *Friends*.

Dreaming of
Jeannie

Fifth Season

114. "Jeannie at the Piano"

Air Date: September 16, 1969

Written by James Henerson

Directed by Hal Cooper

Guest Cast: George Spell

Jeannie grants Tony's casual wish that he had the ability to play the piano. He suddenly plays like a virtuoso, and General Schaeffer decides to send him on a concert tour; Roger books him all over the country. The piano is the key to his abilities, though; Roger decides to plant a bomb in the piano to curtail his talents for good.

115. "Djinn-Djinn, the Pied Piper"

Air Date: September 23, 1969

Written by James Henerson
Directed by Claudio Guzman
Guest Cast: Dick Wilson

Tony mistakenly allows Jeannie to have her violent genie dog, Djinn-Djinn, visit the base. General Schaeffer challenges Tony to a match: Djinn-Djinn vs. Jupiter, his great Dane. Pandemonium erupts on the base as Jupiter goes berserk, tangles the general in his leash, and drags Tony all over the park. The dogcatcher captures Jupiter, but Djinn-Djinn organizes a massive breakout for all the creatures.

116. "Guess Who's Going to Be a Bride?" (Part I)

Air Date: September 30, 1969
Written by James Henerson
Directed by Hal Cooper
Guest Cast: Jackie Coogan, Mickey Morton, Brad Logan, Frank De Vol

The major plays a minor.

Jeannie's granduncle Suleiman arrives and offers Maharani Jeannie I the throne of Basenji. Suleiman misunderstands Tony's intentions regarding Kasha—the enemy of Basenji. Exasperated, Tony says he would not marry Jeannie "if she were the last genie on earth!" Angered and hurt, Jeannie decides to abandon her ungrateful master forever.

Note: Watch Major Nelson in a major blooper. When Uncle Suleiman punishes Major Nelson by zapping him into wooden stocks, the film cuts to a shot of Suleiman, and then back to Major Nelson who is still holding his hands up in the air as if they were locked in stocks—but the stocks are missing. The camera cuts back again and the stocks reappear. Obviously a glitch in continuity, the oversight was probably not caught in time to re-edit.

117. "Guess Who's Going to Be a Bride?" (Part II)

Air Date: October 7, 1969

Written by James Henerson

Directed by Hal Cooper

Guest Cast: Jackie Coogan, Mickey Morton, Brad Logan, Frank De Vol

Dreaming of
Jeannie

Tony is miserable without Jeannie and decides to find her and propose to her. Ordered to the Arctic, he and Roger receive word there that Jeannie is going to be married, so Tony decides to trek to Basenji. Tony risks his own head for Maharani Jeannie I, but at the last moment, she saves her master and blinks them back home.

118. "Jeannie's Beauty Cream"

Air Date: October 14, 1969

Written by Joanna Lee

Directed by Hal Cooper

Guest Cast: Harold Gould, Jim Begg, Jerry Shane, Eric Boles, Laraine Stephens

Jeannie presents Amanda Bellows with a jar of amazing face cream, which transforms her into a beautiful teenager. Unaware of the great metamorphosis, Amanda goes to NASA where Roger innocently falls in love with her. When Tony realizes what has happened, he tries to keep Amanda out of sight until Jeannie can blink up the antidote.

119. "Jeannie and the Bachelor Party"

Air Date: October 21, 1969

Written by Dick Bensfield and Perry Grant

Directed by Hal Cooper

Guest Cast: Judith Baldwin, Richard McMurray, Wright Colbert, Sr., Francine York, Chanin Hale, Judi Sherven, Nancy Fisher, Yvonne Shubert

Roger knows Tony does not want a bachelor party but plans one anyway, smuggling a bunch of girls—dressed as men—into NASA. He orders Tony to a meeting at NASA. Amanda Bellows suspects the men are having a party and takes Jeannie along to NASA to investigate. In the end, it's Dr. Bellows who gets drunk and pops out of a giant party cake. (That busting-out-of-the-top-of-a-cake thing was popular in the sixties. Remember Mrs. Howell on *Gilligan's Island*?)

120. "The Blood of a Jeannie"

Air Date: October 28, 1969

Written by John L. Greene

Directed by Claudio Guzman

Guest Cast: Ned Glass, Ruth McDevitt, Ivor Francis

Tony and Jeannie must undergo a blood test before they are married. Jeannie casually informs Tony that she possesses green corpuscles. Unwillingly, Roger is made to undergo the blood test instead of Jeannie—by shoving his arm out from behind a screen. Meanwhile, Jeannie is anxious to catch the pickpocket who stole Tony's wallet in a jewelry store.

121. "See You in C-U-B-A!"

Air Date: November 4, 1969

Written by John McGreevey

Directed by Hal Cooper

Guest Cast: John Myhers, Pedro Gonzales-Gonzales, Howard Morton, Farrah Fawcett

Tony is set for a flight to Puerto Rico in a new, fully automated T-38 supersonic jet-fighter. Jeannie interrupts the mission and blinks Tony home to help with party plans. The plane takes off without Tony. When Jeannie blinks him back to the T-38, it veers off and lands in Havana, Cuba, where he is eventually taken prisoner.

122. "The Mad Home Wrecker"

Air Date: November 11, 1969

Written by Howard Ostroff

Directed by Hal Cooper

Guest Cast: Michael Lipton, Marvin Silbersher, Robert Munk

As a wedding gift, a mod sculptor known as Helasco is sent to redecorate Jeannie and Tony's home. Kept out until Helasco has finished the remodeling, Tony sleeps on his couch at the office. When Tony returns home, he is appalled at Helasco's style. Jeannie blinks up a newly remodeled home in the end.

260

Dreaming of
Jeannie

Note: The Nelson home underwent a facelift, which debuted in this episode. One noticeable centerpiece on the new living room set was the large white fireplace with an open cubbyhole in front for nesting Jeannie's bottle.

123. "Uncles a Go-Go"
Air Date: November 25, 1969
Written by Ron Friedman
Directed by Russ Mayberry
Guest Cast: Ronald Long, Arthur Malet

Jeannie's zany relatives pop in to approve of the prospective groom. Uncle Azmire and Uncle Vasemir disappear, but warn Jeannie they will be watching Tony. Both uncles pose as other people to test Tony, but eventually they declare their approval.

124. "The Wedding"
Air Date: December 2, 1969
Written by James Henerson
Directed by Claudio Guzman
Guest Cast: Cliff Norton, Jack Smith, Harvey Fisher, Reginald Fenderson, Hal Taggart, June Jocelyn

The widely publicized nuptials of astronaut Tony Nelson and his fiancée, Jeannie, are in jeopardy when it is realized that the bride does not photograph. In pictures, she is invisible. Photographers from *Life, Newsweek,* and major

The Nelson living room, remodeled for the final season.

newspapers are ready to shoot the ceremony when Jeannie comes up with a solution: She clothes a mannequin who will substitute for her during the ceremony as she looks on. The plan is for Jeannie to blink the mannequin out and herself in for the final "I do's" to make it legal. Caught up in an emotional daydream, Jeannie nearly forgets to rejoin her own wedding ceremony.

Note: *TV Guide* (Nov. 22–28, 1969) featured Barbara Eden in her beautiful white wedding gown (designed by Joie Hutchinson) on the cover, with a color spread inside. After this episode, Barbara Eden was finally allowed to diversify her wardrobe, slip

Finally, a blushing bride.
(Steven Colbert collection.)

into civvies, and show off some miniskirted leg. (She is seen considerably less often in the signature pink pantaloons.) Although this remains one of Barbara Eden's favorite episodes, at the time, it signified the end of the show and almost everyone associated with the series knew it.

James Henerson, the show's story consultant, who reluctantly wrote the wedding script, told interviewer Richard Barnes in 1992: "It was a terrible idea in my opinion. Everybody connected with the show fought [the marriage concept] bitterly. Especially Larry. For the rest of us, there came a point when we knew we couldn't win anymore. The network was determined to marry them off. We had many, many conferences. But the network was adamant: We think it's going to be terrific and you have to do it. It made a crazy-man out of Larry. He became really, really difficult that last year. I don't think anybody can blame him. He went from being the most cooperative actor to being part of the problem."

125. "My Sister the Homewrecker"

Air Date: December 9, 1969
Written by James Henerson
Directed by Claudio Guzman
Guest Cast: Michael Ansara, Farrah Fawcett

Jeannie II wants to destroy her sister's recent marriage because she feels Tony Nelson should have been hers. Jeannie II masquerades as her married sister and creates a sensation when she and Major Biff Jellico are caught making out. Dr. and Mrs. Bellows are outraged at Jeannie's behavior and decide to confront her about it.

126. "Jeannie the Matchmaker"

Air Date: December 16, 1969
Written by Don Richman and Bill Daily
Directed by Claudio Guzman
Guest Cast: Janis Hanson, Elaine Giftos

Jeannie consults a computer matchmaking service to find a date for Roger, and the computer indicates Laverne, the computer operator. In a swinging nightclub merry mixup, two women collapse after being slipped a Mickey Finn while Tony and Roger try to conceal the predicament.

127. "Never Put a Genie on a Budget"

Air Date: December 30, 1969

Written by Sidney Sheldon

Directed by Oscar Rudolph

Guest Cast: Noam Pitlik, Stafford Repp, Larry Bishop, Maggie Thrett, Ellen Nance, Sheer Delight (as herself)

After going to jail for charging purchases without a charge account, Jeannie is bailed out by Tony and put on a strict budget. A visiting Russian major is impressed with Tony's typical American home life—until Jeannie serves up a budget supper consisting of half a TV dinner with stale bread on the side. The foreign visitor leaves hungry and disillusioned, assuming the American space program lacks funds.

128. "Please Don't Give My Jeannie No More Wine"

Air Date: January 6, 1970

Written by James Henerson

Directed by Jon Andersen

Guest Cast: Alan Oppenheimer, Mary Grover

At a Bellows dinner party, Jeannie blinks up a bottle of vintage wine—from 1591. Dr. Bellows tastes it and begins to vanish. Busy serving, Amanda doesn't notice that Alfred has disappeared. Amanda tastes the wine and she also becomes invisible. Since Jeannie can't blink the Bellowses back, they must wait for the wine to wear off; meanwhile, Amanda indulges and gets sauced on the ancient nectar.

129. "One of Our Hotels Is Growing"

Air Date: January 13, 1970

Written by Robert Rodgers

Directed by Jerry Bernstein

Guest Cast: Marvin Kaplan, Ned Wertimer, Jimmy Cross, Fran Ryan

Jeannie, Tony, Roger, and the Bellowses all take a trip to California, where they find that their hotel has no vacancies. The hotel clerk wishes there were an extra floor to accommodate them, so Jeannie blinks up an additional level—a thirteenth floor. The hotel bellman and a hotel drunk are confounded by the extra floor, as Tony and Jeannie frantically attempt to contain Dr. and Amanda Bellows in their room.

263

Dreaming of
Jeannie

Note: Guest star Marvin Kaplan (the bellman) recently recalled Larry Hagman's laggard attitude during the production of this episode; Hagman most likely knew the end of the show was near. "Larry Hagman was unprepared," says Kaplan. "He didn't read the script until he was in makeup that morning. I was surprised by that. He didn't know what he was doing, and Hayden [Rorke] scolded Larry because he was wasting time and wasting money. No one else could do that to Larry because Hayden had known his mother and now they were friends. Larry just listened, because I think he respected Hayden. Barbara Eden was completely calm about it. She told me that it was usual procedure for this to happen."

130. "The Solid Gold Jeannie"

Air Date: January 20, 1970

Written by Joanna Lee

Directed by Jerry Bernstein

Guest Cast: Robert Hogan, Shirley Bonn, Jim Galante, Bill McKinney, Robert Gros

Following their moon-landing mission, Roger, Tony, and Commander Wingate are confined to an isolation chamber for observation. Jeannie breaks the quarantine to be with Tony and he insists she must stay because she might become contaminated. Jeannie must shrink herself and masquerade as a small gold trophy. Dr. and Mrs. Bellows spot Jeannie through a window and assume she is a visitor from outer space.

131. "Mrs. Djinn-Djinn"

Air Date: February 3, 1970

Written by Dick Bensfield and Perry Grant

Directed by Russ Mayberry

Guest Cast: Jerry Shane

Jeannie's favorite pet, little Djinn-Djinn, pops in for a visit accompanied by Mrs. Djinn-Djinn (a dainty poodle), who is about to give birth to puppies. Overjoyed, Jeannie prepares for her a nice maternity bed and blinks up a bottle of Vitamins for Pregnancy. Major Healey misinterprets everything he sees and spreads the word around the NASA base that Jeannie and Tony are expecting a baby. A group at the base get together and surprise Jeannie and Tony at home with a surprise baby shower.

132. "Jeannie and the Curious Kid"

Air Date: February 10, 1970

Written by Perry Grant and Dick Bensfield

Directed by Claudio Guzman

Guest Cast: Michael Barbera

Jeannie is trapped in her bottle when the Bellowses arrive to ask if Jeannie and Tony will watch their young nephew, Melvin, for the day. Thinking the coast is clear, Jeannie emerges from her bottle while Melvin is watching. Afraid of Melvin's growing curiosity, Tony warns Jeannie not to use any magic. Melvin steals Jeannie's bottle and Tony and Roger must retrieve it from the Bellowses' house.

133. "Jeannie, the Recording Secretary"

Air Date: February 24, 1970

Written by James Henerson

Directed by Claudio Guzman

Guest Cast: Joan Tompkins, Norma Connolly, Elizabeth Lane

Jeannie becomes the recording secretary for the Officers' Wives Association. Jeannie wants Tony to win the First Annual Good Husband Award. Thanks to an extra-heavy dose of sleeping pills, Major Nelson is a mess when he is interviewed for the Good Husband Award, although Jeannie attempts to cover it up.

134. "Help, Help, a Shark"

Air Date: March 3, 1970

Written by James Henerson

Directed by Claudio Guzman

Guest Cast: Jim Backus

Tony louses up an opportunity to obtain a three-day pass when he jeopardizes General Schaeffer's chance to compete in a billiards match. Tony takes the general's place and Jeannie is set to ensure that Tony wins for the general. General Fitzhugh, however, does not allow Jeannie to remain in the room during the match, so she hides under the table.

135. "Eternally Yours, Jeannie"

Air Date: March 17, 1970

Written by James Henerson

Directed by Joseph Goodson

Guest Cast: Damian Bodie, Denny Miller, Wright Colbert, Sally Ann Richards

When Tony receives a perfumed letter from a high school sweetheart, Bonnie Crenshaw, Jeannie smells trouble. Disguising herself as Tony's former girlfriend to test his fidelity, Jeannie uncovers Crenshaw's ulterior motives. Her masquerade causes confusion among everyone involved.

136. "An Astronaut in Sheep's Clothing"

Air Date: March 24, 1970
Written by James Henerson
Directed by Bruce Kessler
Guest Cast: Don Dubbins

Tony suggests to Jeannie that perhaps a handmade anniversary gift might be appropriate and thoughtful, rather than something extravagant. Jeannie decides to knit Tony a sweater, so she travels to Tibet for a cashmere goat; she has a difficult time trying to shear the animal and conceal it from Tony.

Major Nelson doesn't know how he wound up in Dr. Bellows's house.

137. "Hurricane Jeannie"

Air Date: April 28, 1970
Written by James Henerson
Directed by Claudio Guzman

A hurricane strikes Cocoa Beach, confining Jeannie, Tony, Roger, and Dr. Bellows in the Nelson home. Tony must use the telephone to "talk down" two astronauts who are circling over the storm. The place becomes a madhouse as Tony and Roger attempt to thwart Jeannie from using magic. When the power lines go down, Jeannie restores the electricity, which makes Dr. Bellows extremely suspicious. During the night, Dr. Bellows witnesses some of Jeannie's powers—or does he?

Note: This was the last episode of the series to be filmed. It, and the series, wrapped on January 30, 1970. Although the *Jeannie* ensemble did not officially know the show's fate, they all had a feeling the network was going to blink this baby right off the grid. A sad day in TV Land.

138. "One Jeannie Beats Four of a Kind"

Air Date: May 19, 1970
Written by Perry Grant and Dick Bensfield
Directed by Michael Ansara
Guest Cast: Herbert Rudley, William Wintersole, Tony Giorgio, Walter Burke

Captain Ross attempts to locate the card sharp who is fleecing the men on the NASA base. Congressman Martino, actually the card sharp, sits in on a friendly game of poker at Tony's home. When Tony and Roger win, they become the suspects of the investigation.

139. "My Master, the Chili King"

Air Date: May 26, 1970

Written by James Henerson

Directed by Claudio Guzman

Guest Cast: Gabriel Dell, Dick Van Patten, Lew Brown, Pearl Shear

Tony's cousin, a con man named Arvel, arrives from Texas. Jeannie goes into business with cousin Arvel in order to provide her master financial security for life. Jeannie and Arvel create "Cousin Tony's Texas Chili," with the unconsenting astronaut's image on the label. Amanda Bellows discovers "Cousin Tony's" product and investigates while Tony and Roger attempt to buy out every store's stock of the item.

Major Nelson—"a regular pool trout," Jeannie says. Tony goes wild with the talcum powder during a billiards competition.

25

Strictly Taboo

◆

*And what do you do? You wiggle that beak of yours
and we get into trouble.*

—Darrin Stephens

guess it might have been L. Frank Baum, in 1900, who gave us *good* witches. His tale of Oz—purely an American original—not only captivated the ages but dispelled some myths swirling around witchcraft. Not all witches are ugly.

Bewitched earned respect certainly because of its longevity and appeal—this hugely successful sitcom ran for eight seasons—but it's now considered by many critics and popular culture historians a landmark for women, in part because of the perfect performance of its star, Elizabeth Montgomery. Writer Jess Cagle called *Bewitched* "the most subversively feminist series of its era." During a stretch of the nineties, a *Bewitched* and *Jeannie* renaissance swept through Cable TV Land. After thirty years,

Bewitched: *The supernatural sister-sitcom was a neighboring entity at the studio and in viewers' minds.*

Bewitched *was heavily merchandised—more than its sister show,* **I Dream of Jeannie.**

these shows deserve a second look, a peer into the psyche of these sixties gems.

Both shows traded heavily on the sex appeal of their lead actresses, with Eden opting for a style of va-va-va-voom gaga and Montgomery doing a more sophisticated version of come-hither. But where *Jeannie* offered the male fantasy of an attractive woman obliged to fulfill one's every wish, *Bewitched* always made it clear that Samantha was much smarter than goofy, grinning Darrin.

—Ken Tucker
Entertainment Weekly

At its most moralizing, *Bewitched* served as the Grimm Brothers nursery tale of its era, beginning with enchantment and ending with a lesson. But even then, at most it was fifty parts Magic Carpet to one part Magna Carta—and as such, ideally suited to the ostrich years of early sixties TV.

—Donna McCrohan
Prime Time, Our Time

The notion that anyone chooses—for the sake of taking sides—to admire only *Bewitched* or *Jeannie* is a grostesque one just like the old *Munsters* vs. *Addams* thing. Sure there are similarities and shared traits between *Bewitched* and *I Dream of Jeannie,* but the latter can hardly be labeled a ripoff of the former. That's been suggested. Even *The Munsters* and *The Addams Family* shared similar skeletal structures, but both shows invented a unique product in their era.

Undoubtedly, during production there was a mild competition between the *Bewitched* camp and the *Jeannie* group. But they learned to work the same neighborhood and ended up playing host to many of the same guest stars, utilizing the same sets, writers, and designers. Both shows were produced on the Columbia lot, on nearby soundstages.

Who cares if one show inspires another? If it weren't for *The Honeymooners,* we wouldn't have *The Flintstones.* The pairing of a witch married to a mortal has roots in the motion pictures *Bell, Book and Candle* and *I Married a Witch.* Perhaps the secret of *Bewitched* was not divine inspiration, but rather the stellar cast and the outstanding supporting players. During the program's highly decorated life, the show became a watering hole for countless wonderfully bizarre characters with dimension. The show's guest stars had presence. The supernatural sitcom had one of the largest, most respected casts in television history.

One of the good witches on television was Endora. Acid tongue and all, she had a heart of gold, and her character became a pop icon. It took a special actress, with subtle tones, agility, and perfect timing, to pull off such an acerbic character yet keep her lov-

Best Witches: Elizabeth Montgomery, little Erin Murphy, and Agnes Moorehead during their favorite time of the year. (Courtesy of Erin Murphy.)

able to viewers. Even these days, five-time Academy Award nominee Agnes Moorehead is a favorite of many *Bewitched* connoisseurs. As in *The Beverly Hillbillies,* the matriarch stole the show.

To summon their powers, Samantha Stephens and Jeannie have distinctive methods—both punctuated with cartoonish percussion. When Jeannie folded her arms, blinked, and nodded, a *doyyynnng!* sound effect followed. The piece used to create it was a small instrument similar to a mouth harp. When Samantha twitched her nose (a peculiar little talent of Elizabeth Montgomery's), the twinkle was that from a xylophone. Occasionally, Samantha and Endora waved their arms and vanished with a harmonious chime of several notes on the xylophone or a beautiful scale gliding up a harp.

She didn't intend to. In fact Agnes Moorehead had no ambition of taking on this role and creating such a memorable mother-in-law. Into the first season, she explained her introduction into witchhood for a *New York Sunday News* reporter. "I was trapped," she said, smiling. "I was sent the pilot film script. I looked it over and it was charming and had no violence in it; it was clean and had a smile in it, and a little fantasy and a little romance, so I said, 'This won't sell,' and since they offered me a good sum to make the pilot, I did it. Then I went out on the road to do my one-woman show, and when I came back they told me it was sold . . . and I was committed to do it."

The next seven years were hardly a one-woman show for Moorehead. She loved and missed theater and warned the reporter when the show started its run: "For 17 years I've been in movies and played theater from coast to coast, so I was quite well known before 'Bewitched,' and I don't particularly want to be identified as the witch. When my contract expires, I'll do what I did before."

Into the second year, it was apparent that Moorehead had learned to love the lifestyle, the adulation, and the time to enjoy her Beverly Hills home and shelve the suitcases for a while. Television proved to be hard work, but she handled it gracefully, and kept renewing her contract on *Bewitched.*

She really was the show's pearl, an exemplary actress trained in the theater; her style and professional reputation made her well known in radio, television, and film as well. One of her most famous radio performances was the neurotic wife-victim in *Sorry, Wrong Number,* now recognized as a classic. Her Emmy Award came from a performance in an episode of *Wild Wild West*. Remember the suspenseful *Twilight Zone* episode in which she portrays a woman terrified by an alien, desperate to defend herself and escape?

Moorehead made her movie debut with Orson Welles in *Citizen Kane,* in 1941. She won the New York Film Critics Award for best actress of the year in 1942 for *The Magnificent Ambersons,* and was nominated for an Oscar five times, for her roles in *The Magnificent Ambersons, Mrs. Parkington* (1944), *Johnny Belinda* (1948), *All That Heaven Allows* (1955), and *Hush . . . Hush, Sweet Charlotte* (1964). Her final movie appearance was in the NBC-TV two-parter *Frankenstein: The True Story* (1973).

Following *Bewitched,* Moorehead did go back to what she did before. In 1973 she toured and landed on Broadway in a production of the musical, *Gigi.* But she was forced to cut her New York engagement short because of illness; she died of cancer on April 30, 1974, in a Rochester, Minnesota, hospital affiliated with the Mayo Clinic.

Agnes Moorehead was a charming cohost on **The Mike Douglas Show** *in 1967.*

The Saga of Durwood

Dick York was beautifully frantic. Hilariously frazzled. Totally spellbound in a marriage to a witch with a twitch. If you think about it, it made sense to have Darrin Stephens maintain an antiwitchcraft stance, so his blowups would carry more punch. Somehow, it was still irritating when he vetoed any supernatural assistance.

L.A. Weekly writer Derek Thomas wrote this about the original Darrin: "York *was* Darrin, like Sean Connery *was* James Bond. When York tossed off an exasperated 'Sam!' (the equivalent to 'Bond . . . James Bond'), it wasn't just a cue for the laugh track, but a projection of Darrin's inner turmoil, his need to live a life of normalcy in the midst of the supernatural." Most fans have agreed, over the years, that York made the character stronger and funnier than his successor.

Fact is, producers originally wanted Dick Sargent for the role in the pilot, but the actor's schedule was muddy. Dick York landed the costarring role and fame and sitcom stardom came his way, albeit with a price tag. York's years on *Bewitched* were grueling for him—not because of his relationship with coworkers. York's own physical debilitation, at times, left him in agony.

Dreaming of
Jeannie

Just a few years before playing advertising man Darrin Stephens, the spindly York suffered a back injury, tore ligaments and threw out discs while filming a Gary Cooper motion picture, *They Came to Cordura* (1959). His torn ligaments and thrown discs would become the physical and mental downfall of his professional acting career.

"I fought with that on *Bewitched* for years," York said in 1989 from his home in Rockford, Michigan. "But you work with pain in any job. I had a wife and five children to support. People depended on me, so I hung on to the 'witch' a while longer. Of course they were good years professionally, but not comfortable. We did 35 shows a year, 12 to 14 hours a day, and I can't do pain-killers. Never could. I had to stick it out."

Bewitched's executive producer, Harry Ackerman, painted a slightly different picture in *The TV Collector,* a longtime East Coast fanzine published for the TV generation. In this 1986 interview, Ackerman noted that York was extremely effective on the show, "except for his lapses into illness of one kind or another. Actually he was on drugs. And we were extremely lucky when we finally had to hospitalize him. He collapsed on the set. We knew we had to replace him and because of his various lapses into problems over the years, we had done a number of the shows without the character."

Stirring gently so as not to bruise, Ackerman went forward with a transition. He

275

Dreaming of
Jeannie

TOP: *Darrin Number Two: Dick Sargent joins the cast of regulars Maurice Evans, Elizabeth Montgomery, Erin Murphy, and Agnes Moorehead.* RIGHT: *Voila! Dr. Bellows's home was merely the Shephenses' living room set from* Betwitched *with a few modifications.*

compiled those dozen or so episodes without Darrin and aired them all in a row for the summer repeats of 1969. In the fall, new man Dick Sargent sat behind the drawing table at McMann & Tate.

Ackerman must have felt that viewers' senses had been sufficiently dulled by Darrin's chronic absence. Or maybe the producers assumed that no one in TV Land would care. The sitcom had to go on, so they did what was necessary to keep the show running, short of chopping out the character. Suffice it to say, Dick Sargent, who played Darrin until the show ended in 1972, became an adequate replacement—just not as funny and energetically expressive as Dick York.

Screen Gems' publicist, Bob Palmer, says he really liked Dick York. "He was having his problems, but he never complained. Sometimes he had to take painkillers.

"Anges Moorehead once said to me that he was the one who really held the show together," Palmer says. "And that he was the least appreciated, because the hardest job in the world is to react to crazy situations in a believable way. He made Darrin so believable. I don't think Elizabeth Montgomery ever fully appreciated his contribution.

"Agnes would get impatient with Elizabeth and she didn't like the way they treated Dick York," says Palmer. "She thought Elizabeth was a bit of a 'spoiled little girl,' as she put it."

Dreaming of
Jeannie

Palmer was in his forties when he left ABC—lured to Screen Gems by Elizabeth Montgomery and her husband, *Bewitched* producer Bill Asher. "Studios are more fun than the networks, because you're where the production is. I loved the job," he says. "I liked working with Jackie Cooper. He was a great boss. I think back on that time with great affection now."

As the publicist who roamed the set on occasion, watched filming, and discussed interviews with the cast and producers, Bob Palmer became the liaison between the network and the actors when publicity activities were underway. Operating in producer Jules White's former office—*with* facilities, mind you—Palmer was ringside at the productions for which he created press: *The Monkees, Farmer's Daughter, I Dream of Jeannie,* and *Bewitched* among them. Because of Palmer's close proximity, he could peek into the fishbowls.

"Elizabeth Montgomery didn't like any competition," he says. "She really liked being the queen. Around me, I don't recall her even acknowledging Barbara Eden, so I don't think there was any competition there. She knew *Bewitched* was the big show on the lot. She also liked to be one of the boys in the sense that she liked the crew, and she liked to go over to this place nearby that served great hamburgers. Elizabeth would go over there with the guys on the crew and eat hamburgers. She liked playing the horses and doing her thing."

At the time of this interview in 1989, Dick York was fighting the battle of his life: emphysema. Despite the tubes in his nose, he was slowly compiling notes and audio-recorded memories for his autobiography, which he tentatively titled "Sitcom Stardom and Other American Dreams." In it, he planned to reminisce about his childhood and the inspiring people in his life, his film career (he was in *My Sister Eileen* and *Inherit the Wind,* among others) and years in radio and television.

"I loved *Bewitched*," he said. "I loved the Italian [episode], where I learned to speak Italian. Our show was a good, clean show. We did some razzle-dazzle special effects and it was innovative. The cast had a good relationship. Me, Liz, and Aggie Moorehead. If it hadn't been for my disability, it would have been a ball. The crew helped out and made sure I didn't have any real physical strains and they would put boards under pillows and couches so I didn't sink and freeze up.

"I loved it when I would be changed into an animal or something," he said, "because the goat worked, not me."

In his fifth season, York suffered a seizure on the set and was rushed to the hospital; he never returned to the show. In the years after, work ran out. The actor's weight escalated to 306 pounds, and he lost all but a few of his teeth. He blamed his deterioration on faulty nutrition, lack of calcium, and neglect. Eventually, he cleaned himself up, resurfacing in the late 1980s with a TV guest appearance on *Simon & Simon,* but decided he'd had enough and hung it up. Near the end of his life, York lost weight and he and his wife, Joan (whom he called Joey), lived in Michigan and generously donated their time and money to local organizations which fed the poor. That was an important mission for York, who died in his sixty-third year in 1992.

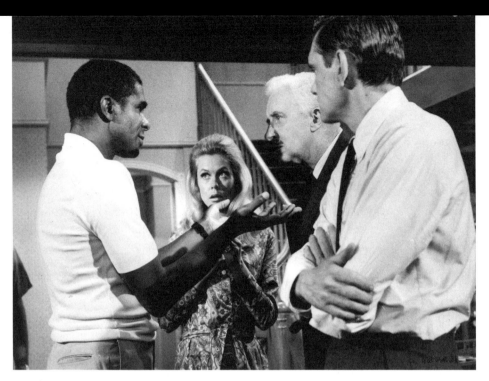

Director Luther James explaining a scene to the actors during production of an episode.

Although Dick Sargent only took on the role of Darrin Stephens for the last few seasons, it's what he'll be best remembered for in the entertainment world.

Sargent's final television appearance, on the daytime talk show *Vicki!*, was in February 1994, just five months before his death. Appearing with a panel of sitcom favorites, the gray-haired Sargent—who appeared healthy—revealed his terminal illness before the tabloids. He soberly told host Vicki Lawrence: "I have cancer of the prostate now . . . and I'm gettin' through it. It's a sentence of death, I suppose, but so far I'm doin' okay. It's what Bill Bixby died of, what Don Ameche died of . . . Frank Zappa died of. It's a very common ailment in mature men. And so far, I'm maintaining, but that's all I can hope for, I guess."

Interview with a Witch

With a manual twitch of her nose, little blonde, blue-eyed Erin Murphy made magic as the young sorceress Tabitha on *Bewitched*. Her appearance at age two on the hit sitcom was not, however, Murphy's first *poof* into television.

"My first commercial was with Ronald Reagan for Borateem [detergent], before he ran for governor," says Murphy, now in her mid-thirties. She was only eleven months old, too young to recall performing with Reagan, but she does recall growing up amid characters like polka-dotted elephants on the studio set she shared with her second family. "Since I grew up on the show, I don't remember anything before the show," she says.

Originally, Tabitha was two children, fraternal twins Erin and Diane Murphy. Both little tykes enchanted viewers beginning in 1966 and were used "interchangeably," says Erin, who eventually took on the bulk of the role. "Diane got a black eye when she was young and couldn't work at all."

Except that she was privately tutored during those years, Erin's childhood was quite normal. She became friends with Elizabeth Montgomery's children, and shared a birthday with Montgomery's daughter, Rebecca, so the two were used to celebrating together. Erin participated in lots of kiddie activities, such as ice-skating lessons, sometimes with other industry children like Susan Olsen and Maureen McCormick. Her second family was the TV cast and the countless recurring personalities. "I knew Elizabeth Montgomery was my pretend mom on the show and I called her 'Samantha Mommy' and Dick York and Dick Sergent were 'Darrin Daddy,'" she says.

And then there was the change in daddies. "The switch was not strange," she says. "It had been explained to me. I knew that Dick York had been so sick that last season he was on the show. His whole last season, practically, they showed him sitting down or lying down. I remember him being in a lot of pain. I didn't resent Dick Sargent. I liked him right away.

Both Elizabeth Montgomery and Barbara Eden were pregnant when their respective shows began filming. Elizabeth Montgomery was eight months along when Bewitched commenced, so director William Asher had to shoot the first five episodes around her and edit in Montgomery's scenes later, after her baby was born. Barbara Eden filmed the first eleven episodes of Jeannie during the initial five months of her pregnancy (a much faster than normal shooting schedule), then resumed after her child was born. Director Gene Nelson (along with Eden's wardrobe mistress) had to do some fancy footwork to avoid catching any revealing shots of a swollen Jeannie during the first batch of episodes.

Johnny Whitaker plays Jack in the episode "Samantha and the Beanstalk." Whitaker escorted little Erin Murphy on a lunch "date" during the production.

"They were completely different people," she points out. "Both were great to me. People always ask who I 'preferred.' It's like comparing your own parents. You can't say you like your mother more than your father."

It's not surprising that Grandmama Endora (Moorehead) cuddled Murphy, spoiled her, sat with her on the stairway, and told stories and drew pictures with her like a loving grandparent. Bumbling Aunt Clara (wobbly-jowled Marion Lorne) actually collected doorknobs, a hobby that was incorporated into the script. "She gave me a crystal doorknob that I kept," Murphy recalls.

During the series' Emmy-winning prime-time spell, Murphy also shone in Barbie commercials, attended the openings of banks, and waved from parade floats. She truly enjoyed the VIP treatment that went hand-in-hand with child stardom, and she promoted *Bewitched* like a little trouper. "They had a special Bewitched Ice Cream at Baskin-Robbins. Oh, the worst thing you could imagine. Vanilla with chunks of orange and licorice. I ended up being the poster child for this ice cream and had to go around to stores and tell everyone how good it was."

Murphy's memories of day-to-day interactions with her television family are sketchy, since the show lasted only until she was eight. "I remember some things, like the crew setting up and spraying wires, so you couldn't see them. They used this special paint so they were transparent to the camera."

One memorable birthday party on the set for Liz Montgomery prompted the crew to wheel on stage an extravagant sheet cake loaded with trick candles, which eventually caught on fire. "It turned out the whole cake was made of wood and they had to bring in hoses and put it out.

"And I had my first 'date' on the show," she recalls. "It was with Johnny Whitaker, who was a guest star playing Jack [and] the Beanstalk. I was four and he was eight. He asked me to lunch and I was really impressed because he had his own checking account and he signed it and paid for it. He was a little gentleman."

Murphy tried her best to sit still for the disappearing act, an essential process to master in this production. "Everyone around the person disappearing would stand still for about thirty seconds," she explains, "while they cut the film. The person would walk away and they'd throw in a smoke bomb, and then the camera would roll again. *Then* you could move. We had it down so we could do it very quickly."

Flash forward a few decades. (Think smoke bomb.) Today, Murphy is a single mom with two young sons, and is

still close to her twin sister. Over the years Murphy kept in contact with some of the cast, especially Liz Montgomery; she cherishes a special conversation she had with Montgomery not long before the sixty-two-year-old star died of cancer in 1995.

ABOVE: *Stuttering Aunt Clara (Marion Lorne) throws a hex in* Bewitched. *In real life, Lorne—like her character—collected doorknobs as a hobby.* BELOW: *Child stars Erin Murphy and Johnny Whitaker reunited at a Hollywood nostalgia show in 1997. (Photo by Steve Cox.)*

The Lost Episodes of Bewitched

BY SCOTT MAIKO

Thought you knew everything there is to know about Bewitched? So did I. Oh, I read all the books, surfed all the websites, watched what I thought were all the episodes. Then I did a little Kravitzing around, and boy, was I surprised at what I uncovered. The following three episodes haven't been seen in over thirty years, nor do they appear in syndication. And, believe it or not, the cast refuses to admit they exist!

"The Cat Came Back"

Samantha takes in a stray cat as a pet. The cat turns out to be Endora in disguise; she is spying on the couple. When Darrin finds out, he blows his top, storms out to his favorite bar, and gets loaded. Driving home drunk, he hits and kills a cat, which he believes to be his mother-in-law. Now he's stuck with a serious dilemma: How does he gently break the news to Sam while concealing his own delight? Upon arriving home, however, he finds Endora very much alive and complaining to Samantha about a certain nosy neighbor. Next, the doorbell rings—it's Abner Kravitz looking for his wife. A guilty-looking Endora vanishes. The tag at the end of the episode features a rare happy moment between Endora and "Durwood," when they laugh over the fact that "curiosity killed the cat."

Note: Rumor has it that this was written as a farewell episode to the original Gladys—actress Alice Pearce—but was never aired because the producers decided to pull a Darrin and simply replace the character with another actress without explanation.

"I Am Darrin, Hear Me Roar"

Endora overhears Darrin tell Sam that women have always had it easy in the world. Angered, Endora zaps away his genitalia and replaces them with their female counterparts to teach him a lesson. Darrin is oblivious to this until

Dreaming of
Jeannie

he, Larry Tate, and their client, Mr. Phillips, step into the men's room after lunch to relieve themselves. Standing at the urinals, both Larry and Mr. Phillips are amazed at what they see—or rather, don't see—on Darrin. Though equally surprised and horrified, Darrin quickly recovers and explains that he has female genitals to prove a point: that he didn't use Phillips After Shave that morning, and without Phillips After Shave, "You're Just Not a Man." The client loves the slogan, McMann & Tate land the account, Samantha gets an apology, and Darrin is reunited with his accoutrements.

Note: Oscar Mayer, one of the show's sponsors, pulled its spots from this episode's one and only airing (November 7, 1968), because it had been previously assured by the producers that the client in the episode would be a lunch-meat executive trying to boost sales of his firm's all-meat wieners.

"The Furor Over the Führer"

Sam and Darrin have to attend a dinner party at a client's house, so they ask Aunt Clara to baby-sit for Tabitha. While entertaining Tabitha with simple witchcraft, she accidentally zaps Adolf Hitler into the Stephenses' living room. Unable to send him back, she alerts Sam to the emergency and they make a hasty exit from the party. Arriving back at home, they find Tabitha safe and asleep in her bed—but Hitler's missing! While Darrin contemplates the far-reaching and possibly catastrophic effects of this, Sam hears screaming across the street and finds Adolf chasing Gladys Kravitz around the backyard with Tabitha's water pistol in one hand and her Easy Bake oven in the other.

Note: ABC shelved this episode directly after its original airing when they were bombarded with calls and letters from angry Jewish viewers incensed at the dinner party scenes showing the client and his wife—the Goldsteins—serving pork chops to their guests.

Scott Maiko is a comedy writer based in Los Angeles.

283

Dreaming of
Jeannie

To Hex with It

Here's the rule: In the realm of Bewitched, *one witch cannot undo another's spell. Incantations, while personal to the witch or warlock conjuring and casting them, are also exclusive. Their rhythms are so elegantly musical and flamboyant in execution. There was no strategic anticipation of witchcraft on* Jeannie, *but there was on* Bewitched. *Confined to the private sphere by Darrin, magic was forbidden fruit for Samantha; the limitation only increased viewers' appetite for magic. Most of the time, Sam obediently curbed her tendencies and used her powers sparingly, not to upset the natural order of things. But that was no fun. Who can deny that practicing the craft was never more romantic than when Endora whipped up a mind-buster and let the forces do their thing? Alas, as dotty Aunt Clara could attest, it's not always easy to reverse the ode. Here are some beauts, from simple to sublime. Hope you enjoy them, each beat and rhyme.*

Sam repairs a broken platter:
Crickory crockory, heed my wishes
Reassemble into dishes.

Aunt Clara summons an electrician
. . . Ben Franklin:
Hark ye, hark ye
Ye witches who live in lamps
Ye powers of watts and oomps and amps
Wizards of AC-DC transmission
Send to me an electrician.

Endora:
Lumpkin, pumpkin, spider's eye
If this mortal he doth lie
Whether told to a friend or told to foe
Each lie will cause his ears to grow.

Samantha:
Fiddle dee dee and fiddle dee dum
Let Witchcraft work and let it hum
Give all the credit to Larry Tate
As Darrin wanted before his hate.

Endora:
Backward, turn backward,
oh time in thy flight
Into the past with the speed of light
To Henry's time, let's check the date
And do not pass Henry, number eight.

Samantha turns humans into toads:
From polliwogs come great big frogs
We'll never know quite how
It's easier to turn a bee into a purple cow.
So hark ye witches, now pay heed:
Reverse this spell with haste and speed
With no regrets, man into toad
He'll hop the straight and narrow road.

Endora:

To avoid the shock of sudden wit
We'll start from scratch, bit by bit
A chime will cause your brain to whirl
Your jokes will cause their hair to curl.

Endora:

Winds blow and stars turn 'round
Into the past with the speed of sound
Take this witch to the time and place
Back to the scene of Salem's disgrace.

Samantha:

Sun, stars, wind and tide
In the heavens where you abide
Before your powers we do bow
Bring Santa's helpers here and now.

Endora:

Your view of life I find quite sick
This spell will change what makes you tick
At serious things you'll laugh and giggle
The graver the note, the more it will tickle.

285

Dreaming of
Jeannie

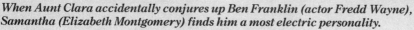

*When Aunt Clara accidentally conjures up Ben Franklin (actor Fredd Wayne),
Samantha (Elizabeth Montgomery) finds him a most electric personality.*

About the Authors

STEVE COX, 33, graduated with a B.A. in communication arts and journalism from Park College in Kansas City, Missouri. He has written a dozen books on film and television, including *The Beverly Hillbillies, The Munsters, The Munchkins of Oz, The Addams Chronicles, The Hooterville Handbook: A Viewer's Guide to Green Acres, Here's Johnny!, The Abbott & Costello Story* (with John Lofflin), and *Here on Gilligan's Isle* (with Russell Johnson). He resides in Los Angeles.

HOWARD FRANK, 43, maintains Personality Photos, Inc., one of the premiere entertainment and historical photograph archives in the United States. He has contributed to more than fifty books on film and television, and his extensive archive has been accessed by almost every major periodical, including *TV Guide, People, Time, Entertainment Weekly,* and *Newsweek*. He lives in New York.